DIVORCE EMPOWERMENT

DIVORCE EMPOWERMENT

What You Need To Know, Do, And Say

Linda E. Power

Legal Advisor – Donna E. Abrams, Attorney At Law

Financial Advisor – Mary Prior, MS, CFP®, CDP

PowerWise Books
New York

This publication is designed to present basic educational material on the subject matter covered. It is to be used as a general guide, not as a substitute for professional advice and assistance. It is sold with the understanding that neither the author nor publisher is dispensing legal, financial, psychological, or therapeutic advice. Furthermore, laws and their application are subject to continual change. Expert assistance or legal, financial, or psychological advice must be secured from qualified, licensed professionals. The author, publisher, and all others involved in any way with the preparation, publication, sale, or distribution specifically disclaim any responsibility for any financial or personal liability, loss, or risk that may be claimed or incurred as a consequence, directly or indirectly, of the use and application of any of the contents of this book.

ISBN 0-9727616-1-6

LCCN 2003090008

Legal Advisor – Donna E. Abrams, Attorney At Law
Financial Advisor – Mary Prior, MS, CFP*, CDP
Proofreader – Tina Tocco

This book is dedicated to

*All those who have lost a dream --- and with determination ---
have gone on to create others.*

And to

Andrew and Mary, my parents --- who taught courage by example.

Acknowledgments

To my friends and family, I wish to express heartfelt gratitude for their unfailing support and encouragement.

I especially want to recognize my sister, Ginny, for her early editorial review and moral support.

My good friend, Olga, deserves to win the lottery for her enduring patience, faithfully helping me master the computer and overcome "cyber-challenges."

To all the professionals in the legal, financial, and healing fields who saw the value of this project and offered encouragement and advice, I am genuinely indebted.

I especially appreciate the guidance of Eleanora, an exceptionally gifted spiritual visionary, who witnessed the planting of the seed and delighted as it sprouted and matured.

I greatly value the help of Ellen Shapiro, a conscientious, principled private investigator of Research Services, in answering questions and offering suggestions on investigatory techniques.

With pleasure, I acknowledge and thank Donna E. Abrams, Attorney At Law for her no-nonsense approach in applying her expertise to the book's legal material and for her enthusiastic support. With exemplary ethical standards and compassion, she is a tribute to the legal profession.

I am deeply grateful to Mary Prior of Financial Priorities for her blend of expertise, logic, and wisdom. Her forthright criticism helped to enhance the book's accuracy, tone, and balance.

I wish to express both admiration and appreciation to my proofreader, Tina Tocco, for her dedication and meticulous attention to detail.

Among those who deserve my deepest gratitude are my clients. As they learned from me, I learned from them, and the book grew richer and more reader responsive. With courage and commitment, they overcame confusion, fear, anger, and frustration --- and were a constant source of inspiration.

And I am eternally grateful to the Universal Spirit that guides each of us.

Contents

Acknowledgments   vi
Easy-To-Use Book Cues   xi

PART I – REALITY OF DIVORCE   1

♥ PRELUDE   3

1 ON YOUR KNEES, BUT NOT FOR LONG   5
    Your Inner And Outer Reality
    Realization And Action
    A Divorce Guide By Your Side

2 ON YOUR FEET, GETTING STEADY   9
    Balance And Focus
    Legal Process – Brief Overview
    Primary Concerns And Adjustments
    Framework For Your Strategy

PART II – STARTING TO GET ORGANIZED   15

3 FIRST THINGS FIRST   17
    Goal
    Immediate Concerns

4 CARING FOR YOURSELF   21
    Physical Well-Being And Safety
    Mental And Emotional Well-Being
    Using Negative Emotions With Positive Intent
    Seeking Professional Assistance
    Starting To Build Strategic Muscle

PART III – WHAT IS THERE AND WHERE IS IT?   25

5 YOUR ROLE   27
    Your Involvement Is Essential
    Timing Is Important
    What To Do
    Keep Documents Organized And Filed

6 FINANCIAL AND PERSONAL DOCUMENTS   31
    Joint Account Alert
    Financial Records
    Personal Records

7 FINDING AND USING INFORMATION   39
    Investigating Credit
    Uncovering Hidden Assets
    Compiling Your Marital History
    Power Of Information

PART IV – LEGAL PROCESS AND TERMS   47

8 SOME LEGAL BASICS   49
    Legal Reality
    Requirements For Filing
    The Three Facets Of A Case
    Court Calendar
    Laws Change

9 FAMILY COURT   53
Basic Function
How Family Court Can Help You
Pros And Cons of Taking Action In Family Court
Procedure

10 LEGAL GROUNDS   57
Introduction
Fault Grounds
Separation Agreement
Annulment

11 STEPS IN THE DIVORCE PROCESS   61
Your Approach To The Legal Process
Basically There Are Two Ways To Attain Your Divorce
Three Phases Of The Legal Process
Handy Clarifications

12 PROBLEMS WITH THE LEGAL SYSTEM   73
Problems
Reform: Integrated Domestic Violence Court

PART V – AREAS OF CONCERN   77

13 DIVISION OF PROPERTY   79
Equitable Distribution
Marital And Nonmarital Property
The Process Is Imperfect

14 LET'S LOOK AT THE TAX BITE   83
Basics
Calculate Real Value

15 WHO GETS WHAT?   87
Principal Residence
Pension
Other Distributions
Your Will

16 CHILD CUSTODY / SUPPORT / VISITATION   95
Your Approach To Custody
Best Interests Of The Child
Contested Custody
Child Support
Visitation

17 REMEMBER THE IRS   101
Real Value Of Property
Support Payments
Advantages To Working Together
Options With Tax Consequences

18 ESSENTIAL PRACTICAL CONCERNS   105
Maintenance
Health Care
Counsel Fees
Financial Planning
Bankruptcy Alert

19 NEGOTIATE LIKE AN EXPERT   109
Preparation
Techniques

PART VI – SELECTING AND WORKING WITH LEGAL COUNSEL 113

20 SELECTING A LAWYER 115
Get Down To Business
Where To Start
Is Pro Se A Possibility?
Attributes To Consider
First Meeting

21 LEGAL PROTECTION 123
Your Rights
Retainer Agreement

22 WORKING WITH YOUR LAWYER 127
Be Prepared And Alert
Save Time, Confusion, Money
Firing Your Attorney

23 DIVORCE MEDIATION 133
How Divorce Mediation Works
Selecting A Mediator
Pros And Cons Of Divorce Mediation
A Workable Alternative

PART VII – LEGAL AGREEMENTS 139

24 PREPARE FOR SUCCESS 141
Introduction
Continue To Develop Your Strategy
Know The Issues And Your Concerns
Psychology Of The Situation
Your Lawyer's Responsibility
Goals
Not Sure You Want To Divorce?

25 GENERAL FORMAT 145
Introduction
Articles
Reminders

26 DESIGN AN AGREEMENT THAT PROTECTS YOU 153
Introduction
General Considerations
Specific Issues
Conclusion

PART VIII – ADJUSTING AND HEALING 167

27 BASIC ADJUSTING AND PLANNING 169
Divorce Frazzle
Reminder – Take Care Of Yourself
Moving Toward Your Future

28 YOUR HEALING 173
Time To Heal
Releasing Negative Emotions
Healing Thoughts
Healing Ceremonies

29 FAMILY HEALING AND CO-PARENTING   **181**
Transition And Co-Parenting
Co-Parents' Relationship
Co-Parenting Your Children
Communication

PART IX – MOVING INTO YOUR FUTURE   **187**

30 FOLLOWING MARITAL BREAKUP   **189**
Wrap Up Documents
Ongoing Concerns

31 LOOKING FORWARD   **199**
Your Finances
Prenuptial Agreements

32 GROWING INTO YOUR TOMORROW   **205**
Know Yourself
Communication Is Key
Life Demands Change
Celebrate Yourself And Your Success

APPENDIX   **213**

A CUSTOMIZING GUIDE   **215**
How To Use
Specifics To Customize

B GLOSSARY – TERMS OF DIVORCE   **227**

C ORGANIZERS   **245**
Action Matters
   How To Start And Proceed
Money Matters
   Monthly Budget
   Financial Puzzle Pieces
   Wrap It Up Right
Mind Matters
   Deposition Primer
   Statement Of Client's Rights And Responsibilities
Agreement Matters
   Pathfinder

D EXHIBITS   **267**
   Summons With Notice
   Verified Complaint
   Order To Show Cause (for pendente lite relief)
   Qualified Domestic Relations Order
   Statement Of Net Worth

E HELPFUL RESOURCES   **291**

F INDEX   **295**

G BOOST EMPOWERMENT! – TELL YOUR STORY   **303**

H EXPRESS ORDER FORM   **305**

I DIVORCE GUIDE VOUCHER for $30   **307**

Easy-To-Use Book Cues

Is This Book For You?

Yes, if you are one of the millions of Americans fearing, facing, or recovering from marital breakup, or if you are a divorce professional who wants a comprehensive, yet easy-to-understand, resource for your clients. The book's fast-find format and reader responsive features make it exceptionally user-friendly. *Divorce Empowerment* can be read cover to cover as a sequential guide or used as a reference for specific concerns.

Goal Focused

Concise chapters with to-the-point sections and subsections inform and guide you.

Preview Pages

A detailed list of contents precedes each of the nine Parts to give you a foretaste of what you will find.

Cross-References

Cross-references (cited next to the text and headings of relevant sections) take you effortlessly from any page to related information elsewhere in the book. Example:

PART VI - in Chapter 21: "Retainer Agreement"
APPENDIX – Customizing Guide

To facilitate the manual's use as a reference for selective research, some data is intentionally covered in more than one Part.

Terms Of Divorce

The Glossary of 325 divorce-related terms will preclude your being "lost for words."

Organizers

Organizers are specifically designed to help you maintain focus and prepare for tough tasks, such as collecting and condensing data into a manageable, inclusive format; succeeding at a deposition; and assembling a comprehensive settlement agreement.

Customizing Guide

The Customizing Guide walks you through how to adapt the legal facts for your state.

Exhibits

The Exhibits are intended to familiarize you with some common legal documents and forms. They are not meant to be working copies. Survey the court orders so you know the format and what can be included. Preview the Statement of Net Worth, so you are aware of the demands of the task. Use the *Money Matters* Organizers (*Monthly Budget* and *Financial Puzzle Pieces*) to help you organize your financial data. When you are ready to fill in your Statement of Net Worth, either download a working copy from *www.courts.state.ny.us/networth.htm* or obtain a copy from your lawyer.

Directory Of Symbols

- ◆ Specific points of information.
- ❐ Material or tasks to check off once understood, included, started, or accomplished.
- ➥ Action-oriented behavior or tasks, such as what to ask or how to develop a strategy. Also, used as sub-bullets.
- ☝ Advantages.
- ❧ Disadvantages.
- ♥ Actions or material of a more personal or sensitive nature.
- ▨ Facts needing further research to be "state specific."

Justice is one of our fundamental values,
but it does not prevail automatically.

Do not unwittingly throw your divorce into
the legal arena and expect evenhandedness.

Just as a seafarer's fate may rest upon knowing about an unseen
iceberg, your fate may rest upon locating and learning what you
do not yet know. As you read this sentence, be reassured that
you hold in your hands much of what you need to learn.

PART I – REALITY OF DIVORCE

♥ PRELUDE

1 ON YOUR KNEES, BUT NOT FOR LONG
Your Inner And Outer Reality
Realization And Action
A Divorce Guide By Your Side

2 ON YOUR FEET, GETTING STEADY
Balance And Focus
Functional Balance
Personal Focus
Your Future Well-Being
Successful Transition
Legal Process – Brief Overview
Marriage As A Legal Issue
Adversarial System
Divorce Lawyers
Your Options
Become Informed
Primary Concerns And Adjustments
Yourself
Your Children
Others' Reactions
Financial
Framework For Your Strategy

Sometimes our fate resembles a fruit tree in winter.
Who would think that those branches would turn
green again and blossom, but we hope it, we know it.

Johann Wolfgang von Goethe

PRELUDE

If you are one of the four million Americans currently in some stage of dissolving your marriage, you need cost-effective, ready-to-use divorce information and guidance. While divorce is a deeply emotional experience, it is also a multibillion-dollar business. With overcrowded matrimonial courts, complex legal procedures, and spiraling attorney fees, attaining a fair settlement is increasingly improbable unless you are adequately prepared. Learn how to design and implement goal-specific financial, legal, and psychological strategies so you can work cost efficiently with legal professionals and complex legal demands.

Divorce Empowerment: What You Need To Know, Do, And Say is an informative, take-charge manual that tells you what you need to know, do, and say to achieve goals and minimize costs. It guides you through all facets of divorce with essential legal and financial facts, practical strategies, empowerment techniques, and healing exercises. Use it as a comprehensive, sequential guide or as a reference for specific concerns and interests. *Divorce Empowerment* is an indispensable pre-lawyer primer. Its collection of fundamental insights and divorce know-how can empower you to become a wise consumer of professional services and to work effectively with legal and financial specialists.

Concise chapters with well-defined subdivisions enhance *Divorce Empowerment*'s fast-find format. Streamlined text simplifies the complicated, addresses realistic needs, and inspires success. Cross-references, cited at the end of paragraphs and sections, direct you to related information. These helpful references and the *Terms Of Divorce* Glossary make this book uniquely reader responsive.

Use the specially designed Organizers (*Money Matters, Mind Matters, Action Matters,* and *Agreement Matters*) to prepare and stay organized. View samples of common legal forms so the process and paperwork feel less intimidating and more approachable. Since matrimonial law is state specific, detailed legal information is presented for one state, New York, to create an instructional legal model. By using the innovative *Customizing Guide,* readers of every state can readily adapt for their home states the specific points, terms, and names introduced in the detailed legal model.

The intent of *Divorce Empowerment* is to educate and inspire. It does not cover individual situations and is not to be construed as legal, financial, or psychological advice. The information presented is not intended to be used as a substitute for retaining a lawyer or for working with a financial advisor or mental health expert. The existence of abuse, violence, or addiction creates special needs and concerns. Under such circumstances, it may be impossible or dangerous to try to work directly with a spouse or gather documents about the marriage. Extra care and caution are necessary with child-related issues. Use the book to become informed and secure the specialized professional assistance your situation may demand.

In every winter's heart there is a quivering spring, and
behind the veil of each night there is a smiling dawn.

Kahlil Gibran

1

ON YOUR KNEES, BUT NOT FOR LONG

YOUR INNER AND OUTER REALITY

Divorce is not something for which people plan or train.

You may be opening this book in disbelief that divorce is happening to you. Most facing the breakup of their marriages experience a similar feeling. People do not marry with the expectation of negotiating a divorce settlement. Some may come to this book with relief that a nightmare is ending. Others come to it with the agonizing realization that they can no longer hold together a charade, no matter how much they might want to maintain certain qualities of their married lives.

The marriage contract is so simple and hopeful; it is blessed with anticipation, joy, and good wishes. In contrast, the divorce contract has none of these features. It is agreed to in an atmosphere permeated by a sense of failure and negative feelings. Divorce is not something for which people plan or train or are readily equipped to handle.

For most, divorce is a debilitating, if not devastating, experience. On the heels of disbelief follow fear and bewilderment. You must cope with increased uncertainty, responsibility, turmoil, and disruption at a time when your effective energy is compromised by emotional, mental, and possibly, financial stress. That which you had held most dear is gone. The realization that the person who, at one time, was your most intimate companion is now your adversary compounds the pain. Your spouse is not only not there for you; he or she is probably working against you.

Recognize what is happening. You are trying to untangle yourself from a married identity while mourning the end of your marriage. You may feel as if you are on an emotional roller coaster regarding how you feel about the situation, your spouse, and yourself. Staying organized mentally can be difficult. Mental wandering often results from the emotional trauma. It is not uncommon to walk into a room with purpose and not remember why you are there. Raw emotions and scattered rational ability can make even the smallest tasks seem overwhelming.

Take care of yourself as well as you can. Strained emotions and worrisome thoughts are likely to deplete your energy. Inconsistent eating and sleeping habits and an overstressed immune system can debilitate you physically. It may be tempting to want to dull the pain with anything that brings relief. Be careful; some choices are more harmful than others. Try to stay away from those choices that may bring temporary relief but could induce addictive behavior.

Your sense of trust and moral beliefs are being fundamentally tested, especially if you had believed in your marriage and trusted your spouse. Having a spiritual foundation at this time can be invaluable. As devastating as your divorce feels, a belief in a grander plan in which all happens as it is meant to happen can offer immeasurable comfort and reassurance. It is during crisis that many people begin to find their spiritual centers and strengthen their faith. As you heal and grow, your perception of trust will take on a renewed fullness.

Life as you have known it is ending. Dissolving your marriage with its familiar structure, behavior, and security can be unremittingly stressful. You are parting from your marriage, from your spouse, and from the person you used to be. Moving into an unmarried life with its uncertainties and financial challenges is no easy task.

You may feel extremely alone, thinking no one could really understand. You are partly right; some aspects of your story may never be understood. There are, however, some common threads in the divorce experience; the most prevalent are emotional rupture, financial upheaval, and the need to terminate the marriage contract legally. According to the United States Department of Health and Human Services, the nation's divorce rate has more than tripled in the last forty years. Approximately fifty percent of marriages end in divorce or legal separation. That means each year about four million American spouses are coping with issues similar to those with which you may be struggling.

REALIZATION AND ACTION
Action generates clarity and motivation.

Eventually, among your emotions you may recognize a deep anger. This can be a good sign, especially if you use your anger in a productive manner as a tool to motivate yourself. Combining the positive use of your emotions with knowledge and informed guidance can empower you to take appropriate action.

You cannot move ahead in a positive manner until you acknowledge what is happening and what needs to be done. Making competent decisions regarding the welfare of your family and yourself demands that you give up denial, accept the facts, and "walk" with your pain and anger. If there is a choice between resolving marital discord or dissolving the marriage, move toward that which is both realistic and best for your family and do all that is feasible to reach your goal. Either way, start to take action.

Take some small action each day to help you move toward your future. If divorce is inevitable, the road ahead may at first appear too difficult to travel. As you initiate action, you will further define what you need to do to make progress. Action generates clarity and motivation. Ultimately, you want to move into your future in a manner that is positive and healthy for you and your family.

Seeking assistance is a measure of your strength and a clear sign you are connected to reality. Find the positive support you need in the forms that best serve you, such as trusted friends, professionals, spiritual guidance, support groups, and reference materials. By opening this book, you have already demonstrated your determination.

A DIVORCE GUIDE BY YOUR SIDE

Use Divorce Empowerment *as a reference or as a comprehensive guide.*

With essential legal and financial facts, practical strategies, empowerment techniques, and healing exercises, *Divorce Empowerment* is designed to guide you through all facets of dissolving your marriage and moving into your future. The manual's easy-to-use format presents practical, precise information with an emphasis on analyzing options and reinforcing proactive conduct. Use *Divorce Empowerment* as a reference for specific issues and concerns, or read it from cover to cover to guide you through your divorce.

Divorce is a fragmenting, life-changing experience. Playing out its emotional, financial, and legal aspects in an adversarial court system provides fertile ground for any individuals involved to take advantage of the circumstances. People who enter into the legal process unprepared with misinformation, half-truths, and naïve notions are powerless to protect themselves and get fair settlements. Those who anticipate "having their day in Court" do not realize the court system may be too overburdened and the process too costly to effectively "right wrongs." Being uninformed and ill-equipped can lead to confusion and irrational decisions, causing additional emotional and financial hardship.

You want to be prepared and in the position to avoid making irreversible mistakes. Approaching the process with realistic expectations, a workable strategy, and practical knowledge will best equip you to avoid problems and influence the outcome. Before becoming too enmeshed in the divorce process, become informed, and in so doing, become empowered. Have *Divorce Empowerment* by your side as your divorce guide. (Locate the *Action Matters* Organizer in the Appendix and use *How To Start And Proceed.*)

PART I – Prelude
APPENDIX – Customizing Guide
     Action Matters: How To Start And Proceed

Start by doing what's necessary, then what's possible
and suddenly you are doing the impossible.

St. Francis of Assisi

Whenever you fall, pick something up.

Oswald Avery

2

ON YOUR FEET, GETTING STEADY

BALANCE AND FOCUS

The Chinese character for "crisis" is a combination of two symbols;
one for "challenge" and the other for "opportunity."

FUNCTIONAL BALANCE

Maintaining a practical approach to the demands of divorce is essential. Separating your emotions from the business aspects of dissolving the marriage is an ongoing necessity. Continue to seek and accept support to release the emotional buildup and begin to prepare and educate yourself to conduct business with your divorce team (lawyer, accountant, other professionals).

PERSONAL FOCUS

➥ Work at releasing your marriage; honor it as you let it go and say good-bye.
➥ Respect your pain; release it in manageable amounts. Thank it for reminding you of how deeply you can care.
➥ Avoid ensnaring interaction with your spouse.
➥ Keep your long-term goals in focus as a beacon toward which to move.
➥ Acknowledge your achievements each day, day by day.
➥ Strive for what you need and deserve but accept the reality of compromise, even when you feel or know you are entitled to a better outcome.

YOUR FUTURE WELL-BEING

Possibly, the divorce itself is serving as an impetus for a beneficial life transformation. It might be a wake-up call for you to make changes about which you have been in denial or feared you did not have the strength to do. It may favorably alter your relationship with your family or be a potential lifesaver in helping you recognize and modify unhealthy behavior.

Ultimately, you will move beyond the breakup of the marriage with a wisdom and determination fitting for the person you are becoming. Hidden desires and talents may surface and energize a redirection in your life. Positive feelings formerly absent, such as hope and self-worth, may emerge and inspire you to rediscover your true essence.

SUCCESSFUL TRANSITION

Accept what you cannot undo or change; take action to achieve what is possible. Consider viewing your divorce as a blessing in disguise. Focus on the ways your life can change for the better. Begin to become the person you want to be. Divorce forces change; use it to your benefit. It might be helpful to remember the Chinese character for "crisis" is a combination of two symbols; one for "challenge" and the other for "opportunity."

LEGAL PROCESS – BRIEF OVERVIEW

Our judicial system encourages combative strategies.

MARRIAGE AS A LEGAL ISSUE

Legally, marriage is a civil contract, dissolvable only by the Court. Our legal system is impersonal, governed by established rules, and has its own language, "legalese."

ADVERSARIAL SYSTEM

Our judicial system is adversarial; its procedures encourage combative strategies. It is not designed to resolve marital discord; on the contrary, it intensifies conflict. The assumption is that opponents entering this justice system will be represented equally.

DIVORCE LAWYERS

Each lawyer's professional focus is on representing his or her own client, with little responsibility for the well-being of the other side. Lawyers know one another. They have histories, as well as futures, in the legal profession. Lawyers' ties to each other and to the assigned Judge may interfere with their commitment to individual clients.

YOUR OPTIONS

The most significant option you and your spouse can exercise is whether to seek an uncontested or contested divorce. With an uncontested divorce, you have considerably more control over the decisions. You can negotiate a Settlement Agreement, Stipulation of Settlement, or Separation Agreement to resolve the division of assets and liabilities, child custody, support, and other key issues. The completed Agreement is submitted to the Court along with, and incorporated into, the final Judgment of Divorce, Judgment of Annulment, or Judgment of Separation, which is signed by the Judge. There is no need for a trial to obtain your divorce decree. A signed Agreement can be the basis for an uncontested divorce, or you can choose to remain married living by the terms of a Separation Agreement. Circumstances regarding children, religion, culture, health, and finances might make the latter choice advantageous.

PART IV - in Chapter 11: "Uncontested Divorce"
PART VII – Legal Agreements
APPENDIX – Agreement Matters: Pathfinder

With a contested divorce, you relinquish your power to decide those issues that you and your spouse cannot resolve. Instead, you hope that your attorney will be able to present a clear, cohesive argument to the Court and that the Judge will make a decision favorable to you. A contested divorce is headed for trial but can be resolved anywhere

along the way by agreeing to a settlement. Contested divorces are unavoidable if either side is entrenched, for example: does not want the divorce for personal, financial, social, health, or religious reasons; is unable or unwilling to compromise further; is stalling while hiding assets; or wants to control or punish.
PART IV – Legal Process And Terms
PART VII – Legal Agreements

BECOME INFORMED

Become empowered with knowledge. You can have immense influence over your case by preparing yourself psychologically, understanding your finances, and learning what the legal process demands. Save time, energy, and money by knowing how to work with the system.
PART II through PART VII

PRIMARY CONCERNS AND ADJUSTMENTS

Rage, fears, memories, and other people can throw you off.

YOURSELF

Releasing your married identity and sorting out who you are, now that you are no longer part of a couple, is hard work. Managing the household and children without a partner will be stressful; safety will take more planning; and social obligations may remind you of the depth of your pain. Allow the mourning process to move through its cycles and accept that your feelings of sorrow and loneliness are natural.

Organizing documentation and fulfilling legal demands require that you function under increased pressure while you are already mentally and emotionally strained. Your work performance might suffer from disruptions and poor concentration. Be practical about what can be accomplished each day; try to stay on schedule and be persistent. Do the most challenging work or planning during the part of the day or week in which you function best. Rage, fears, memories, and other people can throw you off. Recognize when you simply have to retreat into some uncomplicated quiet time in order to reenergize. At the end of each day, recognize what you have done and give yourself credit for your accomplishments.

YOUR CHILDREN

With divorce, children lose much of what makes them feel loved and secure. Sharing a daily routine with caring, responsible parents, including everything from the small, silly, warm moments to the much anticipated, traditional celebrations, provides a sense of stability. Tell them of the divorce in a manner to reassure them that they are loved and will continue to be cared for. Often, children fear neither will be so.

How you and your spouse decide to tell your children depends on the needs and ages of the children and the circumstances of the breakup. Make the explanation brief and devoid of blame and personal details. Emphasize your love for them, even though the two of you will no longer be living together as their parents. Be very clear with your children, stressing that they in no way contributed to the breakup. Young children often blame themselves in some way for their parents' problems. It is best that children be given advance notice of some weeks when a parent will be moving elsewhere; include how and where that parent can be reached.

An ongoing gift you can give your children is to treat their other parent with respect; they deserve to feel they can love both parents. Try to minimize any conflict connected with custody and visitation. For most children, the feeling they must take sides is extremely stressful and hurtful.

PART VIII - Chapter 29: Family Healing And Co-Parenting

Be consistent and realistic in your expectations and guidelines for yourself and for your children. Keep them informed and encourage open dialogue. Your children will need to express their fears and confusion; your adjustment and behavior will serve as a model for them.

OTHERS' REACTIONS

Reactions of family, friends, and acquaintances will vary depending on their comfort level and experience with divorce. Some may provide genuine support, but most will, probably, be uncomfortable to some degree. Anticipate that some family members and friends may simply not accept or acknowledge that your divorce is happening. Others may be uneasy, feeling they are expected to side with you. Still others may either want to avoid you, because you spark in them anxiety about their own marriages, or have no desire to associate with you, now that you are not part of a couple.

Friends with their own personal agendas may not give you the support you need. Those who are insecure about or dissatisfied with their own marriages might see you either as a threat or as eligible. Single friends might view you, or your spouse, as eligible. Unfortunately, you may also have people in your life who appear to be sensitive to your situation, but really only want to encourage you to reveal personal details to use later for a few minutes of self-serving gossip. Others may interfere with well-meaning advice that is not relevant or helpful.

You do not have to discuss your divorce with anyone who asks. Do not let others steal your energy to satisfy their own needs. You need to conserve your strength to focus on the work you must do. Decide what you wish to share, with whom, and when. Have a simple, direct way to respond: *Thank you for asking. The marriage just isn't working. I appreciate your concern. Maybe we could talk about it some other time.* Do not feel you have to explain yourself; it will deplete your energy. As you maintain control over your divorce information, you may also benefit by feeling more in control and appearing so to others.

Those who care will support you by keeping in touch and offering specific information and services. You need one or two true friends or acquaintances who have the maturity and sensitivity to support your efforts. To keep your approach proactive and positive, you need honest reaction to your ideas and plans from supporters who can maintain confidentiality. Attentive listeners can help clarify options and assist in finding resources and professional guidance. If you fear you do not have this kind of backing, you might find some of what you need in a support group.

As part of your strategy for success, develop a "personal presentation" regarding your attitude and communication style. A positive, in-charge attitude and precise, respectful communication can go a long way in helping you get what you want and need. To elicit the respect and treatment you deserve, eliminate any signs of self-pity. Realistically, much of divorce focuses on the monetary value of the marriage; this is business. Give the appearance you are prepared to handle the business of resolving marital issues and moving on with your life.

FINANCIAL

Begin to plan how you are going to support yourself and your part of the household expenses, especially if you are presently unemployed. Managing a budget strained by divorce takes diligence. You will need to become well-informed about your finances, including the amount of income and expenses, as well as the value of marital assets and liabilities. Review your credit ratings and obtain credit in your own name.

PART III - in Chapter 6: "Credit Cards"
*   in Chapter 7: "Investigating Credit"*

Begin developing a strategy on how best to divide the marital assets and liabilities. Foremost in your mind must be that you and your spouse are now in competition for property you once owned together. It would be naïve to believe the Court will have the time or sensitivity to be sure you receive all to which you are entitled. You need to learn what there is, what you are entitled to, and plan how you are going to attain it.

PART III – What Is There And Where Is It?
PART V – Areas Of Concern

FRAMEWORK FOR YOUR STRATEGY

Divorce can free you to become who you are meant to be.

↪ Focus on your goals. Do not share them with your spouse if there is the slightest hint that he or she is not working in good faith with you.

↪ Keep discussions of the issues with your spouse tentative; do not make agreements.

↪ Stay clear of arguments with your spouse. You do not want to be forced into saying something that will reveal "your hand."

↪ Do not sign papers you have not gone over with your legal counsel.

↪ Be selective with whom you share personal and financial divorce information. You do not want to leak anything that could later be used to weaken your position in negotiations.

↪ Remain open, or appear to remain open, to an amicable relationship with your spouse following the dissolution of the marriage.

↪ Be courteous to everyone; you do not need any enemies at this time.

Divorce can be financially disastrous and erosive to your self-esteem, causing a profound identity crisis. It tests your patience and courage and compels you to educate yourself. Ultimately, however, divorce can be an impetus for necessary, beneficial change, freeing you to become who you are meant to be.

What one has to do usually can be done.

Eleanor Roosevelt

Meet the challenges; the Universe loves courage.

PART II – STARTING TO GET ORGANIZED

3 FIRST THINGS FIRST
    Goal
    Immediate Concerns
        Behavioral Issues
            Decision To Move Out Of The House
            Having Sex With Your Spouse While Divorcing
            Strategic Behavior
            Self-Empowerment
        Children
        Abuse / Addiction
        Marital History

4 CARING FOR YOURSELF
    Physical Well-Being And Safety
    Mental And Emotional Well-Being
    Using Negative Emotions With Positive Intent
    Seeking Professional Assistance
    Starting To Build Strategic Muscle
        Basics
        Daily Exercise: Push-Ups For Change

What you must recognize is how you are vulnerable,
not how vulnerable you are.

Thought is action in rehearsal.
Sigmund Freud

3

FIRST THINGS FIRST

GOAL

Adequate preparation will empower you.

Adequate preparation will empower you to make informed, sensible decisions. While collecting your emotional and mental strength, you must also gather information and documentation. Much of getting organized revolves around locating and understanding data and documents regarding income, household expenses, assets and liabilities, child custody and support, and spousal maintenance. This groundwork will help you to assess your situation realistically, so you can attain the best outcome at the least expense. Think about locating and joining a support group so you will receive the ongoing understanding, encouragement, and guidance you need.
PART III – What Is There And Where Is It?
PART V – Areas Of Concern

IMMEDIATE CONCERNS

Putting yourself first is not being disloyal; it's being smart.

BEHAVIORAL ISSUES

DECISION TO MOVE OUT OF THE HOUSE

If one of your goals is to be able to stay in the house following the divorce, especially if you have children, it is best not to leave the house during the divorce process, unless there is abuse. If domestic violence is an issue, you may want to seek an Order of Protection in which the Court orders your spouse to move out for a period of time. If you do leave, most likely it will be difficult to get back in and there can be far-reaching consequences. If you leave property behind, it might be a long time before you can get it. You will have to count on your spouse's goodwill or negotiations or a court order. You are likely to lose bargaining power in negotiating a settlement favorable to your right of possession to the residence or to benefit equitably from its sale. Leaving children behind can have a very damaging impact upon your winning custody.

Consult a lawyer before making the decision to abandon the household. Agreeing upon a "no prejudice" letter might help in your situation. It is a legal device stating neither spouse will hold behavior against the other. For example, one spouse will not

claim "abandonment" if the other moves out. If you leave children behind, however, and custody is an issue, a no prejudice letter is not likely to help you.
APPENDIX – Customizing Guide

HAVING SEX WITH YOUR SPOUSE WHILE DIVORCING
Having sex with your spouse while divorcing can have legal consequences. An adultery charge cannot be used as grounds if you willingly have sex with your spouse after you know of his or her adultery. He or she can plead "condonation," which means by your actions you have forgiven the adultery and it is no longer a legal issue.
PART IV - in Chapter 10: "Fault Grounds"
APPENDIX – Customizing Guide

STRATEGIC BEHAVIOR
Putting yourself first is not being disloyal; it's being smart. Keep communication with your spouse guarded. Do not share your plans or report to him or her about your actions. Do not share written projected budgets or financial agreements. In the initial stages of getting organized, you are educating yourself. You do not want an early written estimate, based on incomplete data, to surface later as an "exhibit" and used against you by the opposing lawyer. Do not agree to anything verbally or sign anything that does not have your lawyer's approval.

Do not say or do anything that could be used against you. Tape recording may be going on or there may be detectives. Small mistakes can be blown up by the opposition into serious accusations, possibly bringing into question your worthiness as a parent and thereby affecting a custody decision. Be polite to everyone.

SELF-EMPOWERMENT
Become a formidable opponent; begin to build psychological muscle. Design an empowerment strategy to effectively alter your behavior so you can have greater control over what is happening. Learn to remain quiet and to "hold your cards close" so that you reveal very little. By staying quiet at chosen times, you will not react in the same way you have in the past. This altered behavior may add to your influence.

Become an observer; be busy absorbing. Listen; absorb every shred of information, every innuendo that surfaces. It might be of value later. Reveal what you know in small amounts only when it has some strategic advantage for you. Act businesslike, positive, calm, and quietly self-assured. Keep the bigger picture in mind: the end result, your goal. Understand there will be some losses along the way in order to win some of what you want.
PART II - in Chapter 4: "Starting To Build Strategic Muscle"

CHILDREN
Plan for the immediate and long-range security of your children. Clarify how they can contact you or another responsible adult if there is need. This is not only a safety precaution, it also helps children feel more secure during a very insecure period of their lives. Be prudent and do what is necessary so that each child can be readily identifiable. Keep on record recent photographs, fingerprints, and signatures. Be sure to have Social Security numbers; they are needed to claim children as dependents for tax deductions and for child support enforcement.

ABUSE / ADDICTION

If your situation involves either addiction or abuse, obtain guidance and support, preferably before the issue of divorce is discussed. In the Government Listings of your phone book, locate the specialized assistance your situation demands. Many organizations providing support have expert counseling and legal services, as well as safe quarters in emergencies.

MARITAL HISTORY

The purpose of a written, chronological history of your marriage is to highlight your contributions to the economic partnership. You want to provide evidence showing that you have been an equal or better contributor to the financial value of the marriage. Your attorney will use this material to argue for an equitable distribution of the assets. Begin to jostle your memory and collect your thoughts; write down every way in which you can remember contributing to the marriage. Just start collecting information; you can organize it into a chronological sequence later. Include what assets you started with, who brought them into the marriage, and what was accumulated during the marriage.

PART III - in Chapter 7: "Compiling Your Marital History"
APPENDIX – Customizing Guide

It is the wounded oyster that mends its shell with pearl.
Ralph Waldo Emerson

Success is a form of awareness.

4

CARING FOR YOURSELF

PHYSICAL WELL-BEING AND SAFETY
Take some basic precautions.

Attend to your body's well-being; it is important for mental strength, emotional balance, and physical health. You will need more rest but will probably have less time for it. It is more important than ever to eat regular, healthy meals, but you will probably feel less inclined to do so. Consider supplementing with vitamins and minerals. Exercise is a great stress reducer and health enhancer.

For safety and peace of mind, take some basic precautions. Consider changing locks and installing outside motion detector lights. Maintain a service contract on the furnace. Keep up with automobile maintenance. Give an extra set of house and car keys to a trusted neighbor or friend. Buy and keep a cell phone with you to connect with your children and for emergencies. Do not reveal to strangers, such as service people who come to your house, that you are alone. Screen incoming calls and get Caller ID. Do not identify yourself on the phone to unknown sources. Have the caller identify the purpose of the call; do not feel you must furnish your name.

Make photocopies of legal documents filed at home. You will need these to negotiate the settlement. If the originals are, subsequently, removed without your consent, you will have access to the information on your photocopies. Also make copies of important papers you normally carry in your purse, wallet, and briefcase, such as driver's license, registration, credit cards, and health insurance cards. They can then be more easily replaced if lost or stolen. This can help to eliminate extra stress at a time when it is easy to lose or misplace things.
PART VIII - Chapter 27: Basic Adjusting And Planning

MENTAL AND EMOTIONAL WELL-BEING

Work with anxiety by seeing it as a messenger.

Most people going through divorce experience pervasive pain and sorrow. The healing process requires that you recognize your pain, let it surface, and let it go. Fortunately, and unfortunately, by necessity, this happens over and over. There are layers; there are cycles. Allow the process to happen. Honor yourself for doing so and know that, eventually, you will heal. The source of your pain may be connected to how deeply you believed in, or were committed to, or were in denial about, the relationship. To deal with your pain and mourn your loss, you will need to release your rage and resentment and recognize and face your fears.

Unresolved fears can burst to the surface and burgeon into bouts of anxiety. Work with anxiety by seeing it as a messenger, revealing to you what yet needs to be resolved. Stay in the present. Focusing on regrets about the past will pull you in the wrong direction. Unchecked anxiety about the future can leave you ineffective.

Stress is likely to be a daily companion. Make some changes to try to minimize it. Simplify your schedule; modify your expectations. Take care of your needs instead of trying to be what others need. When pain, anxiety, and stress overwhelm you, practice ways to balance yourself. Breathe deeply, exercise, speak with a confidant, pray, sing, dance, listen to music, or meditate. Even on bad days, some things go well. Recognize and give yourself credit for your daily accomplishments. Speak them; say them to yourself as you go to sleep at night.

During divorce you learn who your friends are. You will need their support. In all likelihood, you will make new trusted friends having experiences similar to yours. People who have successfully survived divorce can be a motivating, healthy source of support. Express your appreciation to those who help. Be open about how they can further help you by staying in touch, listening and offering feedback, being honest when you seem amiss, and passing on information and resources.

PART VIII - Chapter 27: Basic Adjusting And Planning
Chapter 28: Your Healing

USING NEGATIVE EMOTIONS WITH POSITIVE INTENT

Transform your negative emotions into a creative force.

Use your negative emotions as a creative force to help you achieve your goals and heal. Exercised positively, anger can be a potent tool to stimulate your resolve to be decisive and take action. You will have much to accomplish during the upcoming months. Use your fear to remind yourself to seek guidance, whether it be from professionals, friends, spiritual practices, or books.

When the pain breaks through your bewilderment and immobilizes you, hold onto the part of yourself still functioning and accept that the pain of divorcing can feel utterly consuming. Remind yourself to take it bit by bit: by the minute, the thought,

the task, the day. If you find yourself either crying or in a rage, let it be a reminder of how deeply you believed in the dream of the marriage. With each welling tear or pounding heartbeat, observe and grieve the passing of that dream. Acknowledge how great the loss, and possibly, how great the betrayal or deep your denial.
PART VIII - Chapter 28: Your Healing

SEEKING PROFESSIONAL ASSISTANCE
You need and deserve guidance and support.

Professional support can help you rebuild your self-esteem and revitalize your emotional and mental stamina, and thereby improve your ability to succeed at the tasks ahead. You need and deserve support to:
➥ Manage debilitating pain and guide you through the healing process.
➥ Help identify key emotional issues and work with them in a beneficial, transformative manner.
➥ Unravel extremely mixed feelings about your spouse so you are able to accept a realistic composite of who he or she is.
➥ Clarify your options in negotiating a settlement that minimizes the uncertainties of the future.

STARTING TO BUILD STRATEGIC MUSCLE
Change self-defeating behavior.

BASICS
By recognizing and modifying how you react to your spouse and marital issues, you can begin to build strategic leverage. The opposition will be thrown off by not being able to "push your buttons" and get you to react in a predictable, self-defeating manner. This will be a tremendous, psychological advantage for you in negotiating, because your spouse will no longer know how to control you.

DAILY EXERCISE: PUSH-UPS FOR CHANGE
Concentrate on building psychological muscle. Identify those thought and behavioral patterns keeping you tied to self-limiting, reactive exchanges regarding your marriage. Recognize specifically what makes you react as you do, how it makes you feel, and what you need to do differently to react in a more productive manner. As you work on this, you will cultivate greater awareness and skill.

Begin to change habitual behavior by practicing a daily exercise called "Push-Ups For Change." Each day do one thing differently from how you normally would do it, something as simple as which shoe you put on first, what route you take to work, or how you respond to coworkers. Be aware and committed; alter one routine action daily. It does not matter how simple the changed behavior is, it matters what you do with the action. It is intended to operate like a switch to get the attention of your brain and focus its power. Reinforce your actions with positive, verbal affirmations such as, *I have the power to change and to succeed.*

Each time you exercise with Push-Ups For Change, think of your larger goal: to replace self-defeating thought and behavioral patterns with productive, self-enhancing actions and reactions. Small intentional efforts to alter your everyday routine can begin to condition your brain and prepare it to make far-reaching, meaningful changes. Breaking old reactive patterns and building psychological muscle will enable you to access essential inner strengths. Ultimately, you will be able to negotiate with increased, strategic leverage and succeed.

PART II - in Chapter 3: "Behavioral Issues: Self-Empowerment"
PART VIII - in Chapter 28: "Healing Thoughts" and "Healing Ceremonies"
in Chapter 29: "Transition And Co-Parenting" and "Communication"

PART III – WHAT IS THERE AND WHERE IS IT?

Documents are the nuts and bolts needed to construct a fair settlement.

Please note: Some options presented in Part III may not be applicable to your situation. Trying to gather documents where abuse or violence exists can be dangerous. Use this information to become informed, but secure the specialized professional assistance your circumstances may demand. Consult with an attorney to be sure you stay within the law while gathering data.

5 YOUR ROLE
Your Involvement Is Essential
Timing Is Important
What To Do
Keep Documents Organized And Filed
Necessary Features
Labeled Sections
Emergency
Documents – Financial And Personal
Financial Forms And Inventories
Bills And Receipts
Lawsuit Documents And Communications
Progress Journal

6 FINANCIAL AND PERSONAL DOCUMENTS
Joint Account Alert
Bank Accounts
Credit Cards
Closing Accounts
Applying For Credit
Credit Counseling
Equity Credit Lines
Safety Deposit Boxes
Investments
Material Possessions
Financial Records
Bank Accounts
Income Tax Returns
Loan Applications
Credit Card Statements And Receipts
Investment Portfolios
Life And Disability Insurance Policies
Titles And Deeds
Material Possessions
Retirement Information
Private Business
Statement Of Net Worth
Proposed Budget

Personal Records
    Journals / Calendars
    E-mails
    Telephone Message Machines
    Home Videos
    Prescriptions / Medical Records
    Employment Personnel File
    Telephone Records
    Tape-Recorded Conversations

7 FINDING AND USING INFORMATION
    Investigating Credit
    Uncovering Hidden Assets
        Ways Assets Are Hidden
        Take Action
            Bank Accounts
            Income Tax Returns
            Loans
            Retirement Plans
            Businesses
            Public Records
            Tackle Head On
        Be Focused And Tactful
    Compiling Your Marital History
        Assets
        How You Advanced Spouse's Career
        Role As A Parent
    Power Of Information

5

YOUR ROLE

YOUR INVOLVEMENT IS ESSENTIAL

No one is going to care as much about your well-being as you.

The degree to which you and your spouse can work together at dividing property and providing for the family's needs can greatly impact the quality of your settlement and the amount of money you spend on legal and forensic fees. Keep in the forefront of your mind, however, that aside from providing for the children, you and your spouse now have some competitive interests. Be realistic; no one is going to care as much about your well-being as you.

Unfortunately, most marital breakups stimulate competition and manipulation regarding access to the marriage's financial documents. Some spouses conceal documentation they have in their possession with no intention of honestly sharing it. Others have been hiding records regarding marital wealth for a period of time before the breakup. If you do not have access to documents, and the information contained therein, you will not be knowledgeable about the monetary value of the marriage and will not be able to negotiate for your rightful share. In addition, you will be unable to protect yourself from being held liable for unknown and possibly growing debts generated by your spouse.

Keep in mind that documents verifying your marriage's financial value are the property of both spouses; you have a right to this evidence. If records are intentionally being hidden and your spouse is uncooperative, it is unlikely you will benefit from your legal right to marital property, unless you are able to uncover hidden financial and personal documents. Your role in attempting to do so is essential. The more complete and detailed your findings are, the more leverage you will have in negotiating a satisfactory settlement that reflects what you deserve and provides for what you and your family need.

TIMING IS IMPORTANT

Evidence can disappear.

Be cautious about how you approach the task of gathering information, especially if you think your spouse is likely to hide assets. Develop a safe strategy that has the greatest chance of succeeding. It is most advantageous to locate necessary records before divorce is openly discussed. Evidence can disappear. If you fear a custody dispute, try to document inappropriate behavior before your spouse's lawyer advises him or her to behave like a model parent. Having photocopies and documentation in your possession can facilitate your moving more easily toward a suitable settlement. An uncooperative spouse who is concealing information may force you to use legal discovery to request documents, and then produce them gradually, bit by bit. The intention may be to exhaust you emotionally and financially, thereby forcing you to agree to a settlement not representative of your share of the marital assets. Using legal discovery with a spouse who is bent on hiding assets or concealing information can be time consuming, costly, and ineffective in uncovering missing or hidden documents.
PART IV - in Chapter 11: "Discovery Stage"

If your spouse is transferring or otherwise dissipating assets, or increasing the marital debt, you have little or no time to gather documents. It might be best to start legal action to protect your financial well-being and to request restraining orders be placed on existing assets. The commencement of the lawsuit may also establish the date beyond which debts incurred by either spouse are considered separate and not a marital liability. Consult legal counsel regarding the specifics of your situation.
PART IV - in Chapter 11: "Situations In Which It Is Important To Commence Legal Action"
APPENDIX – Customizing Guide

WHAT TO DO

You may need to act quickly with courage and caution.

You may need to act quickly with courage and caution. A review of the documents to which you need access is covered in *Chapter 6: Financial And Personal Documents.* Photocopy documents and either replace the originals or remove them. When in doubt about a document's value or validity, copy or remove it anyway. Its significance may only be apparent as the whole picture becomes clearer. Save computer-stored financial data on a diskette or CD and print out necessary copies. It is wise to make three copies of each document: one for your personal file kept in a safe place, one for your attorney, and one held by a trusted friend or family member. If you have given your spouse power of attorney over your assets, try to have all copies of the document in your possession, and consult your attorney about how to rescind it.

It might be to your advantage to remove original documents and keep them in a safe place outside of the house. If you feel this is too inflammatory or does not benefit you, return them exactly as you found them after making copies. Do what is safest and will give you the most leverage in negotiations. Copying and replacing originals may be the most strategically advantageous to the outcome of your case, because your spouse might not know to what extent you have been able to inform yourself. This can enhance your bargaining position. If the originals are subsequently altered or disappear, your copies can provide great leverage in revealing the opposition's propensity for deceit. Some documents may be so sensitive for your circumstances that you must put them in safekeeping. If you fear the children could be abducted to your spouse's homeland, it might be best to remove their passports. Consult your attorney on matters as sensitive as this and about whether replacing or removing originals is best for your situation.

If you cannot locate necessary documents at home or in safety deposit boxes, review all incoming mail and keep a list of addresses for insurance companies, savings and lending institutions, brokerage firms, and business connections. Contact each in an effort to obtain the documents or information you need. Most of the information you gather will focus on financial aspects of your marriage, but be alert to any data relating to grounds and child custody that may enhance your bargaining power.

PART III - in Chapter 6: "Personal Records"
in Chapter 7: "Uncovering Hidden Assets"

KEEP DOCUMENTS ORGANIZED AND FILED

Design a filing system that works for you.

NECESSARY FEATURES

Create a filing system that has separate, labeled sections and is large enough or can grow. A box with tabbed manila folders will work. You need about one to two inches of space for one year of papers for each section. Plan more room for sections you designate for "Lawsuit Documents and Communications" and "Progress Journal." Each can become bulky, depending on the complexity of your case. Keep originals in a safe place; use photocopies for your frequently accessed working file. The following are some suggestions of what to include in each section, but design a system of organization that fits your needs and style.

LABELED SECTIONS

EMERGENCY

❑ Phone numbers and instructions.

❑ Medical information for children, pets, and others in the household.

❑ Identification of children: photographs, Social Security numbers, signatures, and/or thumbprints.

❑ Photocopies of legal information you carry in your purse or briefcase, such as driver's license, credit cards, and medical insurance cards. Replacement will be easier in the event of loss.

❑ Location of extra keys.

DOCUMENTS – FINANCIAL AND PERSONAL

☐ Tax returns (including all schedules): federal, state, local.

☐ Income statements.

☐ Investments: stocks, bonds, mutual funds, other.

☐ Banking: checking, savings, CDs, custodial and children's accounts, credit union.

☐ Insurance: health, life, disability, homeowners or renters (including any valuables riders), vehicle, personal property, umbrella, commercial.

☐ Loans: mortgage, automobile, credit card, personal notes, bank loans, past applications.

☐ Ownership: deeds, titles, inheritance, gift documentation.

☐ Retirement: IRA, Benefit Statements, Statements of Account (401(k), 403(b), profit sharing).

☐ Marriage license, previous divorce decree and settlement, and Prenuptial Agreement.

☐ Wills, trusts, and Power of Attorney.

☐ Journals, daily/weekly organizers, and calendars.

☐ Marital history.
APPENDIX – Money Matters: Financial Puzzle Pieces

FINANCIAL FORMS AND INVENTORIES

☐ Statement of Net Worth.
APPENDIX – Money Matters: Financial Puzzle Pieces
Exhibits: Statement Of Net Worth

☐ Monthly budget.
APPENDIX – Money Matters: Monthly Budget

☐ Appraisals: residence, commercial property, businesses, material property.

☐ Itemized lists of household furnishings and collections with accompanying photographs and receipts.

BILLS AND RECEIPTS

☐ Received and paid according to category.
PART IX - in Chapter 30: "Record Keeping / Filing System"

LAWSUIT DOCUMENTS AND COMMUNICATIONS

☐ All copies sent to and received from lawyers and others involved with the case, organized by date.

PROGRESS JOURNAL

☐ Written record of what is discussed or resolved with your lawyer and other professionals on the phone or at meetings, including specific times and dates.

☐ Hearing dates and court dates with purpose of each and results.

☐ Updated list of tasks that have been completed and are to be completed by yourself, your lawyer, and other professionals.

☐ Tape recordings, made for your personal use, of dialogue with those working on the case that provide an accurate record of issues discussed and time spent.
APPENDIX – Customizing Guide

6

FINANCIAL AND PERSONAL DOCUMENTS

Use the *Financial Puzzle Pieces* Organizer in the Appendix to stay focused.

JOINT ACCOUNT ALERT
Protect your financial well-being.

BANK ACCOUNTS

When a marriage is unraveling, it is not uncommon to have to take measures to protect your financial well-being. Once money is removed from an account, it may be impossible to retrieve. If there is a chance your spouse will empty a joint account, you can request that the bank freeze the account so no funds can be removed. Some banks, however, will not freeze a joint account at the request of only one party. With the commencement of legal action, a restraining order can be placed on bank accounts, but it might be too late by then.

If you are a nonmoneyed spouse who will have legal fees to pay, you are in a particularly vulnerable position. It may be in your best interest to withdraw all or some of the funds from a joint account as a loan, and put them in a safe place where your spouse does not have access. If you decide to do so, describe in writing your need to "cover anticipated legal expenses." Include the bank's name, account number, withdrawal date, and the amount of money removed. This written disclosure will have no legal standing, but it will be some evidence of your positive intent to work toward a settlement. Disclose in your Statement of Net Worth the amount remaining after paying bills. Confer with your attorney about the best action for you to take for your circumstances.

PART III - in Chapter 6: "Statement Of Net Worth"
PART IV - in Chapter 11: "Situations In Which It Is Important To Commence Legal Action"
APPENDIX – Customizing Guide

CREDIT CARDS
CLOSING ACCOUNTS

To help protect yourself financially, it might be best to close all joint credit card accounts. Before doing so, establish credit in your name. Write a letter to each credit card company requesting that accounts be closed immediately. Include account numbers, card member names, and Social Security numbers. If your spouse is a primary signer, include that he or she does not have your permission to reestablish the account using either your name or your credit history. Either fax or e-mail a copy of the letter and send another copy via certified mail with return receipt requested.

You may need to borrow on credit cards to cover your anticipated legal fees or other living expenses and fear your spouse plans to cancel the accounts. Borrowing the money before the legal action formally starts means the debt incurred is likely to be considered marital debt and divided between you and your spouse. Money borrowed following the commencement of the legal action is viewed as a separate debt you incurred. You will need to prove that the loan should be considered marital debt based upon the purpose for which the funds were used.

APPLYING FOR CREDIT

Having a good credit history and sufficient income make the task of applying for credit fairly easy. If you have a bad credit rating or no recorded credit history, you will need to reestablish or establish a credit rating and provide evidence of your ability to pay. If you do not have a checking account in your name, open one and apply for a credit card through the bank. A local store where you are known is an option for securing a card. You will need some evidence of employment, support payments, or assets. Once you have been issued a credit card, use it wisely and pay the balances promptly. Over time, you can build a good credit rating that will qualify you for additional credit accounts.

CREDIT COUNSELING

If your credit card debt is beyond your ability to manage, consider seeking credit counseling to help analyze your financial situation and manage the debt. However, do not transfer debt in joint names into an obligation in your name alone, even if the interest rate is attractive. Two organizations offering free or low-cost counseling services are Consumer Credit Counseling Service (CCCS) at (800) 388-2227 or *www.nfcc.org* and Debt Counselors of America at *www.dca.org*.

EQUITY CREDIT LINES

If divorce is not yet apparent, but you fear it is a possibility, do not agree to sign for a home equity loan. If you already have an equity line of credit and divorce is evident, contact the lender of the credit line to find out how to either close or freeze the account. Put the request and necessary information in a letter. After faxing a copy for immediate consideration, send another copy via certified mail with return receipt requested. If you cannot close an equity line of credit on your bank account or home equity loan, you may want to consider taking the balance of the available funds and depositing it into a savings account. This would provide you with the security of having money at your disposal in the event support or credit cards are cut off. It will also ensure that your spouse does not take the funds and deprive you of any liquid assets.

SAFETY DEPOSIT BOXES

If there is reason to believe your spouse would empty the contents of a safety deposit box, you might want to put the contents in a safe place until a settlement is finalized. If this is an action you need to take to safeguard your property and peace of mind, prepare a detailed written survey of the contents you remove. Include your reasons for taking this step and your intent at working toward a fair property settlement. Date and sign the document. You may want to supplement this written survey with photographs.

If removing the contents is too inflammatory or not suitable for your situation, make copies of critical documents you cannot remove. Later, if those papers disappear or are altered, you have evidence to use as leverage in your case. Follow the same procedure of surveying and photographing the contents and compiling the inventory. Inspect the contents periodically. Banks keep records of activity connected with safety deposit boxes that can be made available to you upon request.

APPENDIX – Customizing Guide

Once legal divorce action is started, the Court can issue a restraining order preventing either spouse from having access to a safety deposit box and, in this manner, protect the contents. Consult with your attorney and carefully consider the best action for your situation.

INVESTMENTS

Selling investments and transferring the money out of joint accounts can be done quickly via the phone or Internet. Take action to protect your interests. In situations of heightened distrust, freezing the accounts, including all account-related privileges such as drafting loans, may be necessary. Freezing investments, however, can have some serious drawbacks. You will be prevented from disposing of these assets if the need were to arise.

It might be more advantageous for you and your spouse to agree that both of you must authorize any transactions. In addition to speaking with your broker, send a letter with both signatures, describing the mutually agreed upon arrangement to restrict access to accounts. Fax one copy, immediately, and send another copy by certified mail return receipt requested.

Insist that your broker attach a notation to the online file, showing all who have access to it, that the account has either been frozen or requires the authorization of both parties for any movement of funds. If selling investments is a possibility, consult your accountant to become informed about how the tax consequences will affect your marriage's financial picture.

MATERIAL POSSESSIONS

Depending on your circumstances, you might want to remove some items for safekeeping, such as rare coins, jewelry, antiques, and stamp and other collections. Preparing a written record, accompanied by photographs, describing the items removed and your intent to keep them in a safe place until the settlement is finalized may help prevent adverse reaction. Your document will not have legal value, but it may indicate your good faith at working toward a fair resolution of property matters.

FINANCIAL RECORDS

Gather information; negotiate with muscle.

Your first task is to gain access to documents and records that relate to the financial value of your marriage. Some may not be readily accessible. Suggestions on how to try to uncover hard-to-find or hidden evidence will be addressed in the following chapter. Collecting information can educate you about known assets, business contacts, and possibly, the existence and location of hidden assets. Later chapters will help you organize the data so you can present it to your attorney in a cost-effective manner.

PART III - in Chapter 7: "Uncovering Hidden Assets"
PART VI - in Chapter 20: "First Meeting: Preparation / Questions"
Chapter 22: Working With Your Lawyer

BANK ACCOUNTS

Photocopy bank statements and both sides of checks for a minimum of one year, as well as savings account passbooks and IRA statements. Copy onto a diskette or CD banking records kept on the computer. Reviewing canceled checks and bank statements can reveal where money is going and how much it costs to live. Organizing expenses according to what they cover can help you design a proposed monthly budget, which you will need for support issues.

PART III - in Chapter 7: "Uncovering Hidden Assets"
APPENDIX – Money Matters: Monthly Budget

INCOME TAX RETURNS

Photocopy income tax returns or print copies from the computer for at least the most recent three to five years. Make copies of any documentation you find in your tax file, such as W-2 Forms, 1099 Forms, 1098 Forms, K-1s, and IRA statements. If you do not have access to tax records or fear the copies your spouse provided have been falsified, either contact the person you paid to prepare your returns or the Internal Revenue Service. Obtain a Request for Copy or Transcript of Tax Form (Form 4506) by calling (800) TAX FORM (829-3676) or downloading the form from *www.irs.gov*. Follow the instructions and mail it to the IRS. A fee is required for each tax year. Request a "copy" if a printout of the figures is all you need. If, however, you need evidence of who signed a tax return, be sure to request a "transcript." For married filed jointly, copies can be sent to either spouse with only one signature. Allow six to eight weeks to receive the copies by mail.

Tax returns give you and your legal and financial advisors a place to start by providing a brief review of the family finances. First, be sure all past taxes owed have been paid. Unpaid taxes and the interest due may be viewed as a marital debt. Work with your attorney on how best to negotiate an agreement to pay any debt. Have tax returns from earlier in the marriage if you had income that you later gave up to raise a family. If you brought substantial wealth into the marriage, it is helpful to have copies of income tax returns from before the marriage, documenting some of that wealth. Most states legally view assets brought to the marriage as separate property. About two-thirds of the states recognize that with the dissolution of a marriage, separate property goes with the spouse who owns it, unless it has been comingled with marital property. New York and New Jersey are among these states. In about one-third of the states, separate property is allowed to be divided at the end of a marriage. Examples of these states are Connecticut and Massachusetts.

PART III - in Chapter 7: "Uncovering Hidden Assets"
PART V - in Chapter 13: "Marital And Nonmarital Property"
APPENDIX – Customizing Guide

LOAN APPLICATIONS

Loan applications have value because when people are applying for loans, they usually do not underestimate their financial resources. The Court may take a loan application seriously; it is a sworn financial statement with the charge of perjury for falsifying information. If you are unable to locate a loan application, the lending institution might allow you to photocopy what you need. Have copies of personal notes of money owed by or due to either you or your spouse.

PART III - in Chapter 7: "Uncovering Hidden Assets"

CREDIT CARD STATEMENTS AND RECEIPTS

Credit card statements and receipts often present a picture of a family's lifestyle and standard of living, as well as clarify the extent of the marital liability and the possible dissipation of marital assets by a spouse. Statements can also contain evidence useful in negotiations, such as unusual purchases, a spouse's whereabouts, or personal expenses deducted as business expenditures. Try to obtain a year-end summary that categorizes the annual expenses.

INVESTMENT PORTFOLIOS

If records for your investment portfolio are incomplete, your financial advisor or broker may be able to help you. Be aware of any recent sales or purchases.

LIFE AND DISABILITY INSURANCE POLICIES

Verify beneficiaries of life insurance policies and be sure all insurance policy premiums are paid to date. Request that the insurance company provide you with the cash values. Notify your attorney if payments have lapsed so appropriate action can be taken to try to maintain the policies. Try to determine whether any other life insurance policies have been taken out, and if so, who the beneficiaries are.

TITLES AND DEEDS

Confirm that no property has been transferred such as vehicles, a vacation home, land, or commercial property.

PART III - in Chapter 7: "Uncovering Hidden Assets: Public Records"

MATERIAL POSSESSIONS

Make a record of all your material possessions and include monetary values. Supplement the inventory with photos, videos, and sales slips for expensive items.

RETIREMENT INFORMATION

Photocopy statements for all individual (IRA) and employer-sponsored retirement plans, as well as veteran's benefits. The value of defined contribution plans, such as profit sharing plans, is determined by the amount the employee or employer or both have contributed as shown on the Statement of Account. If the retirement plan is a defined benefit plan where the value is determined by calculating the average pay for a number of years before the actual date of retirement and factoring in the total number of years employed, locate the Benefit Statement. With a professional analysis of the defined benefit plan, you will be able to make an informed decision about the value of this marital asset and your portion of it.

PRIVATE BUSINESS

It can be difficult to obtain essential information about a business if you are not actively involved in running it. Photocopy any records you can, such as telephone bills, bank statements, and both sides of canceled checks. Copy available business records from the computer onto a diskette or CD. Business data about operating expenses, income, and names of vendors might lead to learning more about the volume of business. If your spouse is the sole proprietor of a business or sole owner of a limited liability company (LLC), his or her Social Security number also serves as the business identification number. Business income and expenses are recorded on Schedule C of the personal federal tax return. If possible, obtain tax returns for partnerships or corporations.

PART III - in Chapter 7: "Uncovering Hidden Assets"

STATEMENT OF NET WORTH

You will use some of the documentation you gather to fill out a Statement of Net Worth, which is a summary of your expenses, income, assets, and liabilities. It is usually a long, in-depth form, but unless you and your spouse agree on just about everything, the attorneys need you to provide the financial facts about the marital worth. Your lawyer is likely to provide a form with which he or she is comfortable. Start organizing data early; filling out a Statement of Net Worth takes time. If you are unsure about the value of an item use "TBD" (to be determined) or "EST" (estimate). For accounts that have been wiped out, state the amount and write "wrongfully removed." State this fact again under "Other Data" or "Other Relevant Information."

APPENDIX – Money Matters: Financial Puzzle Pieces
  Customizing Guide
    Exhibits: Statement Of Net Worth

PROPOSED BUDGET

You need to know what it costs to live and the amount of money coming in to cover your expenses. Income may be in the form of employment checks, dividends and interest, unemployment checks, disability, Social Security, lottery winnings, and other sources. If there is income from marital assets or investments, such as rental property or mutual funds, enter the percent that reflects your portion of ownership. Expenses are in the form of everyday items, such as food and housing, as well as unanticipated items due to emergencies, like house repairs or appliance replacement. List non-regular expenditures, for example, insurance, property taxes, medical, and dental. Part of a workable budget needs to account for unexpected expenses, so include costs you anticipate in the near future, like home and automobile repairs, orthodontia, and other unusual expenses. Divide the total sum of these non-regular expenditures and unusual costs by twelve months, so they can be worked into your monthly budget.

By reviewing all sources of monthly income and bills, you will clarify your expenses and how much money you need to cover them. Examine expense information you have available for the past year, such as canceled checks, bank statements, credit card statements, cash receipts, paid bills, and loan statements. To create a more accurate financial picture, go back as far as twenty-four months to identify large unanticipated expenditures. Also allow for postmarital changes in expenses, such as the high cost of individual health insurance. If you anticipate being responsible for purchasing your own medical insurance, factor this into your budget and into your negotiations. You do not want to underestimate either your budget or your future needs.

The *Monthly Budget* Organizer in the Appendix can help you sort out your data. Costs necessary to maintain the family's lifestyle, like household and automobile costs, are commonly referred to as "indirect expenses." "Direct expenses" cover specific needs of individual family members, such as tuition, room and board, lessons, children's clothing, and so on. If child support is an issue, child-related costs need to be separated out. Start keeping an up-to-date record of your current expenses to help prepare yourself and your lawyer for negotiations.

PART IX - in Chapter 30: "Record Keeping / Filing System"
APPENDIX – Money Matters: Monthly Budget

PERSONAL RECORDS

Personal records turned evidence can affect your position.

Please note: Confer with an attorney about how to stay within the law while gathering data.

JOURNALS / CALENDARS

Personal journals can influence your bargaining position, especially in child custody disputes. The contents can be used for leverage or, possibly, as evidence. Business journals can have the same impact, because they may reveal a business schedule keeping a parent away often or for long duration. Home and business calendars and organizers, filled with commitments that take a parent away from home or take up too much time, can reflect on appropriateness as a primary custodial parent.

E-MAILS

Making copies of accessible e-mail addresses and communications to or from your spouse or his or her business might lead to hidden assets and to business contacts or improve your negotiating leverage in some way.

TELEPHONE MESSAGE MACHINES

Leave nothing but the most basic, businesslike messages on the answering machine for your spouse such as, *Please call regarding....* Make a copy of messages your spouse leaves for you that might affect your case, such as evidence of abusive language, signs of addiction, or lack of care for the children. It might also be helpful to copy pertinent incoming messages left for your spouse if he or she is still living in the same residence. The information collected might lead to hidden assets or be valuable in improving your negotiating leverage. Store a back up of any taped messages in a safe location.

HOME VIDEOS

Home videos can capture powerful evidence. Inappropriate or neglectful behavior with children may reflect an attitude toward or lack of aptitude for parenting. Addictive and abusive behavior comes across vividly on video. Since home videos do not usually involve hidden cameras and people are aware of the taping, the visual and, possibly, the audio may be acceptable as evidence in New York State. To be sure you are in compliance with the law, consult your attorney.

APPENDIX – Customizing Guide

PRESCRIPTIONS / MEDICAL RECORDS

Medical records can reveal health conditions that limit a spouse's ability to be self-supporting or to pay maintenance. Evidence of or the implication of addiction may impact custody decisions. With child custody issues, medical and mental health records may be subpoenaed for the Judge to read in his or her chambers and, possibly, be presented in Court.

EMPLOYMENT PERSONNEL FILE

Personnel files can be central in contested child custody cases. Information about job performance, treatment for substance abuse, time away on business trips, and promotion possibilities might influence the Court's view of a parent's suitability as the primary custodial parent.

TELEPHONE RECORDS

Telephone records may help locate hidden assets or reveal the dissipation of marital assets. Out-of-area numbers are automatically itemized on your monthly bill. For a few dollars extra a month, you can have the telephone company list all local calls. Telephone records are stored and available for about four to five months, and you can request a copy of numbers called during the past billing periods.
APPENDIX – Customizing Guide

TAPE-RECORDED CONVERSATIONS

Watch what you say. Admit to nothing; promise nothing. Possibly, voice activated or telephone taping devices are being used to capture statements that could empower your spouse in negotiations. Remember, information is being collected and you and your spouse probably have competitive interests. If you are the one doing the taping, even if you do not use the tape as evidence or admit to having dialogue on tape, it may add to your confidence in negotiations. You can subtly bring up information at appropriate times by responding to your spouse during negotiations, *You know you told me differently when we spoke about this on* _date_.

Taped conversations can be used as evidence in New York State, as long as you are a participant in the conversation or have the approval of the other person being taped. The most common and effective use of information caught on tape is its leverage value in negotiations. Tactfully using taped information may have the effect of jarring the opposition into being more amenable to settling. Confer with your attorney about your specific circumstances. Become fully knowledgeable about laws regulating taping others without their permission and comply with the law.

Taping exchanges for personal use can provide a reality check, giving you feedback about what you are handling well and what to improve. Listening to yourself in taped dialogue can help you monitor your emotional progress and remind you to give yourself credit for hard work. Tapes help you track the issues you are covering and scrutinize your success at keeping negotiations moving without inflaming the situation.
APPENDIX – Customizing Guide

7

FINDING AND USING INFORMATION

Please note: As you plan to search for hard-to-find assets, confer
with an attorney about the legality of your approach and actions.

INVESTIGATING CREDIT
Your spouse's debt could be viewed as marital debt.

In the early stages of gathering documentation, it is a good idea to check credit card balances of all accounts. You want to have a clear understanding of the marital debt and see if there are debts about which you are unaware. You also want to be sure that what has been reported is accurate. If you know all the credit cards issued to you and your spouse, you can obtain current data about your liability for each account by calling the Customer Service 800 number on the back of each card or on the billing statements.

Your spouse's credit card debt is likely to be viewed as marital debt, unless you can prove the charges were solely for his or her enjoyment or a result of wastefulness. The burden of proof will rest with you. If the debt is not clearly marital or separate, it becomes a bargaining item in negotiations. A dividing line between marital debt and each spouse's separate debt is often established with the commencement of legal action.
PART IV - in Chapter 11: "Situations In Which It Is Important To Commence Legal Action"
PART V - in Chapter 13: "Marital And Nonmarital Property"
APPENDIX – Customizing Guide

If a credit account is in your name with your spouse as an authorized user, you can have the lending institution remove his or her authorized signature by requesting it in writing. Consider closing all joint accounts to avoid future charges made by your spouse for which you will be held responsible by the lending institution. If you are an authorized user of your spouse's credit card accounts, you can use them, but there may be no recorded credit history for you in your name. If you have no credit history, you will have to prove your ability to pay in order to obtain credit in your own name.
PART III - in Chapter 6: "Credit Cards"

It is important to know the status of each of your credit ratings in case one or both of you are required to refinance property as a result of the divorce. If debt on a joint account is not paid, your credit rating will suffer, despite which spouse incurred the debt. To obtain a credit report for yourself and your spouse contact one of the credit reporting agencies:

◆ Experian, P.O. Box 2002, Allen, TX 75013
(888) 397-3742
www.experian.com
◆ Trans Union Consumer Disclosure Center, P.O. Box 1000, Chester, PA 19022
(800) 888-4213 / (800) 916-8800
www.transunion.com
◆ Equifax, P.O. Box 105873, Atlanta, GA 30348
(800) 997-2493 / (800) 685-1111
www.equifax.com

Send the required information via mail or by following the online instructions.
☐ Legal names, including Jr. or Sr. and middle initial.
☐ Social Security numbers and dates of birth.
☐ Present addresses and zip codes.
☐ Previous addresses and zip codes, if either of you moved within past five years.
☐ Signatures.
☐ Copies of two recent utility bills or copies of driver's licenses to verify present addresses.

Seek help if your spouse will not cooperate or sign the request form to secure a credit report and you think he or she is hiding something. There are businesses that can secure your credit reports without the other spouse's permission. Look in the local Yellow Pages; call numbers that appear to offer this service; ask questions until you find the necessary contact. Be prepared to pay a fee; it will be greater than if you had been able to obtain the report through traditional methods. In New York State, if divorce action has commenced, a private investigator is legally allowed to obtain the credit report of your spouse without his or her permission. In the past, credit bureaus routinely released this information, but they have tightened up for security reasons. Remember, this is information about you and your marital debt that can significantly effect the settlement and your future.

UNCOVERING HIDDEN ASSETS
Do not deceive yourself into believing....

WAYS ASSETS ARE HIDDEN
Do not deceive yourself into believing your spouse will act rationally or fairly regarding the division of the assets. Your spouse may have been hiding assets for a long time. A spouse planning to leave often begins hiding assets before the issue of divorce is brought into the open. Assets can be hidden by:
◆ Inflating expense accounts.
◆ Deferring salary increases or bonuses.
◆ Having bank accounts in other names or in other countries.
◆ Selling assets but the money does not show up in a marital account.

- Incurring liabilities such as a debt to a friend or a business.
- Making secret purchases such as real estate, collectibles, or luxury items.
- Not recording as business income cash payments or "in kind" compensation, which is something of value exchanged for services rendered.

Legal discovery tools can be used to try to uncover hidden assets. For example, employers can be required to supply information about salary, bonuses, or commission that may have been intentionally deferred to reduce a spouse's income. To decide whether to subpoena sources, analyze the available documentation and try to figure out where to look for what is missing.

TAKE ACTION

Take practical steps to uncover hidden assets. Analyze accounts; compare recent activity with past activity. Look for sources of income or causes for growing marital debt. Keep a detailed account of your spouse's transactions, such as assets sold or liabilities incurred and large purchases bought with cash.

BANK ACCOUNTS

The signatures and places of deposit shown on checks can be valuable leads. Look for unexplained deposits and withdrawals. Try to determine where the money came from and where it went. An unknown deposit of significant size might indicate something has been sold. Regular deposits might point to other sources of income, such as rent from commercial property, about which you are unaware. Unknown purchases might mean money is being hidden in some way. Be sure you have all of the canceled checks for an account by matching them with the bank statements.

Watch accounts closely. Possibly, the savings are being withdrawn or used for current expenses while new income is being diverted elsewhere. Check to see if a custodial account has been opened in the name of a child, or if there is unusual activity in existing custodial accounts. If you fear money is being hidden in a safety deposit box or in bank accounts in other names, document your reasoning so you have a record.

INCOME TAX RETURNS

Careful review of tax returns may reveal income or interest and dividends from unknown sources. If there are tax returns for a partnership or a closely held corporation of which your spouse is a major shareholder, seek expert assistance in examining the returns for possible ways that profit is being hidden or cash accessed.

LOANS

Loan applications filled out during the past few years might quote relatively high values for assets that are now being undervalued in your spouse's Statement of Net Worth. When people apply for loans, they usually do not underestimate their financial resources. Review of these applications might also lead to assets about which you had no previous knowledge.

Try to confirm the amount of money that has been loaned to or borrowed from others. Be especially aware of recent debts or your spouse's claims of owing money to a friend or relative. This adds to the marital debt and may be a way of hiding money. If you have already discussed divorce, or you fear it is a possibility, it might be in your best interest to commence legal action to establish a legal dividing line between the marital and separate debt. Also, once a Summons is filed, you can arrange to have restraining orders served on financial institutions and on private businesses to freeze assets.

PART IV - in Chapter 11: "Situations In Which It Is Important To Commence Legal Action"
APPENDIX – Customizing Guide
            Exhibits: Summons With Notice

RETIREMENT PLANS

If your spouse will not share information about the company retirement plan, try to locate a company handbook or ask a co-employee for a copy. It is unlikely that your spouse's employer or the company's Human Relations Department will share information with anyone other than the employee.

PART V - in Chapter 15: "Pension"

BUSINESSES

If you have access to private business records, compare present activity to the previous year. Be alert to exaggerated expenses, cash payments, large inventory changes, loans to the business, sudden payment of debts, and a decrease in reported volume of orders or contracts. Payment of debts to out-of-state creditors, who are not readily available for deposition, could be a sign of phony debts. Review the business checking account. You may find cancelled checks written to cover expenses or purchases of property about which you were unaware. Possibly, personal expenses have been recorded as business expenditures.

Examine the telephone records for leads to vendors and volume of business. Long distance calls are itemized on the monthly bill. Telephone records are kept in the computer for a few months and then stored for several weeks in some form. You can request an itemized list of local calls for past billing periods. If possible, collect numbers and names left on the message machine and e-mail communications.

Some of the phone numbers may be those of other companies. You might want to use the Dun and Bradstreet's site at *www.dnb.com* to plug in the numbers to see if they belong to business entities. At the site click "Search Options" under "Business Search." Once you find a company connection, search the public records at your County Clerk's Office to learn more about it.

PART III - in Chapter 7: "Uncovering Hidden Assets: Public Records"

Each connection could lead to a source of income or related business owned by your spouse about which you had no previous knowledge. You may need to include professionals certified in business valuation as part of your legal team. It might be worthwhile to hire a forensic accountant or certified fraud examiner (CFE), or possibly, a private investigator to look for hidden cash and financial manipulation. Consult with an attorney to be sure you stay within the law while collecting data.

PART IV - in Chapter 11: "Situations In Which It Is Important To Commence Legal Action"
            in Chapter 11: "Discovery Stage"
APPENDIX – Customizing Guide

PUBLIC RECORDS

Searching the public records at your County Clerk's Office is not difficult. If you suspect your spouse may have established a business entity, such as a corporation or sole proprietorship, and you can come close to guessing its name, you may be able to locate specific information in the county records. Most offices are staffed with helpful personnel or equipped with user-friendly computer systems and clear instructions.

A simple way to do a limited search for a business entity is to use a couple of Web sites. Start with Dun and Bradstreet's site at *www.dnb.com*. Enter names or words you think could be part of the company name. Keywords such as "construction," "beauty," or "consulting" will connect you with a list of businesses in those categories. Each entry shows the name of the company, address, and telephone number. The site lists business entities in the United States and in foreign countries. Use the same technique to search for corporations, limited liability partnerships (LLP), and limited liability companies (LLC) at the New York State Division of Corporations site at *http://www.dos.state.ny.us/*. Available information includes current company name, date of organization, county location, service of process address, current status of activity, and sometimes, the name of an officer.

If you believe your spouse may own real estate about which you have not been informed, search the land records at your County Clerk's Office. Real property in your county is on record by the owner's name. You can also search by address. Review deeds and mortgages for purchase dates and liens. Be sure there have been no transfers of property about which you are unaware. If you think your spouse owns real property in another county, call the county or town Tax Assessor's Office. Ask the person who answers the phone to conduct a search by name; it is a fast and simple way to gather information.

UCC (Uniform Commercial Code) records are indexed under the debtor's name. Financial institutions file UCC statements when they make loans. Documenting the asset put up as collateral prevents it from being used repeatedly as security. UCCs are filed with your County Clerk's Office and with the New York State Department of State. Use your spouse's name to search UCC records; they may provide valuable data on marital assets. Since behind every UCC record there is a credit application, your search may lead to unknown bank accounts and may further clarify debts.

TACKLE HEAD ON
Be careful with whom you share information. The opposition may employ an operative such as a private investigator to befriend you. You do not want to unknowingly reveal your strategy or what you have discovered about marital assets. Be prepared to legally protect yourself from accusations by your spouse that you have hidden assets. Keep accurate records and documents. Keep a detailed, dated record of how money or assets you have removed are being used to cover the costs of maintaining the family's lifestyle or for legal expenses.

You may be struggling with the desire to maintain your ethical standards while feeling an urgency to take certain steps to safeguard your well-being. Situations in which there is withholding of information, imbalance of power, or betrayal can elicit and, possibly, demand behavior that is out of character. You may simply have to give yourself permission to act out of character in order to protect yourself and your future. For example, under normal circumstances you might never consider reading or photocopying your spouse's personal journal or looking through the paper recycle bin or trash for information. If this evidence is still in the house, most likely the legal interpretation is that it is marital. If so, you have a right to it. Confer with your lawyer about what actions are legal for your circumstances. If the chance to gather evidence slips away, you add to the strength of the opposition. Whatever is in your possession can empower you. Later, you can decide whether or how to use what you have gathered.

If you feel the need to hire the services of a licensed private investigator, try to get a reference from a reputable source. Think through what you need and what you want to accomplish. Prepare for the interview. Be able to concisely describe your situation; ask how the investigator would obtain the desired results, the amount of time needed, and the cost.

BE FOCUSED AND TACTFUL

Timing when to reveal what you know about hidden assets can be critical to your success. If your spouse wants to negotiate, the timely acknowledgment of your awareness of hidden assets could encourage a faster settlement. Holding back some information and using it selectively may strengthen your bargaining position. If your spouse has no interest in negotiating, because he or she realizes the legal process of discovery is unlikely to uncover all the hidden assets, you will have to skillfully use what you know as the process unfolds. Let your spouse be deluded into thinking he or she holds the winning cards while you work with your attorney to design deposition questions that focus on unreported income and hard to find assets. If information about hidden assets is either revealed in the questions or surfaces due to skillful questioning, your spouse may become concerned and be more receptive to settling.

Deposition questions focus on areas where there are unresolved issues such as grounds, property, support, and custody. Some examples of questions focusing on uncovering hidden assets are:

➥ *Your business has shown a significant profit for three of the prior four tax years. To what do you attribute that success?*
➥ *During the most recent tax year, the business activity of your sole proprietorship appears to have greatly diminished. What economic factors seem to be causing this downward turn in income?*
➥ *Has there been any income not included on your tax returns for _year_ ?*
➥ *Have you transferred any assets to a third party during the last two years?*
➥ *Do you have any outstanding loans made to friends, family, or other third parties? If so, describe to whom, the amount, and the date of the loan.*

If your spouse has not been cooperative and forthcoming with documents and information about marital assets, it is unlikely he or she will answer deposition questions informatively or truthfully. The answers are given under oath and recorded by a court reporter; you may be able to use these responses to your benefit in the future. It can be valuable to have answers on record, especially if you know or think all income has not been reported, and you can possibly produce evidence that contradicts your spouse's sworn testimony.

PART IV - in Chapter 11: "Discovery Stage"
APPENDIX – Customizing Guide
      Mind Matters: Deposition Primer

COMPILING YOUR MARITAL HISTORY

Highlight your contributions to the economic value of the marriage.

The purpose of compiling your marital history is to highlight your contributions to the economic value of the marriage. The Court measures the marriage in dollars and cents and determines your portion.

ASSETS

Most states legally consider separate property to be assets brought to the marriage, such as material property, savings, degrees, and professional licenses, as well as any inheritances, gifts given to one spouse, and compensation from personal injury or disability settlements or lawsuits received during the marriage. About two-thirds of these states recognize that at the end of the marriage the separate property goes with the spouse who owns it, unless it has been comingled with marital property. A few examples of these states are New York, New Jersey, Pennsylvania, Maryland, and Maine. Clearly describe your separate property; support your statements with documentation. You need to prove to the Court that your separate property is not marital and, therefore, is not divisible.

Record in your marital history what you gave up to raise a family, such as employment positions, salary, and a career including a pension, health insurance, and other benefits. Back this up with an employment record if it indicates that you had a promising future. Be detailed about your role in helping to increase the value of assets your spouse brought to the marriage. These enhanced assets or their active appreciation might be interpreted as marital property due to your contribution. If your in-laws gifted to you and your spouse money to buy your home, make that clear so it will not be represented as a loan by your spouse and interpreted as a marital liability. Possibly among your papers, there is a copy of a gift letter submitted to the mortgage company or bank holding your mortgage. If so, remove it or make a copy before it disappears.
PART V - in Chapter 13: "Marital and Nonmarital Property"
APPENDIX – Customizing Guide

HOW YOU ADVANCED SPOUSE'S CAREER

Detail how you contributed to advancing your spouse's career and professional reputation and, thereby, enhanced his or her earning power. Describe how you:
- ❑ Worked to put him or her through school.
- ❑ Entertained business associates and clients.
- ❑ Labored by his or her side building a business and goodwill.
- ❑ Assumed primary responsibility for the children and household, so your spouse could devote time and energy to his or her career.

ROLE AS A PARENT

If child custody is an issue, detail your positive role as a parent and your involvement in your children's activities and interests. If you have been the primary caregiver, highlight that fact. Be prepared to support your statements with convincing testimonials

from teachers, therapists, religious instructors, and neighbors providing evidence that
you are the most appropriate custodial parent. Problems of spousal addiction, abuse,
or unusual behavior that have affected the children's well-being should be documented.
Describe and document the other parent's frequent absences from home for business or
other reasons or insufficient support of the children, if either exists.

PART V - in Chapter 16: "Contested Custody"
APPENDIX – Customizing Guide

POWER OF INFORMATION

Gathering data about the monetary value of the marriage and the suitability of either
parent as a primary custodial caregiver is the nuts and bolts of the process. The quantity
and caliber of evidence you collect will impact your bargaining position, amount of
time and money spent, fairness of your settlement agreement, and ultimately, the
quality of your life.

PART IV – LEGAL PROCESS AND TERMS

Part IV uses New York specific information to create a legal model. It can be customized for any state by substituting home state legal details such as residency requirements, grounds, titles or names of specific forms. Use the *Customizing Guide* in the Appendix.

8 SOME LEGAL BASICS
   Legal Reality
   Requirements For Filing
      Residency
      Jurisdiction
      Legal Grounds
   The Three Facets Of A Case
      Grounds
      Child Custody, Support, Visitation
      Assets And Liabilities
   Court Calendar
   Laws Change

9 FAMILY COURT
   Basic Function
   How Family Court Can Help You
      Order Of Protection
      Child And Spousal Support
      Child Custody
      Other Child-Related Issues
         Person In Need Of Supervision (PINS)
         Juvenile Delinquency (JD)
         Child Protective Services (CPS)
         Paternity
   Pros And Cons of Taking Action In Family Court
   Procedure

10 LEGAL GROUNDS
   Introduction
   Fault Grounds
      Abandonment For One Or More Years
      Adultery
      Cruel and Inhuman Treatment
      Imprisonment For Three Or More Years
   Separation Agreement
   Annulment

11 STEPS IN THE DIVORCE PROCESS
   Your Approach To The Legal Process
      If Possible, Work Together With Your Spouse
      You Continually Have Choices
      Advantages To Establishing Yourself As The Plaintiff
      Situations In Which It Is Important To Commence Legal Action

48 ·

Basically There Are Two Ways To Attain Your Divorce
   Uncontested Divorce
   Contested Divorce
Three Phases Of The Legal Process
   Pleading Stage
      Summons And Complaint Served
      Answer
      Pendente Lite Motions
      Preliminary Conference
      Motions And Hearings
   Discovery Stage
      Informal Discovery
      Formal Discovery
      Negotiations / Pretrial Conference
   Trial Stage
Handy Clarifications
   Going To Court
   Legal Fees
   Frivolous Actions
   Forensics
   Copy Of Transcript
   Certified Copies

12 PROBLEMS WITH THE LEGAL SYSTEM
Problems
   Legal Reality
   Adversarial System
   Regulation Of Professional Conduct
   Judicial Bias
   Discretion Of Judges
   Perjury
   Awarding Legal Fees
   Children Used As Bargaining Chips
   Law Guardians And Experts
   Temporary Relief
   Enforcement Of Orders
   Client's Right To Be Present At Conferences
   Pressure And Stipulations
Reform: Integrated Domestic Violence Court

8

SOME LEGAL BASICS

LEGAL REALITY

Your case can take on a life of its own.

Once you enter the legal system, your case can take on a life of its own and be provoked and controlled by others. The legal system is cumbersome, crowded, expensive, and impersonal. It does not care how you feel; one of its priorities is to decide cases as expediently as possible. Before commencing legal action, become informed. Educate yourself with reality-based information about what could happen. Learn the terminology, the legal language called "legalese." Most of the divorce procedure is governed by state law with the exception of the federal Family Support Act of 1988, which addresses issues such as interstate custody, medical coverage, taxation, and bankruptcy. Becoming knowledgeable about the process and prepared for what could happen can make an immense difference in the outcome of your case. You will be able to tailor your expectations and focus your energy on what is probable, not improbable.

APPENDIX – Glossary: Terms Of Divorce

REQUIREMENTS FOR FILING

To file for divorce, you must fulfill requirements.

RESIDENCY

You satisfy the New York State residency requirements **if** either spouse has lived in the state for at least one year immediately preceding the beginning of the legal action, **and** either your marriage took place in New York, **or** you lived as a married couple in the state, **or** the grounds for divorce occurred in the state.

If you do not meet any of the previously stated requirements, you can qualify to file for divorce in New York **if**:

- either you or your spouse have lived in the state for two or more years immediately preceding the commencement of legal action, **or**
- grounds for divorce occurred in New York State, and both spouses reside in the state when legal action begins.

APPENDIX – Customizing Guide

JURISDICTION

Filing a "Summons with Notice" or a "Summons with Verified Complaint" and serving a copy on your spouse, the defendant, provides the Court with jurisdiction (the legal authority to make decisions) regarding the dissolution of your marriage.
PART IV - Chapter 11: Steps In The Divorce Process
APPENDIX – Exhibits: Summons With Notice

LEGAL GROUNDS

To sue for divorce you must have grounds, a legal reason recognized by the state.
PART IV - Chapter 10: Legal Grounds

THE THREE FACETS OF A CASE

This nutshell introduction will be expanded upon in subsequent chapters.

GROUNDS

Marriage is a civil contract that must be dissolved legally. New York is a "fault" state in which there has to be a valid legal reason to dissolve the marriage contract. The spouse seeking to dissolve the marriage must prove in a Supreme Court of the State of New York that grounds exist, or the married couple must either agree on grounds or live apart for at least one year in substantial compliance with the terms of a legal Separation Agreement or Judgment of Separation.
PART IV - Chapter 10: Legal Grounds
APPENDIX – Customizing Guide

CHILD CUSTODY, SUPPORT, VISITATION

CUSTODY

If you fear any disagreement over custody, ask lawyers you interview if they handle contested custody cases. Some lawyers do not.

SUPPORT

Support applies to children under the age of twenty-one in New York State; the Court, however, will not entertain custody cases for a child beyond the age of eighteen. In some states support applies only to the age of eighteen. According to New York State law, the parent who has custody or with whom the child lives receives child support payments until the child is twenty-one years, unless the child has been legally emancipated at an earlier age. The guidelines used apply to the first $80,000 of combined parental income. Some judges apply the guidelines to the first $170,000 of income; in some cases it has been applied up to $300,000.

VISITATION

The noncustodial parent has visitation/access rights. Be prepared to develop a schedule appropriate for your family.
PART V - Chapter 16: Child Custody / Support / Visitation
PART VII - in Chapter 26: "Child Support" and "Custody And Visitation / Access"
APPENDIX – Customizing Guide

ASSETS AND LIABILITIES

Start planning immediately:

☐ What is there? The Statement of Net Worth can serve as a road map.
PART III - Chapter 6: Financial And Personal Documents
Chapter 7: Finding And Using Information
APPENDIX – Money Matters: Monthly Budget and Financial Puzzle Pieces
Exhibits: Statement Of Net Worth

☐ What is it worth? Some items, like pensions, are relatively easy to evaluate. Others, such as businesses, medical or legal practices, licenses, degrees, and goodwill, are more difficult. Appraisers, brokers, accountants, and other experts may be necessary.
PART V – Areas Of Concern

☐ Who gets it? Either negotiate or the Judge will decide.
PART V - Chapter 19: Negotiate Like An Expert

☐ Separate property is property you brought to the marriage, inheritances, gifts from someone other than your spouse, and awards resulting from a damage suit or settlement. To legally remain separate property, it must not have been comingled with marital property.
PART V - Chapter 13: Division Of Property
APPENDIX – Customizing Guide

COURT CALENDAR

The process is slow, so prepare yourself.

To prevent delay, be sure your attorney puts your case on the court calendar. Hopefully, all will proceed without too much confusion and be over within a year. New York is making an effort to have uncomplicated divorce cases follow a fast track. Other states are enacting new rules in an effort to expedite matrimonial litigation. One of the Court Rules New Jersey recently enacted provides for the assignment of divorce cases to different tracks, depending on their complexity, such as "priority" or "standard." Nonetheless, the process is slow, so prepare yourself. If both you and your spouse are knowledgeable about the marriage's economic value and can work together on a fair settlement, you can avoid getting bogged down in the slow-moving matrimonial legal system.
PART III – What Is There And Where Is It?
PART IV - Chapters 9, 10, 11 and 12
PART V – Areas Of Concern

LAWS CHANGE

Be alert to changes in your state's statutes.

Laws are continually changing. While new laws are created through legislation, the meaning of established laws can shift over time through judicial interpretation. As cases are decided by individual judges, modifications may occur in how a law is viewed and enforced. As a consumer of legal services, you want to be alert to changes in your state's statutes, especially if judicial interpretation alters the original intent of a law so significantly that it no longer provides the fundamental protection intended.

Clarify your concerns so you know what you need to learn. Local Bar Associations can be a good source of information to help you stay current with recent developments in your jurisdiction.

An example of a New York State law affected by judicial interpretation is the Child Support Standards Act (CSSA) of 1989. At issue is a reduction of the noncustodial parent's basic child support obligation while a child is away attending college. There had been no set rule; instead, judicial discretion was exercised case by case to decide the matter. When a credit had been granted, it was generally limited to the noncustodial parent's contribution to room and board expenses. The Second Department (Kings and Richmond County), however, shifted from precedent with *Reinisch v. Reinisch* by ordering a credit "up to the full amount of his child support obligation" against the amount the noncustodial parent contributed to higher education expenses while the child lived away from home. This meant the noncustodial parent's basic child support obligation was cut one dollar for each dollar he or she contributed to the college costs. In a subsequent decision, *Rohrs v. Rohrs*, it was decided that only fifty percent of the amount the noncustodial parent contributed toward just the cost of room and board is to be the allowable deduction.

PART V - in Chapter 16: "Child Support"

The effect of these decisions is to create a disproportionate financial burden for child-related costs. The "shelter allowance" is one of the biggest parts of the child support payments, and shelter costs basically remain constant when a child is away. The custodial parent is not only paying the household expenses with less support from the other parent but is also contributing to the college expenses with no credit in return. Under these circumstances, the custodial parent does not receive the basic support as set forth in and intended by New York's Child Support Standards Act (CSSA).

There is likely to be continued concern and reaction to this shift in judicial interpretation. Some jurisdictions may base their decisions on the most recent precedent or establish new precedents; others may continue to follow the original precedent of granting credit where appropriate against the noncustodial parent's basic child support for specific college costs. It may be necessary to either pass new legislation to clarify the credit entitlement or rely on appellate rulings to clarify the Court's discretionary role in this matter.

9

FAMILY COURT

BASIC FUNCTION

Get help with family issues in the Family Court.

The New York Supreme Court and Family Court have some different functions.
The Supreme Court has the authority to divide marital property and grant divorces,
separations, and annulments. The Family Court has none of these powers. Both the
Supreme Court and Family Court have the authority to decide custody, support and
visitation, and to issue Orders of Protection. In addition, the Family Court addresses
matters concerning juvenile delinquency and PINS (persons in need of supervision).
You can get help in the Family Court without having to first file for divorce.
APPENDIX – Customizing Guide

HOW FAMILY COURT CAN HELP YOU

Resolve issues of safety, support, and custody.

ORDER OF PROTECTION

You can obtain an Order of Protection from the Family Court if you or your children
are being abused or harassed **and** you:
- are legally married to, legally separated from, or divorced from the abuser, **or**
- have never been married, but the abuser is the parent of one or more of your
  children.

The Family Court also has jurisdiction over Orders of Protection against other family
members. A temporary Order of Protection can be obtained within a few hours in an
emergency. Include in your request a list of any expenses for medical care, property
damage, and lost income resulting from the abuse for which you want the Court's help.
In New York, you can also apply for an Order of Protection at your local criminal
court.
APPENDIX – Customizing Guide

CHILD AND SPOUSAL SUPPORT

If your spouse has deserted the family or cut off support while residing in the household, and you have not yet filed for divorce in the Supreme Court, you can petition the Family Court for the financial support you and your children need. Bring as much of the following financial documentation to Court as you have available and be prepared to use the information to support your claims.

☐ Federal and state tax returns for two years.

☐ Pay stubs for four to six months.

☐ Proof of expenses: housing, clothing, child care, medical, school expenses.

☐ Financial disclosure statement summarizing expenses and income. Call your Family Court to see if it has a specific form.

☐ Identification documents: birth certificates of children, Social Security numbers of all involved, last known address and employer of the other parent, your own photo identification.

APPENDIX – Customizing Guide

CHILD CUSTODY

If you are unable to locate a deserting spouse and you have not yet filed for divorce in the Supreme Court, you can petition the Family Court to decide the issue of custody. The Court will explain the necessary steps to take to try to locate your spouse and serve him or her with the paperwork. You will automatically be awarded custody if your spouse, the "respondent," does not appear, and you can prove that he was served with the petition. At the same time, file a petition requesting that the Family Court order the noncustodial parent pay necessary child and spousal support. It is expedient to file the petitions at the same time. Even if you have been unable to locate your spouse, the child support order will be on record and any financial relief you ultimately receive will be retroactive to the date of filing. If divorce proceedings have started and the issues of custody and/or support have been raised in the pleadings, custody and support issues are to be decided in the Supreme Court.

PART IV - in Chapter 11: "Pleading Stage: Pendente Lite Motions"

OTHER CHILD-RELATED ISSUES

PERSON IN NEED OF SUPERVISION (PINS)

It is not uncommon for a family going through divorce to be in crisis. It is a time when children may act out in destructive or even dangerous ways. A youngster under the age of sixteen who acts dangerously or gets into trouble may be a Person In Need Of Supervision (PINS). A PINS petition can be filed in Family Court by a parent, guardian, injured party, or some authority such as the police or the child's school. If the Court finds that supervision or treatment is necessary, the Judge can order that the child be placed in some type of residential facility or allowed to live at home under a Probation Officer's supervision.

JUVENILE DELINQUENCY (JD)

The Family Court hears Juvenile Delinquency cases. A juvenile of at least seven years old but not yet sixteen who is found guilty of an act that would be considered a crime if committed by an adult is legally a "Juvenile Delinquent."

CHILD PROTECTIVE SERVICES (CPS)

To promote intervention on behalf of abused and maltreated children, the Child Protective Services Act of 1973 mandated the establishment of Child Protective Services in each New York State county. Child abuse and neglect petitions charging a child has been harmed, has not been protected from harm, or has been neglected are filed in the Family Court.

APPENDIX – Customizing Guide

PATERNITY

If you are seeking to document the father of your child, you may bring a paternity proceeding in the Family Court.

PROS AND CONS OF TAKING ACTION IN FAMILY COURT

How successful you can be with your efforts in the Family Court depends on your situation, your strengths, and the atmosphere and attitude prevalent in the Court itself.

- If you need help with family issues, you can represent yourself in Family Court. It is more client friendly than the Supreme Court. Based on your financial circumstances, you may be eligible for assigned counsel, an attorney appointed to represent you free of charge.

- However, depending on the atmosphere of your Family Court, the dynamics of your situation, and your personal makeup, you might not be able to adequately represent yourself and will have to be prepared to hire a lawyer.

- Establishing your rights with custody and support petitions in the Family Court, before filing for divorce in the Supreme Court, might put you in a stronger position as you go through the divorce process. Your spouse will have to show that changed circumstances exist to warrant changes in existing orders, and he or she will have to pay legal fees to have the necessary motions filed.

- However, if your spouse has the desire and money, he or she can challenge decisions previously made in Family Court by having motions filed with the Supreme Court for hearings and new court orders.

- Stalling tactics such as unnecessary motions and "continuances" (postponement of a pending court action to a future date) are more prevalent in the Supreme Court. Using the Family Court before filing for divorce may enable you to accomplish more at less cost in less time.

- However, once the divorce papers are filed in Supreme Court, any ongoing legal action in the Family Court can be delayed or stayed by actions brought in the Supreme Court or can be consolidated with the Supreme Court action.

- If the Family Court has not ruled on your petitions by the time divorce action is commenced, the Supreme Court Judge can determine whether all issues are to be decided by the Supreme Court or whether the Family Court is to finish deciding those issues before it.

APPENDIX – Customizing Guide

PROCEDURE

Represent yourself in Family Court or hire a lawyer.

Call your Family Court to clarify what documents and evidence you need to bring.

☐ Financial information for support issues.

☐ Information supporting your parenting ability for custody.

☐ Medical records, police reports, and material evidence for protection.

An efficient way to get the help you require from the Family Court is to start legal action for all the types of legal relief you need (protection, support, custody) the first time you go to the Court.

APPENDIX – Money Matters: Monthly Budget

Family Court is designed to help people obtain court orders without a lawyer. County clerks, probation officers, or court-trained volunteers can help you fill out the required paperwork to "petition" (written request for particular relief) the Court to help you with specific claims. These petitions must be notarized, signed before a notary. Be sure to bring photo identification as proof you are who you claim to be. There will be a notary at the Court.

When you file these official papers with the Court, you are referred to as the "petitioner." The person responding to these petitions is the "respondent." A hearing will be scheduled, generally two to three months in the future. In an emergency, a temporary Order of Protection or order of custody can be obtained within a few hours. A subsequent hearing then determines whether there is just cause to make a temporary order permanent. Become familiar with the rules in your local Family Court. For example, you may be able to obtain a temporary support order in conjunction with an Order of Protection and follow up with a more formal support petition at a later date.

Some say it is best to have a lawyer represent you because the Court will listen to your lawyer and your case will be handled properly. This is a serious decision, deserving careful consideration. Hearing Examiners, conducting the support proceedings, and Judges, conducting the custody and other child-related proceedings, are legal professionals who often prefer the expediency of working with experienced lawyers rather than inexperienced petitioners. The results of a hearing can have lifelong ramifications.

If you are comfortable with and understand the legal procedure, Court setting, necessary paperwork, and have little money to hire a lawyer, you can represent yourself. You would be a "pro se" (for oneself) litigant. You would state your case before the Judge or Hearing Examiner, presenting your evidence and witnesses and cross examining the respondent and his or her witnesses. Many hearings are not very complicated but you must be prepared. After listening to each side, the Judge or Hearing Examiner will decide the disputed issue. Remember, take into account the established attitude and reputation of your Family Court before you decide to go pro se. If, however, you have no money for a lawyer, it might be in your best interests to represent yourself than to do nothing at all.

APPENDIX – Customizing Guide

10

LEGAL GROUNDS

Unless otherwise stated, information presented in *Legal Grounds* is
New York State specific. See the *Customizing Guide* in the Appendix.

INTRODUCTION

Attorneys and Judges don't really care about grounds.

To dissolve marital contracts, valid legal reasons called "grounds" must exist. In fault
states, the spouse seeking to end the marriage must prove to the Court that fault exists.
Most fault states have some less inflammatory grounds, such as living apart for a
specified period of time or irreconcilable differences, where neither spouse is held at
fault for the breakdown of the marriage. New York is a fault state and, in theory, the
spouse suing to dissolve the marriage must prove in the State Supreme Court that fault
exists. In practice, most couples usually agree on grounds. New York's less
inflammatory approach of dissolving a marriage is to live apart for more than one year
while abiding by the terms of a Separation Agreement or Judgment of Separation; fault
is not an issue. New York State does not grant divorces for "irreconcilable differences"
(the breakdown of a marriage due to no fault of the spouses).

New York State Fault Grounds:

◆ Abandonment for one or more years.
◆ Constructive abandonment for one or more years.
◆ Adultery.
◆ Cruel and inhuman treatment.
◆ Imprisonment for three or more years.

Domestic Relations Law Section 170

New York State Grounds Where
Fault Is Not An Issue:

◆ Separation Agreement.
◆ Judgment of Separation.

Connecticut and New Jersey are referred to as "no-fault" states because each has
no-fault grounds. Connecticut recognizes "irretrievable breakdown of the marriage" as
grounds, and New Jersey recognizes living separate and apart for eighteen consecutive
months with no reasonable chance of reconciliation. Occasionally, a New York resident
will move to Connecticut or New Jersey, fulfill the residency requirements, obtain a

divorce, and then return to New York to resolve property, custody, visitation, and support issues. This can put the other spouse at a disadvantage if he or she did not want the divorce and was using that as leverage in negotiating. Nevada is a no-fault state with a six-week residency requirement. No-fault states also have fault grounds.
Connecticut General Statutes Annotated; Title 46b, Chapter 51
New Jersey Statutes Annotated; Title 2A, Chapter 34-2
Nevada Revised Statutes; Chapter 125; Section 0201

Some no-fault and fault grounds for New Jersey:
◆ Separation for eighteen consecutive months. The spouses must live in separate homes with no reasonable possibility of reconciliation. Neither party is at fault; the divorce can be granted even if one spouse does not want it.
◆ Extreme physical or mental cruelty.
◆ Adultery.
◆ Willful desertion for at least one year.
◆ Habitual drunkenness or addiction.
◆ Institutionalization for mental illness for at least twenty-four consecutive months.
◆ Imprisonment for at least eighteen consecutive months.
New Jersey Statutes Annotated; Title 2A, Chapter 34-2

The emotional upheaval of ending a marriage, especially when one spouse appears to be more to blame, causes some spouses to be greatly concerned about getting the grounds "right." Some seem to have a burning need to make it clear who is to blame and what he or she did. This can be an extremely sensitive issue for both spouses and can add to creating a confrontational, even vindictive, stage for negotiations. If you are the "innocent" spouse, subtly using fault as a leverage technique may be of more value than taking a firm outspoken position. In certain circumstances, fault can impact custody cases and equitable distribution. Generally, however, attorneys and Judges don't really care about grounds, and in practice, fault rarely has a bearing in how the Court decides the issues.

As difficult as it may be, try to release the marriage. If it is over, work at accepting that reality. Recovering from some things that happened may be extremely difficult, but try to agree upon grounds with which you can both live. Focus your energy on designing a settlement agreement that protects you and your family and then concentrate on your healing.
APPENDIX – Customizing Guide

FAULT GROUNDS

Either agree on grounds or be prepared to prove fault.

ABANDONMENT FOR ONE OR MORE YEARS

"Abandonment" means one spouse has purposely left the marriage without justification or consent and does not intend to return. To be grounds for divorce, abandonment must exist for a continuous period of at least one year prior to the commencement of the divorce action. The refusal of a working woman to move with her husband who has been transferred is not considered abandonment.

"Constructive abandonment" means a spouse has left the marriage in spirit by refusing without justification to have sexual relations for one or more years prior to the commencement of the divorce action. Constructive abandonment is commonly used as grounds for divorce. It is a form of abandonment and may also be considered "cruel and inhuman treatment."

ADULTERY

Emotionally, adultery feels like strong, clear grounds upon which to file for divorce. In practice, it may be a difficult charge to substantiate unless the accused spouse agrees to it. Proof usually rests on circumstantial evidence that a party had the intent and opportunity, backed up with physical evidence such as credit card statements, tapes (audio/video), written communications, or journals. Witnesses who do not really want to be involved can be evasive, poor witnesses on the stand. Sworn affidavits from witnesses might provide realistic accounts but affidavits take time, persuasion, and money to obtain. A spouse accused of adultery can deny it, admit to it, or do neither. Technically on the books, adultery is still considered a criminal offense in New York, and those accused of it do not have to respond. They are protected from incriminating themselves and a third party.

To pursue adultery as the grounds for divorce may create further animosity in an emotionally raw situation and can be time consuming, costly, and probably, impossible to prove. Some spouses start with the charge of adultery for psychological leverage and agree to switch to a lesser provocative charge as negotiations progress.

In addition, be aware that if you have sexual relations with your spouse after you have learned about his or her adultery, you cannot use adultery as grounds. In the eyes of the Court you have "forgiven" your spouse for the wrongdoing, legally referred to as "condonation." If you also have committed adultery and both you and your spouse prove the other at fault, the Court will not grant a divorce on these grounds. Lastly, there is a statute of limitations of five years from your discovery of the first "unforgiven" act of adultery. If more than five years has elapsed, you cannot use it as grounds.

CRUEL AND INHUMAN TREATMENT

"Cruel and inhuman treatment" means either physical or mental cruelty of the degree that makes it unsafe or improper for the parties to reside together as husband and wife. Generally, the abusive acts or conduct must have occurred within five years prior to filing an action for divorce. Cruel and inhuman treatment is more than incompatibility; it is physical, emotional, or financial abuse such as:

◆ Physical or emotional attacks.
◆ Gambling away funds or unreasonable control of marital funds.
◆ Unexplained absences from the home for too long or too often.
◆ Dating someone else.
◆ Abuse of children witnessed by the other parent.

Constructive abandonment and adultery may also be considered cruel and inhuman treatment.

PART IV - in Chapter 10: "Adultery" and *"Abandonment For One Or More Years"*

The most effective approach for handling situations where alcoholism, addiction, or mental illness are evident may be to focus on the abusive behavior that results from the condition, instead of trying to prove the condition itself exists. In some cases of abuse, criminal charges can be brought or civil cases prosecuted. For example, getting a sexually transmitted disease can be cause for bringing a separate civil case requesting the Court award monetary compensation for damages. This proposed action can have a powerful leverage effect in negotiating the matrimonial settlement.

IMPRISONMENT FOR THREE OR MORE YEARS

A spouse must have served three or more consecutive years in prison before a divorce action can be brought using "imprisonment" as grounds.

APPENDIX – Customizing Guide

SEPARATION AGREEMENT

A less inflammatory approach is to legally separate.

A Separation Agreement is a written contract setting forth the rights and duties by which the separated parties will live for the remainder of their lives. It covers custody, visitation, support, and the distribution of assets and liabilities. You can design a Separation Agreement without resolving equitable distribution issues. Instead, you and your spouse may agree to resolve them in a future divorce action. Consult your attorney with regard to the benefit or detriment of leaving equitable distribution decisions unresolved until a later date. According to New York law, living apart without a formal signed Separation Agreement is not being legally separated and is not recognized as grounds for divorce.

Generally, each spouse obtains his or her own legal representation for advice and guidance in negotiating a Separation Agreement. Once the Agreement has been finalized, it is filed with the County Clerk. One year after filing the signed Agreement, either spouse may commence an action to have the Separation Agreement converted into a divorce decree. The divorce does not occur automatically after the year has ended; legal action must be taken. The Court will issue the divorce decree based on proof that the Agreement was duly executed, filed properly, the parties lived apart for one year, and the plaintiff substantially compiled with the terms of the Agreement.

APPENDIX – Customizing Guide

ANNULMENT

A marriage can be voided or annulled. Some grounds for a legal annulment:
- The spouse under eighteen years of age requests the annulment.
- Either spouse is incapable of having sexual intercourse.
- Either consented to the marriage as a result of force.
- A spouse's consent was obtained by fraud.

APPENDIX – Customizing Guide

11

STEPS IN THE DIVORCE PROCESS

*How you approach dissolving your marriage is as important
as understanding the legal steps involved.*

Please note: Trying to work with a spouse where abuse, violence, or addiction exists can be dangerous or unproductive. Use this information to become informed, but secure the specialized, professional assistance your circumstances may demand.

YOUR APPROACH TO THE LEGAL PROCESS

You do not have to relinquish your divorce decisions to the Court.

IF POSSIBLE, WORK TOGETHER WITH YOUR SPOUSE

Make every effort to maintain control over your divorce instead of handing it over to attorneys. Since each marital breakup has unique features, it can benefit you and your spouse to cooperate in designing a settlement addressing your family's needs. Financially and emotionally, it will be less costly and the outcome is apt to be more satisfying. You can work together to resolve the issues by using lawyers, either as coaches behind the scenes or as active participants.

YOU CONTINUALLY HAVE CHOICES

Just because you start formal litigation does not mean you have to relinquish your divorce decisions to the Court. Generally, the more you rely on the legal system to resolve the marital issues, the more expensive and time consuming the process becomes. Misunderstanding, posturing, and confrontation can escalate as the number of bureaucratic variables influencing your case increases, such as attorneys, financial professionals, hearing examiners, and law guardians. Going through the legal steps and then to trial cannot only take years out of your life and most of your assets, but also deplete you emotionally and spiritually. Remain open to negotiating a settlement at any stage of the process.

ADVANTAGES TO ESTABLISHING YOURSELF AS THE PLAINTIFF

The plaintiff (party who initiates lawsuit) has some control over where the case is to be decided. The strategic move of serving the Summons to determine where the case is to be litigated is sometimes referred to as "forum shopping." Some local practices and state laws may be more favorable to your circumstances than others. There are residency requirements to fulfill, but in some situations the jurisdiction in which the case is decided can make a big difference. For example, New York State recognizes that separate property remains with the spouse who owns it, whereas according to Connecticut law, all property can be divided with the dissolution of a marriage. New York recognizes licenses and degrees as marital property, whereas many states do not.

New York Domestic Relations Law Section 236
Connecticut General Statutes Annotated; Title 46b, Chapter 81
PART V - in Chapter 13: "Marital And Nonmarital Property"
APPENDIX – Customizing Guide
Exhibits: Summons With Notice

SITUATIONS IN WHICH IT IS IMPORTANT TO COMMENCE LEGAL ACTION

APPENDIX – Exhibits: Summons With Notice
Order To Show Cause (for pendente lite relief)

Start the lawsuit with serving the Summons to:

- Establish a "from this time forward" dividing line between separate and marital property and debt where a spouse is spending or transferring assets. At the time the Summons is filed, arrange to have restraining orders served on financial institutions, brokers, and any private businesses to freeze assets so they cannot be removed, transferred, or sold.
  PART V - Chapter 13: Division Of Property
  APPENDIX – Customizing Guide
- Catch the defendant before he or she leaves the state.
- Establish the jurisdiction where custody is to be determined.
- Force a spouse to negotiate, especially when there is a custody dispute.
- Apply for pendente lite (while litigation is pending) relief. Once the lawsuit has commenced, the Supreme Court can order necessary monetary support and legal protection from abuse. Remember, you can obtain relief from the Family Court for family issues regarding protection, support, custody, and other child-related issues without filing for divorce.
  PART IV - Chapter 9: Family Court
- Ensure that the state in which you reside becomes the home state for litigation purposes. This will prevent your having to litigate "long distance," using an attorney with whom you may not be able to have regular contact.

BASICALLY THERE ARE TWO WAYS TO ATTAIN YOUR DIVORCE

Maintain decision-making power over your life or surrender it to strangers.

UNCONTESTED DIVORCE

With an uncontested divorce, you and your spouse resolve the marital issues and sign a Settlement Agreement, Stipulation of Settlement, or Separation Agreement. The Agreement or Stipulation is incorporated into a Judgment of Divorce that is signed by the Judge or Special Referee. When incorporated into a Judgment, an Agreement is converted from a contract between two people to a court order. This is beneficial for enforcement purposes.

Prepare yourself; know your legal rights and understand your finances. Focus on the whole picture. Be attentive to what is most important to you and your family and know what to fight for and what to give up. Start with matters about which you and your spouse can agree and narrow down the unresolved issues. After resolving custody and grounds, much of it is a numbers game. Analyze your long-term needs regarding your future financial picture and necessary support.

PART V – Areas Of Concern

If you wish to secure a divorce as soon as possible, you can do so by agreeing on the grounds, deciding who is to be the plaintiff, and filing with the Court the required legal papers along with a copy of your Settlement Agreement or Stipulation of Settlement for a Judge or Referee to sign. For economic or emotional reasons, such as a favorable tax filing status or time to adjust, you might not want to move quickly to finalize the end of your marriage. If so, you can design a Separation Agreement by which you live as legally separated spouses. You can remain legally separated as long as it fits your needs, or after one year, either party can go to Court to convert the legal separation into a divorce. The necessary filing papers along with a copy of your Agreement are to be submitted for approval with the grounds being "lived separate and apart pursuant to a Separation Agreement." The Court is mainly concerned with the division of assets, support issues, and custody; the legal divorce is almost like an afterthought, a formality. If you have agreed not to resolve equitable distribution issues in your Separation Agreement, you will need to do so in a subsequent divorce action. Both Separation Agreements and Judgments of Separation are revocable, if done so in accordance with the applicable laws.

Domestic Relations Law Section 200

You can commence a lawsuit for a legal separation if you have little desire to be divorced, but it is necessary to clarify the issues of support and custody and the issue of equitable distribution is not paramount to your situation. You must have grounds for an Action for Separation. In addition to those required for a divorce is the ground of "neglect/refusal to support."

PART IV - Chapter 10: Legal Grounds
APPENDIX – Customizing Guide

CONTESTED DIVORCE

With a contested divorce, each party employs many legal devices to try to force its adversary to compromise. It can be a lengthy, expensive, frustrating experience. If you do not settle somewhere along the way, you ultimately relinquish the power to decide the outcome of your marital issues, and the Judge decides for you. Decisions regarding assets, liabilities, custody, and support are set forth in a court order determined by the Judge after a trial. That order then becomes part of your Judgment of Divorce. If a case is settled after a contested divorce is commenced, the parties may enter into a Stipulation of Settlement or Settlement Agreement, which are incorporated into the Judgment of Divorce and enforceable as a court order.

THREE PHASES OF THE LEGAL PROCESS

The following describes the documents and procedures of the divorce process.

This legal model uses New York State as an example. Steps in the divorce process are similar among the states. Terminology, names, time schedules, and requirements may differ. Use the *Customizing Guide* in the Appendix.

PLEADING STAGE

SUMMONS AND COMPLAINT SERVED

To initiate a matrimonial lawsuit, the plaintiff has the defendant served with a Summons and Complaint or only with a Summons with Notice, waiting to serve the Verified Complaint at a later time. One copy of the document is filed with the County Clerk's Office; then another copy is served on the defendant within a certain period of time by either a process server, a nonparty to the action over eighteen years, or through the party's lawyers. The latter method can be the least awkward.

APPENDIX – Exhibits: Summons With Notice and Verified Complaint

Before entering into the pleading stage, attempt to work out a settlement. If you have to commence an action to "stop the clock" with regard to assets and debts, you can withhold service of the Summons for 120 days while you attempt to negotiate a settlement. If possible, speak with your spouse and agree to work directly together. If doing so is too difficult, try to agree to work toward resolving the marital issues in the most positive fashion with your lawyers' assistance. If a settlement is not achieved, you must serve the Summons within 120 days of filing, in order to preserve those rights which you sought to protect with the initial filing.

PART IV - in Chapter 11: "Your Approach To The Legal Process"

How and when a matrimonial lawsuit is started can be provocative. Initiating a legal action can be an agreed upon decision or a surprise attack. If started too early, it can inflame the situation. Once the action has commenced by sending a Summons, the case can take on a life of its own, get out of your hands, and go through many steps of litigation when it really was not necessary.

Serving the Summons with Notice can start the legal action and is less inflammatory than sending the Summons and Complaint together. The Summons with Notice notifies the defendant of the lawsuit, simply states the grounds, and lists the relief being requested such as custody, the marital residence, maintenance, health insurance, and so on. The relief requested has to be part of the Summons with Notice to put the other side on notice for what he or she is being sued. A Verified Complaint, stating the grounds and detailing the allegations, can be sent later.

The contents of the Complaint can be shocking to the recipient, setting the stage for confrontation and making it more difficult to negotiate a reasonable, cost-effective settlement. This is a particularly sensitive area where cruel and inhuman treatment or adultery is alleged. Including numerous, descriptive details of your spouse's wrongdoing is unlikely to benefit you. The effect is more likely to be so offensive to the defendant that he or she becomes resistant. Lengthy, costly litigation may be the outcome from which only the lawyers will benefit. If your situation is not overly antagonistic and you want to try to prevent further discord, be clear with your attorney that you prefer to simply state the grounds and only include basic supportive facts in the Complaint. Be certain, however, that you have sufficient allegations in your Complaint; your spouse might require that you prove there are grounds. Review what has been included before it is sent; demand it be toned down if it feels too inflammatory. You want a good settlement, not a costly fight.

APPENDIX – Exhibits: Summons With Notice and Verified Complaint

ANSWER

The defendant has twenty days to respond by filing an Answer in which he or she either admits to or denies the various allegations in the Complaint. Usually, the Answer consists of a counterclaim, which is the defendant's own version of events and claims against the plaintiff, listing the relief requested. If you are the defendant and realize the dissolution of the marriage is inevitable or want it, filing a counterclaim may increase your psychological and practical leverage in bargaining. On the other hand, if your spouse has no grounds and you do not want to divorce, you can deny the charges and not counterclaim. Either your spouse will be moved to propose settlement terms more favorable to you or you will remain married, probably living apart with the Court ordering temporary support and custody arrangements but not the distribution of assets. Clarify your options with an attorney.

PENDENTE LITE MOTIONS

If you and your spouse have not agreed upon temporary living and financial arrangements, interim relief or Court intervention can be obtained by filing formal motions. Once your matrimonial lawsuit has commenced, your lawyer can request, among other things, temporary relief with pendente lite motions to:

❑ Determine child and spousal support.

❑ Establish custody and visitation arrangements.

❑ Freeze assets if they are disappearing, or there is reasonable fear they will, or if equity is turning into debt.

❑ Remove an abuser from the marital residence.

❑ Be allowed either to relocate with the children or to prevent the relocation of the children.

❑ Prevent health and life insurance from being canceled or to reinstate lapsed coverage.

❑ Seek counsel fees. The Court has the power to order the moneyed spouse to pay the legal fees of the nonmoneyed spouse.

PART IV - Chapter 12: Problems With The Legal System
APPENDIX – Exhibits: Summons With Notice and Order To Show Cause (for pendente lite relief)

To minimize the chance of a dismissal, have adequate information with you so the Judge is informed well enough to make a decision.

❑ Federal and state tax returns for two years.

❑ Summarized monthly expenses and income, including pay stubs for four to six months and proof of expenses for housing, clothing, child care, medical, and school. Include this information on your Statement of Net Worth.

APPENDIX – Money Matters: Monthly Budget and Financial Puzzle Pieces
Exhibits: Statement Of Net Worth

❑ Identification documents such as birth certificates of children, Social Security numbers of all involved, addresses, employers, and photo identification.

Be realistic. It can take up to three months to get a decision for temporary support, so make the motions early and put money aside. If your spouse is no longer residing with you or has threatened to leave the jurisdiction with your children and you feel custody is going to be an issue, it might be best for your lawyer to make a motion for temporary custody when the initial legal papers are filed. Timing is a delicate consideration. This may be a good move to establish your custodial rights or it may be too provocative. You know the psychology of your situation; work closely with your attorney to make this decision.

PART IV - Chapter 9: Family Court

The defendant must be given notice of pendente lite motions except in extreme emergencies or when irreparable physical or financial injury is probable. An ex parte motion (by or for one party) can be filed with no notice given to the other side when abuse exists or there is fear assets will be or are being hidden, sold, or wasted. A restraining order (prohibiting some specific action until a hearing can be held) is served on the defendant with notice of a hearing date when he or she has an opportunity to object to the order.

Usually, temporary orders include the phrase "without prejudice," which means an order can be modified without having to prove a change in circumstances. The implication is that the provisions of pretrial orders do not automatically become part of the final Agreement. Take temporary orders seriously, however; they can permanently affect your life. For example, when a child has done well under a pretrial custody arrangement, the Court may not want to disturb it by granting custody to the other parent.

A contempt of court motion can be filed if a party does not comply with temporary orders. The resulting Order to Show Cause requires the accused to provide a justified explanation for not obeying a court ruling or be held in contempt of court.

Remember, if you have not started the matrimonial lawsuit in the Supreme Court and you need relief, you can petition the Family Court.

PART IV - Chapter 9: Family Court

PRELIMINARY CONFERENCE

Within 120 days of filing the Summons and Complaint, a Preliminary Conference regarding your case is to be held. The Conference is either attended by all those involved (Judge or his or her law secretary or clerk, lawyers and clients) or, if it is the Judge's preference, only the Judge and lawyers. It is to your benefit to be present at conferences, but it is not uncommon for the Judge to prefer to confer initially or solely with the lawyers. Be sure your attorney has made the motions for the relief you need while litigation is pending, such as support and payment of legal fees.

PART IV - in Chapter 11: "Pleading Stage: Pendente Lite Motions" and "Motions And Hearings"
APPENDIX - Exhibits: Summons With Notice and Verified Complaint

Uncomplicated cases with simple financial circumstances and no custody issues might be settled during the conference. With complex cases, a discovery schedule is established with six months to determine the value of the marital assets. If custody is an issue, the Judge is likely to assign a law guardian (a lawyer to represent the children's interests) and may also require forensic (psychological) evaluations of the parents and children.

PART IV - Chapter 12: Problems With The Legal System
in Chapter 16: "Contested Custody"

Be prepared for the Preliminary Conference. Have a clear understanding with your lawyer regarding the issues of your case, such as the assets that need to be appraised and the reality of disputed custody issues. Unresolved issues will be identified. You might be asked to sign a stipulated agreement on those issues recognized as not being disputed. If so, it is unlikely you will be allowed to raise those issues later for negotiation.

MOTIONS AND HEARINGS

As you file motions with the Court requesting what you need, your spouse may file counterclaims on the same issues requesting what he or she needs. Dates for hearings will be set at which the Judge, Special Referee, or Judicial Hearing Officer will make decisions regarding the disputed issues. Often spouses or their attorneys come to an agreement prior to the actual hearings. If there is an important reason to do so, you have the right to a continuance, a postponement of a hearing.

As previously mentioned, it would be in your best interests to be present at conferences to hear what is being said. In practice, however, some Judges meet with the lawyers in their chambers without either of the spouses being present. Become informed, act professionally, and make it clear to your lawyer at the outset that you want to be included in conferences. Be prepared, however, to assess when this request might work to your disadvantage if it were to irritate a Judge who might not want you to be present.
PART IV - Chapter 12: Problems With The Legal System
APPENDIX – Customizing Guide

DISCOVERY STAGE

One objective of discovery is to determine the marriage's economic value. Compiling data about assets, income, expenses, and liabilities is meant to provide a true picture of the financial worth of the marriage. If child custody is an issue, evidence and testimony of experts and witnesses regarding each spouse's parenting ability, psychological well-being, and employment stability may be gathered during this time.

Each party is to produce financial documents such as tax returns and a Statement of Net Worth, accompanied by supporting evidence. If your spouse is uncooperative and either does not submit all of the necessary documents or does so piecemeal, the discovery process can become excessively expensive and not comprehensive. If discovery is incomplete or distorted, a poorly prepared or inadequately represented spouse may be confronting a losing battle in attaining a just settlement.
PART III – What Is There And Where Is It?
Appendix – Exhibits: Statement Of Net Worth

INFORMAL DISCOVERY

You will have to ask your spouse for whatever records you are unable to obtain from files at home or from your accountant, broker, or banker. The more information you and your spouse can voluntarily exchange, the less costly your divorce is likely to be. You can share the necessary documents and data with each other personally or through your attorneys. Whatever is not voluntarily made available will have to be acquired through formal legal channels.

FORMAL DISCOVERY

Formal discovery using legal devices such as interrogatories, depositions, and subpoenas is time consuming, expensive, and often inaccurate or incomplete. "Interrogatories" are written questions for which you must provide written answers under oath. Your lawyer can help you answer the questions. A "deposition" or "EBT" (examination before trial) is a session during which you are required to answer questions orally under oath in the presence of the lawyers and your spouse. The opposing attorney asks you questions and your attorney asks your spouse questions. All answers are recorded by a court reporter. This sworn written record may be used at the trial to test your credibility. Even though your lawyer is present, you are basically on your own as you answer the questions, so be prepared. Your attorney can demand that the opposition produce and bring documents such as bank records, deeds, financial agreements, insurance policies, and credit card statements.

Questions can cover a wide range of concerns such as marital misconduct, property issues, support, and to a limited extent, custody. An interrogatory might produce sufficient information at a reasonable cost. A deposition is more expensive but offers the opportunity to clarify vague responses and pursue questions that might be initially sidestepped. There is also the possibility that during active questioning some new or valuable information may surface. If you decide the expense of a deposition is worth it, use the time wisely by assisting your lawyer in preparing questions that focus on key issues. In most situations, fighting over grounds is not a profitable use of your resources, unless one spouse has dissipated marital assets, committed fraud, or acted in an extremely improper manner so as to influence the Court adversely.

Some questions are designed to elicit basic information, such as a job description or amount of income. Other questions focus on situations and problems. Examples:

➥ *Describe the nonmarital property you claim to own, including the date acquired, its present value, and its location.*
➥ *Is it true that during the years of your marriage, your spouse took over the responsibility of managing the investments and helped to increase the value of the mutual funds you brought to the marriage by fifty percent?*
➥ *Your credit card statement for the past year shows some sizable cash advances. How did you use the money?*
➥ *State the names and addresses of all persons who have worked on your private or business financial records and tax returns during the last three years.*
➥ *You have had the opportunity to review a monthly budget prepared by your spouse. Are there entries that appear to be inaccurate?*
➥ *Your job demands long hours and at least one three-day business trip a month. If you are awarded primary custody, how do you plan to provide for the children's care in your absence?*
➥ *When did you last attend an event at your child's school and what was the event?*
➥ *As primary caregiver, what can you do better than your spouse?*

Usually, a series of questions focuses on a specific issue, and attorneys are precise about dates instead of simply referring to "the past year."

If you decide the benefits of experiencing a deposition are worth the cost, prepare yourself adequately. It can provide a way for you to evaluate your case and how well you and your adversary perform as witnesses. Know the facts of your case, answer only questions asked, and keep your answers simple. Do not offer any information that has not been specifically requested. Design your responses to serve your own purposes. Having the truth on your side may not be enough. New information that is brought to the surface or, possibly, the stress involved, may be an incentive for the opposition to be more receptive to negotiating a settlement. Testimony is taken under oath, recorded, and preserved; you may be able to use these responses to your advantage in the future.

PART III - in Chapter 7: "Uncovering Hidden Assets"
APPENDIX – Mind Matters: Deposition Primer

"Subpoena power" can be used to call witnesses, specialists, and representatives of institutions, such as banks, and to obtain documents that have not been produced by your spouse. You may need accountants, appraisers, actuaries, past and present business partners, associates, and employees to testify regarding the division of property and support. When custody is contested, the testimony of child care personnel, housekeepers, doctors, neighbors, mental health professionals, Social Services personnel, and police can be critical.

NEGOTIATIONS / PRETRIAL CONFERENCE

During the discovery stage, negotiations are going on at some level. When you actively participate in structuring the settlement, you retain some control over what you are willing to give up in order to get what you most want or feel you need. A divorce decree embodies the terms of your Agreement and converts it from a contract into an enforceable court order. If you are unable to arrive at a settlement, you move toward trial where the Judge will decide the unresolved issues.

A Pretrial Conference, also referred to as a Trial Readiness Conference (TRC), is scheduled at the time of the Preliminary Conference. Generally, it is held in a conference room or the Judge's chambers with the lawyers going in first without their clients to give the Judge a summary. Disputed issues are summarized, and the Judge may "lean on" the lawyers for a compromise. Then each client and his or her lawyer, or both clients together with their lawyers, meet with the Judge in an effort to try to resolve the outstanding issues. Prior to the Trial Readiness Conference, sit down with your attorney and go over the unresolved issues and your options for settlement.

At this time, it is not uncommon in some jurisdictions to try to wrap up the case by doing oral stipulations. These are oral agreements made before the Judge in Court in the presence of a court stenographer. The transcript of the proceedings is incorporated into the Judgment of Divorce and signed by the Judge, thereby converting the agreement to a court order. Oral stipulations may be treated differently in the various departments or jurisdictions; in some they may not be allowed. Be aware and alert to the possibility. If your money is gone and your lawyer wants to get rid of the case, or if the Judge is pressuring the lawyers to resolve the case so he or she can "clear the calendar," you may be in a particularly vulnerable position.

Usually, the plaintiff and defendant are asked if they have used alcohol or drugs that day to be sure they are clearheaded. It is at this point that oral stipulations may begin. Be careful. You may answer to something that you will not be able to overturn. You may be thinking that when you see it in writing, you will understand it. It will be too late by then if you have already agreed to it. Oral stipulations become reduced to written stipulations when they are dictated into the transcript, and they can last forever once recorded. To protect yourself, do not agree to any oral stipulations you do not completely understand. Say: *I'll have to think about it*. Request that your lawyer put the proposed oral stipulations into writing for you to read and approve before they become part of the final settlement.

PART IV - Chapter 12: Problems With The Legal System
APPENDIX – Customizing Guide

TRIAL STAGE

Most divorce cases can be resolved long before the trial stage. The drawbacks of going to trial are many. It is expensive, emotionally draining, and unpredictable. It is unlikely that the Judge, who has the power to decide major issues affecting the rest of your life, will have the time to learn all the important details about your case.

Unfortunately, there are some cases where going to trial cannot be avoided, but they are few. If you are one of those few, familiarize yourself with the courtroom setting, its atmosphere, what happens, and how the Judge reacts. Go over your concerns with your attorney before the day of the trial. Know the types of questions you may be asked and practice your responses. Review important papers connected with your case to be freshly informed. Present yourself appropriately in dress, manners, punctuality, respect, organization, and professionalism. Do not be defensive. Take notes. Keep your emotional reactions to yourself.

HANDY CLARIFICATIONS

GOING TO COURT

What does it mean if your attorney says, *A date has been set and we are going to Court*?

- If you have just started a matrimonial lawsuit, "going to court" probably, means going to a Preliminary Conference where you, your spouse, and the attorneys are scheduled to meet with the Judge or his or her law secretary or clerk. Ask to be present, not waiting in the hall.
  PART IV - in Chapter 11: "Pleading Stage: Preliminary Conference"
- If your legal action is not new but not yet settled, you are probably going to a conference to discuss unresolved issues.
  PART IV - in Chapter 11: "Pleading Stage: Motions And Hearings"
- If the discovery phase has been completed and there is still no settlement, you may be going to court for a Trial Readiness Conference (TRC) to be held in a conference room or the Judge's chambers or for a trial to be held in the Courtroom.
  PART IV - in Chapter 11: "Discovery Stage: Negotiations / Pretrial Conference"

LEGAL FEES

New York State law says the Judge "may" award legal fees to the financially dependent spouse. If you are unable to pay the cost of legal representation, ask your attorney to make a motion requesting legal fees at the outset of your case.

PART IV - Chapter 12: Problems With The Legal System

FRIVOLOUS ACTIONS

According to New York rules, "frivolous actions" are not allowed. They are legal actions that are without substance, usually intended to wear down the opposition and stall the case.

FORENSICS

The application of scientific knowledge to solve legal problems is referred to as "forensics." Examples of different areas of forensic evaluation are financial, medical, and psychological.

COPY OF TRANSCRIPT

For an appeal and, usually, for an objection, you need a copy of the transcript. This can get expensive. Call the Court for the current cost per page. If the information you need was recorded on a specific day, you can save money by getting a copy of the transcript for that particular day.

APPENDIX – Glossary: Terms of Divorce

CERTIFIED COPIES

Legal records delivered from one Court to another Court must be certified, not just photocopies. A certified copy of a court or government document guarantees that it is a valid copy of the original. A certification on your copy of the document can be obtained at the County Clerk's Office.

APPENDIX – Glossary: Terms of Divorce

Wisdom consists of the anticipation of consequences.
Norman Cousins

Nine-tenths of wisdom is being wise in time.
Theodore Roosevelt

12

PROBLEMS WITH THE LEGAL SYSTEM

PROBLEMS

LEGAL REALITY

Matrimonial courts are crowded with little time to learn important facts about cases. Insensitive procedures may not always address the seriousness of family issues. The majority of the work is done by adversarial attorneys, representing their individual clients. There is a lot of money to be made structuring divorce settlements.

Be well primed with realistic information before entering the legal arena. It will have a great impact on your expectations and experiences and on the outcome of your case. With foresight, preparation, and active participation, you can prevent your case from being controlled and, needlessly, escalated by others.

PART I - in Chapter 2: "Legal Process – Brief Overview"
PART IV - in Chapter 8: "Legal Reality"

ADVERSARIAL SYSTEM

The adversarial judicial system can intensify conflict; it is not well designed to resolve marital discord. Strategies are used to win. It is assumed that opponents entering this justice system will be represented equally. Often this is not so, because one spouse may be less advantaged financially or without access to essential marital information and documentation.

Intentional use of tactics to wear down the opposition, forcing him or her to run out of money or endurance, is not uncommon. Distorting the facts is a widespread stratagem. If your case is being hampered by the excessive filing of motions or requests for continuances, you might want to contact the Administrative Judge of the Court. This higher-ranking Judge oversees the matrimonial judges and can have influence on professional conduct within the Court. For this action to benefit you, however, the atmosphere in your jurisdiction has to be receptive to responding to litigants' concerns.

REGULATION OF PROFESSIONAL CONDUCT

The legal profession has the power to review the conduct of its own members and discipline them. A litigant who feels he or she has experienced unethical or illegal behavior from a judge or lawyer can file a grievance with the appropriate disciplinary committee. Most of the complaints are dismissed due to "lack of merit." Often lack of funds rules out the possibility of adequate investigations.

JUDICIAL BIAS

Subtle bias involving gender, money, power, and image is not uncommon in family law litigation. Presently, a litigant has no effective way to have a judge recused from a case. "Recusal" means disqualification of a Judge for lack of impartiality. The litigant is required to file a recusal motion with the same Judge about whom he or she is alleging prejudice or ill will. If the motion is denied, the litigant is left with a more hostile judicial atmosphere. Appealing is usually time consuming, costly, and futile.

DISCRETION OF JUDGES

Many statutes dealing with family law use the word "may," which means the Judge is not required to do something but may do so at his or her discretion. Judicial discretion means the Judge has the choice to decide cases as he or she feels, in good faith, is appropriate. This gives the Judge enormous decision-making power that has a far-reaching impact on divorce and child custody issues. Depending on the Judge, judicial discretion can be used wisely or carelessly.

PERJURY

Perjury is hardly ever prosecuted in divorce cases. If you are up against an unethical adversary, the truth can be greatly distorted. You may find you are continually defending yourself against deliberate falsehoods in Court papers. This tactic is designed to enhance your adversary's position and to wear you down psychologically and financially.

AWARDING LEGAL FEES

According to New York State law, the Judge "may" award legal fees to the financially dependent spouse by requiring the moneyed spouse pay an amount equal to his or her own legal fees. The statute, however, does not require the Judge to make the award. The practice of postponing decisions on awarding counselor fees until the end of litigation, or awarding insufficient amounts, puts the nonmoneyed spouse at an extreme disadvantage in securing adequate legal representation.
APPENDIX – Customizing Guide

CHILDREN USED AS BARGAINING CHIPS

New York does not have a "primary care standard," requiring the Court to award custody to the long-term caregiver, so a primary care parent in litigation may be confronted with a custody battle. Most often, the primary caregiver is the financially dependent spouse. Without funds for adequate legal representation, the nonmoneyed parent may be coerced into giving up rights to marital assets in order to win custody of the children.
PART V - in Chapter 16: "Contested Custody"
APPENDIX – Customizing Guide

LAW GUARDIANS AND EXPERTS

Law guardians are court-appointed lawyers who represent the interests of children whose custody is being contested. Usually, a Judge appoints law guardians and mental health professionals with whom he or she is familiar and comfortable. Not all law guardians have the training, experience, or natural skills to protect the interests of children in an emotionally charged atmosphere. If you anticipate contested custody, be sure to retain an attorney who has skill, sensitivity, and experience with child-related issues. A lawyer with these qualifications is likely to have had prior experience with the assigned law guardian and forensic evaluator and can guide you appropriately through the process.

PART V - in Chapter 16: "Contested Custody"
APPENDIX – Customizing Guide

TEMPORARY RELIEF

The Court is to make decisions about pendente lite motions within thirty days, but there are often delays in awarding temporary relief. Family emergencies, such as the lack of money for heating fuel or mortgage payments, can result when court-ordered funds are not paid. Judicial decisions resolving emergencies may be slowed down by the required motions and orders to show cause.

PART IV - Chapter 9: Family Court
       in Chapter 11: "Pleading Stage: Pendente Lite Motions"
APPENDIX – Customizing Guide
       Exhibits: Order To Show Cause (for pendente lite relief)

ENFORCEMENT OF ORDERS

When court orders regarding child or spousal support or any other court-ordered requirement are not obeyed, litigants have to start new litigation in an attempt to get enforcement. There have been some new measures introduced in New York to try to cope better with the problem of delinquent child support. Upon notification by the Department of Social Services, the Department of Motor Vehicles can suspend driver's licenses of those who are more than four months behind in child support payments. Travel to work is an exception. Some professional and business licenses such as law, real estate, teaching, medical, and liquor licenses can be suspended for nonpayment of court-ordered child support. The custodial parent needs to file a petition with Family Court and a hearing is required before suspension. Federal and state income tax refunds of parents proven to owe back child support can be intercepted. Jail time for those willfully delinquent in their payments is rarely ordered with the first contempt charge.

For help with child support, call the office of Child Support Enforcement of your county's Department of Social Services (*www.acf.dhhs.gov*). It might fit your circumstances to call Support Kids (*www.supportkids.com*) at (800) 801-KIDS. This national private company provides assistance with collecting delinquent court-ordered child support in exchange for a percentage of the amount collected.

PART IX - in Chapter 30: "Child Support Payments"
APPENDIX – Customizing Guide

CLIENT'S RIGHT TO BE PRESENT AT CONFERENCES

With the Judge's permission, you have the right to be present at conferences regarding your case. In practice, however, the Judge often meets with the lawyers in his or her chambers without the litigants. Make it clear to your lawyer that you want to be present; you need to know what is being discussed. It is clearly in your best interest to be included, but you do not want to annoy the Judge handling your case. What is said at these closed conferences is not recorded, so you will have no access to that valuable exchange unless you are in the room.

PART IV - in Chapter 11: "Discovery Stage: Negotiations / Pretrial Conference"
APPENDIX – Customizing Guide

PRESSURE AND STIPULATIONS

Oral stipulations are verbal agreements made before the Judge in Court. They become written stipulations once they are dictated into the transcript. Sometimes, it appears that the most expedient way to settle unresolved issues is to do oral stipulations, especially when there is pressure to conclude the case. This can work to your disadvantage. In the rush of the moment, you might agree to something you do not fully understand or is inappropriate for you and your family. Once oral stipulations are read into the record, they can last forever. Request that your lawyer put any proposed oral stipulations into writing for you to see and approve. Then, once you understand them and give your approval, they can become part of the final settlement. In some jurisdictions, oral stipulations are not allowed.

PART IV - in Chapter 11: "Discovery Stage: Negotiations / Pretrial Conference"
APPENDIX – Customizing Guide

REFORM: INTEGRATED DOMESTIC VIOLENCE COURT

An example of an initiative designed to make the judicial system more responsive to people's needs is a model court referred to as an Integrated Domestic Violence Court (IDVC). It has been established in the Westchester County Supreme Court with the purpose of having one Judge hear all of a case's criminal, family, and matrimonial issues. In addition to handling criminal charges filed due to domestic violence, the IDVC handles the Family Court aspects such as custody and visitation. Support issues are still heard by a Hearing Examiner, but objections to decisions are decided by the IDVC Judge.

PART V – AREAS OF CONCERN

If you and your spouse cannot agree,
state laws will determine how your property is to be divided.

Much of the information in Part V is generic to residents of all states. Details regarding equitable distribution, separate and marital property, and the Child Support Standards Act are specific to New York State. The data presented provides an informational foundation upon which to build by adding the specifics for any state. Use the *Customizing Guide* in the Appendix.

13 DIVISION OF PROPERTY
  Equitable Distribution
  Marital And Nonmarital Property
    Marital Property
    Separate Property
    Conversion Of Separate Property Into Marital Property
  The Process Is Imperfect

14 LET'S LOOK AT THE TAX BITE
  Basics
  Calculate Real Value
    Mutual Funds
    Commercial Real Estate
    Value Of Cash
    Summary

15 WHO GETS WHAT?
  Principal Residence
  Pension
    Plan Carefully
    To Divide A Pension
    Drafting A Qualified Domestic Relations Order
  Other Distributions
    Businesses
    Degrees / Licenses / Goodwill
    Distributive Awards
    Liabilities
  Your Will

16 CHILD CUSTODY / SUPPORT / VISITATION
  Your Approach To Custody
    Amicable
    Less Than Amicable
  Best Interests Of The Child
    Custody Arrangements
    Relocation Disputes
  Contested Custody
    How The Legal Process Resolves Custody Disputes
    Custody Cues

Child Support
  Basics
  New York's Child Support Standards Act (CSSA)
    Basic Formula
    Additional Expenses
Visitation

17 **REMEMBER THE IRS**
  Real Value Of Property
  Support Payments
  Advantages To Working Together
    Tax Return Status
    Exemptions And Credits
    Professional Help
  Options With Tax Consequences

18 **ESSENTIAL PRACTICAL CONCERNS**
  Maintenance
    Is Maintenance A Possibility?
    Special Considerations
  Health Care
  Counsel Fees
  Financial Planning
  Bankruptcy Alert

19 **NEGOTIATE LIKE AN EXPERT**
  Preparation
    Inner Work
    Basics For Success
    Listening
    Inequality
  Techniques

13

DIVISION OF PROPERTY

EQUITABLE DISTRIBUTION

Do not assume property distribution will be equal or fair.

Marriage is legally viewed as an economic partnership in which spouses combine income and labor with the intention of sharing the benefits of such. A couple can divide their assets and liabilities pretty much as they wish when the marriage ends. If they cannot agree, the Court has the power to determine how the marital property is to be divided. In New York State, fault has no impact unless a spouse is guilty of dissipating assets, fraud, or extremely improper behavior, often referred to as "egregious fault."

Most states are equitable distribution states, meaning that property is to be divided "fairly" by using certain criteria. Among these states, however, there is variation regarding the interpretation of what property qualifies as divisible. Some state laws allow all property of a married couple to be divided; others differentiate separate from marital property and allow the separate property to continue to be held by the spouse who owns it. For example, both New York and Connecticut are equitable distribution states, but New York defines separate property and allows it to stay with the owner, while Connecticut allows separate property to be divided.

The general principles for the distribution of property in New York State are set forth in Domestic Relations Law Section 236 (1980), also known as the Equitable Distribution Law. It defines marital property as all property acquired by both or either spouse during the marriage until the day divorce action is started or a legal Agreement is signed. The marital assets and liabilities are to be divided equitably between the spouses. Deciding what is equitable is a judgment call; a fair outcome is contingent upon judges being impartial and informed. With overcrowded matrimonial courts, there may be little time for judges to learn the facts of each case.

Some factors the Court uses to determine equitable distribution of property are:
- Length of marriage.
- Health and age of each spouse.
- Contribution and services to the marriage.
- Future earning ability.

- ◆ Liquid and nonliquid nature of the assets.
- ◆ Possibly, the income and property each brought to the marriage.
- ◆ Loss of inheritance and pension rights. By law, married persons automatically get one-third or more of the estate of their spouses. With the dissolution of a marriage, spouses lose their right of inheritance to their former spouses' estates. The Court takes this loss of inheritance into account when distributing property.

Equitable distribution means fair distribution, not necessarily equal. It is not an automatic fifty-fifty split, but presently there tends to be an equal split of many of the assets with marriages of ten years or more. Interests in businesses and the value of degrees and licenses are often difficult to divide, regardless of the length of the marriage. Do not assume the division will be equal or fair. Be prepared to prove and negotiate for your rightful share of the marital property. For the less advantaged spouse with questionable earning capacity, even an equal split of the property may be unfair when the earning capacity of each spouse is realistically analyzed. Do the math; calculate the amount of income each of you can generate during your working years. This can be especially disturbing if you helped your spouse earn a professional degree or build his or her career or business. Try not to think "equal"; think "fair" in terms of your future financial well-being.

Divorce has become more business focused as a result of equitable distribution, because time-consuming investigation into the existence and value of marital assets is often required. Professional fees can consume a large part of a couple's equity. From the outset, clarify your priorities about those assets you most want and need. At the first meeting with your lawyer, know the basics of the Equitable Distribution Law. Be informed about the financial value of the marriage and clear about what you desire and what is reasonable to expect. Be psychologically prepared to lose some property. Dividing property is viewed as an economic necessity; try to keep the emotions out of it. The Court sees it as business. Judges do not have the time to care about how you feel. The Court does not concern itself with morality or fault, unless there is extreme dissipation of assets or egregious fault.
PART VI - in Chapter 20: "Get Down To Business"

Remember, you and your spouse can decide how you want to divide your property. Except for adhering to the child support guidelines, you have great freedom in how to distribute assets and liabilities. If your agreement on distribution fits your needs and appears to be fair to each party, the Court is likely to accept it.
APPENDIX - Customizing Guide

MARITAL AND NONMARITAL PROPERTY

Marital property is to be divided.

MARITAL PROPERTY

In New York State, marital property is considered to be any asset you and your spouse acquired while you were married, regardless of who made the money and acquired it or whose name is on the deed, title, or account. Basically, marital property is anything that is not separate property.

Examples of marital property:
- Principal residence, vacation homes, business real estate, vehicles, bank accounts, investments, pensions and other retirement accounts, royalties, and professional degrees and licenses acquired and earned during the marriage.
- Gifts between spouses during the marriage.
- Active appreciation (increase in value as a result of active participation) of both separate and marital property. If both you and your spouse worked on a property or paid a mortgage from your incomes, the increase in value becomes marital property, even if the asset belongs to one of you.
- Property acquired by using marital property. If during the divorce proceedings you use marital property to buy more property, the new property is also marital.
- Businesses, including professional practices. You may need to employ experts to determine values. With a short-term marriage where a license has been earned due to the efforts of both spouses but a profitable practice has not yet been established, the license itself may be viewed as having little value as marital property.
- Celebrity status as an artist.

In summary, title does not control distribution of property; it does not matter in whose name the property is. The trend of the Court is to view most of a couple's assets as marital.

APPENDIX – Customizing Guide

SEPARATE PROPERTY

The spouse who claims to own separate property has the burden of proving that it should be separated out of the marital pot.

Examples of separate property:
- Property you brought into the marriage.
- Inheritances you received.
- Gifts given solely to you from someone other than your spouse.
- Gifts given to you by your spouse prior to the marriage.
- Compensation from personal injury/disability settlements or lawsuits, except for the compensation for lost earnings, which is marital.
- Assets listed as "separate" in a valid Prenuptial Agreement.
- Passive appreciation of separate property during the marriage.
- Property you acquire after commencing divorce action or signing a legal Agreement, except bonuses earned during the marriage or any asset acquired with marital assets.

APPENDIX – Customizing Guide

CONVERSION OF SEPARATE PROPERTY INTO MARITAL PROPERTY

Unknowingly, spouses often convert separate property into marital property. It happens when you comingle or combine your separate property with marital in some way, such as putting a gift of $50,000 given solely to you into a joint bank account. If your spouse actively contributed to your separate property by paying part of the mortgage on the home you brought into the marriage or by giving you advice on how to invest money awarded to you in a damage suit, it could be interpreted that your separate property has been converted into marital property.

There are many gray areas with the conversion of separate property to marital property. If you feel you have contributed to a separate property and it should qualify as a divisible asset, you will need to argue it and negotiate. Possibly, just the increase in value caused by your participation may be divisible; this is referred to as the "active appreciation" on the asset. The burden of proving whether specific property has become marital or remains separate rests with you.

THE PROCESS IS IMPERFECT

Experts will vary; it can become a matter of negotiating numbers.

Ultimately, each spouse goes over the other's Statement of Net Worth and supporting documentation. Each is entitled to rely on professional financial evaluations. The cost of the divorce goes up with the services of accountants, appraisers, actuaries, and other professionals. It can become a numbers game; especially with appreciation.

It is easy to value bank accounts and stocks and bonds. To value real estate, antiques, and jewelry is relatively easy with appraisals. Pensions can be valued with information from an employer or by an actuary, using a set of parameters to estimate the value.

Small businesses are harder to value, especially if all records and day-to-day management are under one spouse's control, but there are professionals certified in business valuation. The assistance of a forensic accountant or certified fraud examiner (CFE) or, possibly, a private investigator might be appropriate.

You may be encouraged to get the highest value placed on the assets your spouse wants and the lowest value on those you want. You each can get your own appraisals, but since expert valuations often differ, it can become a matter of negotiating numbers. Be prepared to negotiate.

Career assets such as degrees, professional licenses, business reputations, and celebrity status are vital aspects of your marital value but are very difficult to measure in money. The enhanced earning power provided by these is often more valuable than the house or pension. These assets have precious value and are extremely important in negotiations.

APPENDIX – Customizing Guide

14

LET'S LOOK AT THE TAX BITE

BASICS

Do not be fooled about the real value of an asset.

Estimating the amount of taxes you will be required to pay when you sell a property or withdraw income from a retirement plan will enable you to determine the asset's real value. Income tax must be paid on income withdrawn from retirement plans, such as 401(k) or IRA accounts. Be aware of penalties associated with early withdrawals. Capital gains taxes must be paid on gains you make when you sell stocks, real estate, businesses, and possibly, a residence that has appreciated significantly. Taxes can substantially impact an asset's apparent value. To calculate taxes due for assets other than income, first determine a dollar value the property in its present condition is expected to bring in the market, its "market value."

CALCULATE REAL VALUE

Even if you are not good with numbers, this is not hard; stay with it.

MUTUAL FUNDS

Let's say your spouse proposes a split of two hundred shares of ABC stock. You can have one hundred shares (Group A), and he or she will take one hundred shares (Group B). Each has a present market value of $30,000. It sounds like a decent proposal, but do not agree until you do some figuring. Let's look at how taxes affect the real value of what appear to be two assets of equal value.

GROUP A		GROUP B
$ 30,000	Market Value	$ 30,000
- 5,000	Basis	- 20,000
$ 25,000	Capital Gain / Taxable Profit	$ 10,000
x 20 %	Capital Gains Tax (not including state)	x 20 %
$ 5,000	Tax Liability	$ 2,000
$ 30,000	Present Value	$ 30,000
- 5,000	Tax Liability	- 2,000
$ 25,000	**Real Value**	**$ 28,000**

What superficially appears to be an equal trade awards you investments worth less than the stock your spouse would get. Taxes can have a significant impact on the real monetary value of an asset.

COMMERCIAL REAL ESTATE

Calculating the true value of investment real estate is more complicated; you must account for more factors. To find the after-tax value, begin by calculating the "adjusted basis" of an asset. Knowing the adjusted basis and doing some math may enable you to figure the profit you are likely to make, the capital gains tax due on that profit, and the real value of the asset.

To determine the adjusted basis, you must work with the "original basis" and other factors, such as the cost of improvements and amount of depreciation allowed or allowable. With commercial real estate, a certain amount of depreciation is expensed yearly on tax returns, allowing you to deduct the cost of the asset over its life. When you sell the property, you must include the amount of depreciation you have been allowed during the previous tax years. If you are unable to determine the up-to-date depreciation, contact your tax preparer for an accurate figure.

Do your calculations as follows:

◆ **Adjusted Basis = Original Basis plus Improvements minus Depreciation plus Selling Expenses** (advertising, legal, other).

◆ **Sales Proceeds minus Adjusted Basis = Capital Gain** (profit on which you must pay tax).

◆ **Capital Gains Tax = 25% x Capital Gain on amount of Non-excess Depreciation.** If depreciation in excess of straight line was used, it can be subject to ordinary income tax.

◆ **Capital Gains Tax = 20% x Capital Gain on profit other than Depreciation.**

◆ **Real Value = Net Sales Proceeds minus Tax and Mortgage due.**

Let's say during the settlement negotiations your spouse proposes to transfer to you a commercial property with a current value of $200,000. Its original cost was $100,000; the remaining mortgage is $22,000; improvements were $10,000; depreciation has been about $50,000. What you are trading to your spouse for the commercial property should be of equal value or greater. It is not enough to just know the "equity" (current market value minus the outstanding mortgage or debt). You must know how the taxes will impact the value; you must know the real value. You might have $178,000 in equity in the property, but the real value after taxes might be closer to $145,000. Tax laws regarding depreciation can be complicated; seek financial advice and guidance.

APPENDIX – Customizing Guide

VALUE OF CASH

If you have a choice between a $100,000 401(k) account and a $100,000 CD account, which would you take? The CD is like cash; there are no taxes on cash. Withdrawals from the 401(k) are taxed; so if you are in the 28% tax bracket, the 401(k) is worth about $70,000. Remember, one dollar of cash in the bank equals one dollar. A dollar of retirement plan funds must be reduced by the tax liability.

SUMMARY

When negotiating to divide your assets, be aware of the tax consequences so you can calculate the true value of each asset. What superficially appears to be an equal swap can be significantly less than equal. Consider working with an accountant who has experience with the financial issues connected with divorce.

Opportunities are never lost. The other fellow takes those you miss.

Anonymous

What is more mortifying than to feel that you have missed
the plum for want of courage to shake the tree?

Logan Pearsall Smith

15

WHO GETS WHAT?

PRINCIPAL RESIDENCE

The marital residence is often the biggest emotional and financial issue.

Often, the single most valuable marital asset is the principal residence. You can opt to sell and divide the proceeds or trade other assets for your spouse's share of the property's value. Without any other assets, the Court can order the house to be sold and the money divided. A spouse who wants to stay in the residence with the children may decide to give up his or her right to the other spouse's pension as a trade. If you are thinking about negotiating for the house, be sure you can handle the financial burden of the monthly mortgage payments, taxes, and upkeep. You may also be required to qualify to refinance the mortgage in your own name if your spouse wants his or her name removed from the original mortgage.

Some couples are able to work out joint ownership for a specific period of time, possibly until the children have graduated from school. To succeed, the ex-spouses must trust each other and work well enough together to cover expenses and maintain upkeep. This type of arrangement is not likely to work well for young families who would have joint ownership for a long time. One spouse might want to remarry or relocate and not keep the agreement.

PENSION

The pension can be one of the most secure assets.

PLAN CAREFULLY

To learn about your spouse's pension plan, you either have to be provided the information voluntarily or have your lawyer request or subpoena it. You need to know the rules, options, and benefits of the plan so you can best provide for your future financial needs. Express that, as a result of a pending lawsuit, you are "pursuing an interest in the retirement plans provided for the employees of company's name" and need information regarding specific regulations for the approval of a Qualified Domestic Relations Order (QDRO). Request a Summary Plan Description (SPD) and a copy of the text of those plans for which your spouse is eligible; include his or her

Social Security number. Ask for information on how to contact the Plan Administrator, such as name, address, phone number, and e-mail. Request a copy of your spouse's account statement and/or benefits statement. If you are unable to secure what you need directly, work through your lawyer.

APPENDIX – Exhibits: Qualified Domestic Relations Order

Types of retirement plans:

- ◆ Defined contribution plans – the most common of which are the 401(k), 403(b), and profit sharing plans. Some defined contribution plans allow for a lump sum transfer to the nonemployee spouse at the time of divorce. The use of a QDRO will avoid the imposition of a 10% penalty, when an interest in the plan is assigned to the other spouse. A current statement shows a plan's value.
- ◆ Defined benefit plans – company plans promising to pay a certain amount per month to the employee after retirement. An actuary can determine a plan's value.

Division of pensions is often a sensitive issue and can be used as a bargaining tool, but be certain any assets you accept in place of a portion of your spouse's pension are equal in value. Giving up your portion of the pension for the principal residence might not be a fair trade and may cause you unexpected financial hardship. If you plan to receive your share of your spouse's retirement at the time he or she retires, be sure that your share is secured by life insurance or that you are named as the beneficiary of the funds to the extent of your interest therein.

PART V – Chapter 14: Let's Look At The Tax Bite
PART VII – in Chapter 26: "Property"

Be aware of the "time value" of money. The present value of a defined contribution plan may appear to be insignificant, but when you consider its tax deferred benefit, the pension's value in the future can be significant. For example, the present amount of $50,000, allowed to grow taxed deferred at eight percent, will have a value of more than $233,000 in twenty years. The divisible portion of the pension is only that which had accumulated during the marriage, but the nonparticipating spouse can still benefit from the tax deferred growth on that amount.

Go over the value of the pension carefully. It is not something to give up lightly. It can be one of the most secure assets. Project into the future to try to determine your financial needs and the value of the pension when it starts to pay you. Take into account the affect of inflation. With a steady three percent inflation rate, prices will double in twenty-four years. If the rate were to jump to six percent, costs would double in twelve years. You want to have sufficient assets to support yourself during retirement.

Find out about your Social Security Retirement Benefits. You may be eligible to start receiving payments at the age of sixty-two. These benefits are based on your earnings and the number of years you worked. With a marriage of at least ten years prior to divorce, you are eligible to have your benefits calculated according to your former spouse's earnings history, as long as you have not remarried and are not eligible for a higher benefit on your own earnings history. You may be eligible to fifty percent of your ex-spouse's amount, and he or she still receives his or her full benefit. Be sure to get updated specifics about this; there are some limitations. If divorce seems to be inevitable and you have been married close to ten years, consider waiting until you pass the ten-year mark in order to increase your retirement options.

To find out what the records show for you, complete a Request for Social Security Statement, Form SSA-7004. To get this form:

➥ Call your local Social Security office or the Tele Service Center at (800) 772-1213.
➥ Connect with *www.ssa.gov* via the Internet.
➥ Write to Social Security Administration, Office of Public Inquiries, Windsor Park Building, 6401 Security Blvd., Baltimore, MD 21235.

A Social Security Statement will be sent to you showing your Social Security earnings history, amount of money you have paid in, and an estimate of your future benefits.

TO DIVIDE A PENSION

A pension legally belongs to the spouse enrolled in the pension plan, hereafter referred to as the "Participant." With divorce, each spouse loses his or her rights to the other spouse's pension. To divide a pension between divorcing spouses, a domestic relations order, called a Qualified Domestic Relations Order (QDRO), needs to be drafted by an attorney or a pension specialist and then filed with the Court. The QDRO must also be qualified (approved) by the administrator of the pension plan to be sure it conforms to the plan's requirements. The divisible portion of the pension is that which had accumulated during the marriage up to the commencement of a divorce action or the filing of an Agreement. Pension benefits accrued before the marriage and following the commencement of legal action remain with the Participant.

The Qualified Domestic Relations Order states how the pension is to be distributed according to the couple's Agreement. The court order directs the pension administrator to divide the pension and pay each spouse directly. It divides the pension into two separate retirement accounts, often fifty-fifty. The nonemployee ex-spouse, hereafter referred to as the "Alternate Payee," is treated like a participant in the pension plan. There are no tax penalties. If you are the Alternate Payee and divorce without a QDRO, the plan is not authorized to pay you.

Qualified Domestic Relations Orders apply to defined benefit plans and to defined contribution plans. The amount of a defined benefit plan is determined at retirement. An actuarial formula is used to estimate the pension's value. Your QDRO will include words similar to "With the retirement of name of Participant, name of Alternate Payee will begin to receive payments, representing fifty percent of the qualifying divisible amount of the pension, and these payments will continue for life." Defined contribution plans like 401(k) and profit sharing plans have a specific value and can be divided as of the date of divorce or legal separation.

Individual Retirement Accounts (IRA) can be divided at the time of divorce or legal separation without tax penalties, as long as the transfer of funds is made directly into the spouse's IRA account. This distribution does not require a Qualified Domestic Relations Order. Government pension plans such as United States Civil Service, state public employee pensions, and military pensions require special court orders.

APPENDIX – Customizing Guide
Exhibits: Qualified Domestic Relations Order

DRAFTING A QUALIFIED DOMESTIC RELATIONS ORDER

Qualified Domestic Relations Orders basically state the amount or portion the Alternate Payee is to receive, how payments are to be figured, when payments are to begin, and what she/he is to receive if the Participant dies prior to retirement.

Research the pension thoroughly to find out what you need to know so you can assist your lawyer in designing a QDRO that protects you sufficiently within the limits of what the pension allows. The pension administrator might not willingly volunteer information but might answer questions. Two key questions to ask are: (1) *Is the Alternate Payee allowed to start to receive benefits at the earliest retirement age for the Participant, even if the Participant does not retire at that age?* (2) *Does the plan provide for "survivor's benefits?"* If you are inquiring about a defined contribution plan, ask if the plan allows for a lump sum payment to be made.

It can take several months for the plan administrator to qualify the domestic relations order. During this time, the plan is supposed to separate out the Alternate Payee's agreed upon share. Check to see that this is done. It might be wise to state in the QDRO that the Participant is not allowed to borrow against the Alternate Payee's portion during this time. Also, you might want to provide for the Alternate Payee to share in any appreciation of his or her share of the retirement monies until the date of transfer. Be mindful that the Participant may want to include a provision requiring that any decrease in the funds, until the date of transfer, be shared proportionately by the parties.

If not otherwise prohibited, draft the order to allow the Alternate Payee to withdraw money from the plan at the earliest allowable retirement age, usually fifty-five years, even if the Participant does not retire at fifty-five years. The reason for doing so is that the Alternate Payee cannot take money from the plan until the Participant is eligible to do so. If the Participant is eligible at fifty-five but chooses to continue working, it may be interpreted that the Alternate Payee must wait for the Participant's actual retirement before drawing a pension. Do not leave it to interpretation.

Include wording to cover the event of early retirement, often accompanied by a monetary incentive, so the Alternate Payee can share in this enhanced benefit. If the plan allows the Participant to borrow from the plan, be sure to include in the court order that the Alternate Payee is to be assured the same right.

Arrange for the protection of your portion of the pension in the event the Participant dies. Learn from the pension administrator what options the plan allows for setting up survivor's benefits, so you can clarify this in your settlement agreement and be protected. The QDRO must specifically detail how the Alternate Payee is to share in the death benefits and is limited by the terms of your Agreement. If the company does not provide death benefits, try to include in your Agreement that a life insurance policy is to guarantee the Alternate Payee's portion of the pension in the event of the death of the Participant.

PART VII - in Chapter 26: "Property"
APPENDIX – Exhibits: Qualified Domestic Relations Order

Be sure any lump sum amount being sent to you from a qualified retirement plan is transferred directly to your Individual Retirement Accounts (IRA). If it is not, taxes will be withheld and a penalty imposed for premature distribution.

There is an Internal Revenue Service rule that might help you if your finances have been overly stressed by the divorce. It states that money received from a qualified retirement plan as a result of divorce can be withdrawn without your having to pay the ten percent penalty for early distribution. An IRA is not considered to be a qualified plan; therefore any monies that are distributed to you from an IRA are subject to the 10% early withdrawal penalty, unless you are fifty-nine and one-half years of age. The penalty, however, does not apply to distributions made by a QDRO from qualified plans, but you will have to pay income taxes on the amount you take out. You have to separate out the amount of money to be used before it is transferred directly into your IRA. There are also certain timing restrictions; withdrawing the funds cannot be done before the divorce and must be done within a certain time after the divorce. Work closely with your accountant or financial advisor to be sure your circumstances qualify you for this benefit. Also laws change; you need professional guidance and up-to-date information.

Tax Code Section (72)(t)(2)(D)

OTHER DISTRIBUTIONS

*When it is impractical or impossible to divide an asset,
a distributive award can be allocated.*

BUSINESSES

A business is difficult to divide. It can be sold and the proceeds divided but often this is not a viable option. One spouse can buy out the other spouse but must have the assets to trade or cash to do so. For negotiating, be prepared to prove how you contributed to building the business.

PART III - in Chapter 7: "Compiling Your Marital History"

DEGREES / LICENSES / GOODWILL

New York State law views professional licenses and degrees earned during the marriage as marital property. Most states, however, claim these assets are not property and cannot be transferred. Measuring the value of the enhanced earning power degrees and licenses help to generate is imprecise at best. The same is true with valuing the income producing capacity of celebrity status or a recognized name or professional reputation, often referred to as "goodwill." Degrees, licenses, and goodwill are often more valuable than the house or pension because of the elevated earning power they create.

To prove and negotiate your economic right to a portion of the value of degrees, licenses, business reputation, and celebrity status acquired during your marriage, provide details about:

❐ Contributions you made to your spouse's education, training, or career and professional reputation.

☐ Potential value of the career you gave up to be a wife/husband or primary caregiver.

☐ Benefits you gave up such as a pension, medical insurance, and career or earning potential.

☐ Service as a homemaker and/or social director.

Outcomes of matrimonial actions involving licenses, degrees, and goodwill are unpredictable because the Court has a great degree of discretion in deciding how to divide these assets.

PART III - in Chapter 7: "Compiling Your Marital History"
PART IV - Chapter 12: Problems With The Legal System
APPENDIX – Customizing Guide

DISTRIBUTIVE AWARDS

When it is impractical or impossible to divide an asset, such as a business or professional license, a distributive award can be allocated. It is an amount of money equal to the fair share of another asset, usually paid out over a period of years. The sooner your distributive award can be paid, the better. Since this transfer of assets is not taxed, it may be to your advantage to agree to a lesser amount in exchange for a lump sum payment. Instead of waiting for periodic payments, you would be able to invest the full amount and make it start working for you. The payments you are to receive in the future will be worth less due to inflation. A $50,000 distributive award is worth that amount today and something less as time passes. You can negotiate that interest be included interest when the award is to be paid over time. If you fear your spouse might declare bankruptcy, agreeing to a distributive award may not be a financially secure decision. Work closely with an attorney knowledgeable about bankruptcy.

PART V - in Chapter 18: "Bankruptcy Alert"
PART VII - in Chapter 26: "Options And Their Consequences"
APPENDIX – Customizing Guide

LIABILITIES

You will be liable for joint debts until they are paid, regardless of what your legal Agreement says. Creditors will hold you both responsible. Have your name removed from any mortgages or liens on property going to your spouse. Be very clear about this in your Agreement and follow up to see that it is done. When one spouse's name is to be removed from a loan commitment, the bank usually requires the remaining spouse to refinance the loan in his or her name only. If you are the custodial spouse and want the house for the sake of the children, be sure you financially qualify for a mortgage. Some lending institutions do not count maintenance and child support as income for the first year or two.

PART IX - in Chapter 30: "Wrap Up Documents"

Significant credit card debt or other large bills can pose a difficult problem. If possible, pay off all debt before divorcing. If you cannot do so and your spouse is responsible for paying some portion of the debt and defaults, the creditors will not only come to you for payment, but your credit rating will be damaged. Try to negotiate either that some marital property is to be sold to pay the debt, or that you assume the responsibility for paying it in exchange for more marital property. In addition, some creditors are willing to lower the total amount of the debt in return for a sizable lump sum payment.

PART VII - in Chapter 26: "Property" and "Debts And Liabilities"
APPENDIX – Customizing Guide

YOUR WILL

Your spouse is entitled to one-third or more of your estate.

You should draw up a new will. If you have a will that leaves most or all of your estate to your spouse, it would be wise to make a new will. In New York State, until you are divorced or have signed a legal document such as a Settlement or Separation Agreement, waiving your inheritance rights to each other's estates, your spouse has the right to one-third of your estate or $50,000, if the latter is greater. Find out the specifics for your home state.

If you do not have a will and there are no children, your spouse is entitled to your entire estate according to New York State law. If you do have children and no will, your spouse is entitled to $50,000, plus fifty percent of the balance of the estate. The remainder goes to the children. A simple will is neither complicated nor costly to do. It could give you much peace of mind. You may also need to change the beneficiary of your life insurance policy, if there is not a temporary restraining order limiting your right to do so.

APPENDIX – Customizing Guide

Knowing is not enough, we must apply.
Willing is not enough, we must do.
Johann Wolfgang von Goethe

If you are patient in one moment of anger,
you will escape a hundred days of sorrow.
Chinese Epigram

16

CHILD CUSTODY / SUPPORT / VISITATION

YOUR APPROACH TO CUSTODY

With contested custody, take nothing for granted,
even if you have been the primary caregiver.

Please note: Trying to resolve child-related issues with a spouse who is abusive, violent, or addicted may be impossible or dangerous. Use this information to become informed, but secure the specialized professional assistance your circumstance may demand.

AMICABLE

Cooperate with your spouse to decide custody, support, and visitation issues. You know better than others what is best for your family. It is less unsettling for children to know that their parents, and not strangers, are making the decisions that affect them. Reassure your youngsters; tell them: *We are working it out.* View your agreement as a "living document" that is able to accommodate your children's changing needs. Design it to satisfy both present and future circumstances. Co-parenting is a long-term obligation. You want to be able to work with your former spouse to manage and resolve family issues, instead of going back to Court.
PART VII - Chapter 26: Design An Agreement That Protects You

LESS THAN AMICABLE

In New York State, unless a parent has been proven unfit, both parents are considered to be equally qualified to care for the children. The Court generally feels it is best for a child to have access to both parents. Domestic violence or safety issues such as parental carelessness, neglect, and abuse may leave you no choice but to fight for custody. Many custody battles, however, are not over what is best for the children, but instead, are motivated by revenge or used as a financial strategy. Often the children become pawns for money. If there are contested issues regarding the children, be prepared for the worst and secure a lawyer who has successful experience handling custody cases.

Take nothing for granted, even if you have been the primary caregiver and your spouse has not demonstrated a genuine interest in or involvement with the children. The Judge might decide to award custody to your spouse, based on financial status or some other reason that appears to be more significant than your continuing as the primary caregiver. Abusive spouses are more likely to precipitate custody battles as a way of continuing to dominate and punish. If either desertion or abuse exist and you are commencing a divorce action, you might want your attorney to file a motion for temporary custody at the same time he or she files the papers to start the lawsuit. If you want to protect your custodial rights without also filing for divorce, you can arrange for a hearing in Family Court to obtain a court order for temporary custody. Having a lawyer with you in Family Court is not necessary, but it is advisable.

PART IV - Chapter 9: Family Court
in Chapter 11: "Pleading Stage"
APPENDIX – Customizing Guide

BEST INTERESTS OF THE CHILD

The Court determines custody
based on serving the "best interests of the child."

CUSTODY ARRANGEMENTS

If you and your spouse are unable to work out a custody arrangement, the Court will decide the issue based on serving the "best interests of the child," as interpreted by the presiding Judge. The Court considers:
◆ Stability of the parents and needs of the child.
◆ Relationship each parent has with the child.
◆ Ability of the parents to communicate with each other regarding the child.
◆ Present residence of the child and the effect of a change in the living arrangement.
◆ Degree of care and concern demonstrated by each parent.
◆ Capability and availability of each parent to care for the child.
◆ Importance of keeping siblings together.
Warning: Do not assume anything.

There are two parts to custody. The legal aspect is the decision-making power regarding major matters of a child's life such as religion, education, and health. Residential custody addresses the day-to-day care and living arrangement of a child. According to an agreed upon schedule, the daily care may be the primary responsibility of one parent or the shared responsibility of both parents. When you design your own agreement, you have greater flexibility in creating an appropriate arrangement.

There are a variety of labels used to describe custody arrangements. For example, with "joint legal custody," both parents are authorized to participate in making major decisions for the child. With "sole legal custody," only one parent is authorized to do so. With "joint physical custody," the child lives with each parent part of the time. One version of this is for the child to remain in the principal residence, and the parents alternate living there. Do not let labels get in the way of your designing the best arrangement for your family's needs. Courts rarely impose joint custody following a trial. Joint custody means both spouses are friendly enough with each other so they can make decisions together. If parents are in Court arguing, a Judge reasons they cannot work together with joint custody and will usually award sole legal custody.

APPENDIX – Customizing Guide

RELOCATION DISPUTES

Little research has been done regarding the effects of relocation on children, and the courts are being forced to decide cases where it is unclear what constitutes the best interests of the child. Generally, if the relocation is disputed and is not a financial necessity, but just for financial betterment, the custodial parent will not be allowed to move with the children from the state or area where both parents live. There is no agreed upon criteria for making these decisions; each case is judged on its own merits. If you feel it is necessary for you to move with the children, try to work out an agreement with the other parent. You can reorganize the visitation schedule to allow the noncustodial parent visits of longer duration to compensate for less frequent visits. Any informal agreement with your ex-spouse must have Court approval; do not relocate without it. If you do, you could be forced either to move back to litigate the issue or to send your children back while the case is pending.
APPENDIX – Customizing Guide

CONTESTED CUSTODY

Once you file a child custody motion,
many other people become involved.

HOW THE LEGAL PROCESS RESOLVES CUSTODY DISPUTES

To resolve custody disputes, the Judge receives assistance from forensic investigative reports from a variety of sources. A probation officer or social worker may make announced home visits and meet with the child alone and with the child and each parent. The Probation Officer's report does not look behind the answers given. It is a basic "He says…; she says…." type of report. The psychiatrist or psychologist, appointed by the Judge, is usually someone with whom the Judge is comfortable. Evaluative reports are made on each child and on each parent. This is expensive due to hours of interviewing and compiling the findings. The Judge determines how the fee is to be paid based upon the parties' respective incomes and the available liquid assets. The investigation includes psychological testing and appraises parenting ability, the household routine, and the home atmosphere. It evaluates parental involvement in the daily activities of the child with school functions, academic enrichment, religious instruction, and home care. Balancing a career with parenting can be a sensitive area.

A law guardian is assigned by the Court to act as an advocate for the child. This appointee is a lawyer whose interpretation of the child's best interests may be different from what a parent feels is best. It is common for the state to pay the law guardian's fee in Family Court. However, when both parents retain counsel, the Court may require them to pay. In Supreme Court, the parents are almost always responsible for paying the fee. The law guardian reviews necessary papers, meets with the children and parents, speaks with third parties involved in the family's life, and attends all court appearances.

Your meetings and interviews with legal and health care professionals are extremely important. The Judge relies heavily on the position of the law guardian and forensic evaluator and on the forensic investigative reports they generate. Make a good initial impression. Remain focused; act naturally. Do not speak negatively about the other parent, with the exception of being honest about any form of abuse and unreasonable use of drugs and alcohol. Prior to meeting with the Court-appointed psychiatrist or psychologist, it might be helpful to schedule a private visit with a mental health professional to become informed about what to expect with the forensic examination and how to best present your strengths. It is extremely important to be viewed as a caring, stable parent, involved with your youngster's daily activities and committed to raising a well-adjusted child. With custody battles, everything about your life can be examined, including confidential meetings with your own mental health professional.

Be prepared with convincing documentation, providing evidence that you are the most appropriate custodial parent. If you have been the primary caregiver, highlight that fact. Include evidence of enrichment activities for the child and testimonials from teachers, therapists, religious instructors, and neighbors. Describe the stability of the home and include a statement regarding the child's care when you are not available. The moneyed parent can overpower a more suitable, but nonmoneyed, parent in a custody battle if the latter is overconfident or underprepared. Organize documentation focusing on why your spouse should not be awarded custody, if there are clear reasons such as frequent trips away from home, abusive behavior, or excessive use of alcohol or drugs. If you are the designated custodial parent while litigation is pending, keep a dated record of actions or incidents that reflect on your spouse's parenting ability. Late payments and irregular visitation may help to suggest your spouse would not be the suitable choice as a primary caregiver.
APPENDIX – Customizing Guide

CUSTODY CUES

- Custody can be heard in Family Court or Supreme Court. Family-related issues such as custody, visitation, support, and Orders of Protection can be decided in the Family Court if you have not yet started divorce action in the Supreme Court. Otherwise, those issues are handled by the Supreme Court, which also rules on the status of the marriage and property division.
  APPENDIX – Customizing Guide
- Avoid including children as part of a package deal. Litigate the money issues, if necessary, but not custody, if possible.
- If you leave your home and children, it creates the presumption that the one left behind with the children is suitable to be awarded custody.
- A child's preference to be with one parent is not binding on the Court, but it is, usually, given more weight with older children.
- There is no rule on this, but the custodial parent with small children is often allowed to stay in the residence if the mortgage and taxes are not more than a rental, and there are other assets with which to negotiate.

CHILD SUPPORT

If you and your spouse cooperate,
you are more likely to design a workable arrangement.

BASICS

You and your spouse can make your own agreement regarding the support of your children, but it must comply with the Child Support Standards Act. Your attorney can advise you on the details. If you cooperate, you are more likely to design a workable arrangement with the support being paid on a regular basis. The Family Court can award child support as part of a child support proceeding, or the Supreme Court can do so as part of a legal separation action or a divorce action. You are financially responsible for your children until they reach the age of twenty-one, unless they emancipate earlier by marrying, joining the military, becoming self-sufficient through full-time employment, or by maintaining a separate permanent residence, not including school or travel. In negotiated agreements, child support is often paid until the twenty-second birthday, because it is rare for a child to graduate from college by the time he or she turns twenty-one. A stepparent is not legally responsible for the financial support of a stepchild, unless he or she has legally adopted the child.

APPENDIX – Customizing Guide

NEW YORK'S CHILD SUPPORT STANDARDS ACT (CSSA)

BASIC FORMULA

New York's Child Support Standards Act (CSSA) of 1989 has established guidelines for the minimum amount of court-ordered child support. A percentage of your combined income is to be allocated for support; it varies depending on the number of children, as follows:

- 17% for one child.
- 25% for two children.
- 29% for three children.
- 31% for four children.
- No less than 35% for five or more children.

The amount is proportionally divided between you and your spouse according to your individual incomes. The noncustodial parent pays his or her portion to the custodial parent. The guidelines allow for deductions, for example: maintenance payments would be calculated as a deduction to the payer's child support obligation.

The Court is required to apply the guidelines for the first $80,000 of combined income, but it is not limited to $80,000. The Court of Appeals has reinterpreted this law by ruling the ceiling of $80,000 no longer applies. The Court can vary from the guidelines when it is evident that the specified percentage amounts are not appropriate. Some influencing factors are:

- A child's physical and emotional health and needs.
- The financial resources of the child and of the parents.
- The financial burden of a parent with children in multiple households.

In addition, a portion of income derived from insurance claims, inheritances, gifts, and lottery winnings can be allotted to child support.

PART IV - in Chapter 8: "Child Custody, Support, Visitation"

The Child Support Standards Act establishes guidelines for court-ordered child support; it does not take away your right to design your own agreement. Your support arrangement must, however, meet minimum requirements, unless there is a legal basis for deviating from the guidelines. In the future, either parent can go into Court to request child support payments be adjusted upward or downward based upon legal criteria, such as a substantial, unanticipated change in circumstances.

PART VII - in Chapter 26: "Child Support"
APPENDIX – Customizing Guide

ADDITIONAL EXPENSES

Other child-related expenses such as child care, health, special needs, and education are to be determined and included. When the custodial parent is working or obtaining an education, reasonable child care costs are to be divided proportionally and added to the child support amount. Non-reimbursed health expenses, not covered by insurance, such as deductible premiums, prescription drugs, orthodontist, optometrist, ophthalmologist, eye glasses, and psychotherapy, are to be considered and divided proportionally. It is your responsibility to document a child's special needs and inform your attorney and the Court. Detail any emotional or physical disability and the educational, therapeutic, and medical attention required. Although not a statutory requirement, try to provide for the extras during the younger years, such as tutoring, enrichment programs, lessons, sports equipment, and camp. The Court may also award educational expenses where appropriate for private school and for the costs of higher education, such as tuition, room and board, and travel to and from school. Take into account the effect of inflation and provide in your Agreement for a periodic cost of living adjustment (COLA), based on changes in the Consumer Price Index.

PART IV - in Chapter 8: "Laws Change"
PART VII - in Chapter 26: "Child Support"
APPENDIX – Customizing Guide

To provide for children, it is wise for each parent to take out a life insurance policy on his or her life and to have disability insurance. Write a new will. With divorce, you and your ex-spouse automatically lose all rights to each other's estates. If you die without a will, your property is to be distributed according to the laws of your state. Be prudent and take the necessary steps to assure security for your children.

PART V - in Chapter 15: "Your Will"
PART IX - in Chapter 30: "Wrap Up Documents"

VISITATION

Design a visitation schedule that fits your family's needs.

The noncustodial parent has visitation/access rights. Parents can design a visitation schedule that fits their needs and those of their children. This includes weekday and weekend access including overnights, alternating holidays and school vacations, and reasonable and unobstructed telephone, mail, and e-mail contact. Visitation rights can be legally suspended or curtailed if there is documented evidence of parental neglect, drug use, undue influence of alcohol, criminal activity, inappropriate sexual behavior in front of children, or violence toward them or in their presence.

PART VII - in Chapter 26: "Custody And Visitation / Access"

17

REMEMBER THE IRS

Good tax advice can empower you to make wise decisions about tax options. Learn how future taxes can impact the proposed financial settlement. Three ways assets are transferred when a marriage is dissolved are property division, child support, and spousal maintenance. Each of these is treated differently by federal income tax laws.

REAL VALUE OF PROPERTY
Be knowledgeable about the impact of future taxes.

With divorce or legal separation, property such as real estate, stocks, Individual Retirement Accounts, and other retirement funds can be transferred tax free. Property settlement payments, such as one spouse trading half of a commercial property to the other spouse, are neither taxable to the recipient nor tax deductible to the payer. When the asset is sold, however, tax is due on the profit made, called "capital gain." You may have substantial capital gains taxes to pay on stocks or commercial property when they are sold. Also, income tax must be paid on withdrawals from retirement funds.
PART V - Chapter 14: Let's Look At The Tax Bite

With the sale of your principal residence, there may be no capital gains taxes due on the profit up to $250,000 for an individual tax return and up to $500,000 for those who file jointly or as divorced or legally separated. To qualify as the "principal residence," you must have owned and lived in the home for at least two out of the five years preceding the sale. You and your spouse qualify, providing you both used the house for two of the past five years, or either you or your former spouse lived in it for two of the past five years as a result of a divorce judgment or legal separation agreement, and neither of you took this exclusion during the past two years. This exemption can be used again on subsequent principal residences. Consult your tax advisor to be certain you are up to date with the most recent tax laws and that you qualify according to the interpretation of the law.

SUPPORT PAYMENTS

The IRS has a specific definition regarding tax deductible maintenance.

Maintenance can be taxable as income to the recipient and deductible for the payer. An overall tax savings can occur, because the payer is usually in a higher tax bracket than the recipient. Some couples work together to take advantage of this tax deduction and share the monetary benefit. If you are the recipient of maintenance, estimate the amount of taxes that will be due, so you can negotiate an adequate gross payment to cover your living expenses, as well as the tax bill. Check with your accountant to find out if you are required to file quarterly estimated tax returns; you want to be prepared to pay on time and avoid a penalty. You and your spouse can choose to file your tax returns so that maintenance does not qualify as either tax deductible and or taxable. If this seems to be an appealing option, discuss it with your tax advisor.

To deter tax payers from declaring other types of payments as if they were tax deductible maintenance, the Internal Revenue Service has a specific definition for "maintenance." Neither property settlement payments nor child support are taxable income to the recipient or tax deductible to the payer. Tax deductible maintenance must satisfy specific requirements. The payments can be in cash or by check or money order. The obligation to pay spousal support must be declared in a final divorce decree, legal Agreement, or temporary court order, and include that the payer's obligation is to end with the recipient's death. Even though your divorce may not be final, you and your spouse cannot file a joint tax return. You and your spouse cannot be living in the same household, unless the divorce is not yet final and the payments are being made under a temporary court order.

If the Internal Revenue Service considers part of the payment to be child support, that portion will not be treated as maintenance. Basically, the Internal Revenue Service treats the payment as child support if it is to end or be reduced within a specific time of the child's emancipation age. The rules can be complicated; work with a competent tax advisor to be properly informed regarding your circumstances.

The IRS Web site (*www.irs.gov*) can help to inform and prepare you to work with a tax advisor or certified divorce planner (CDP). You want to be fully informed and kept up to date regarding limits and requirements affecting what you are trying to accomplish. Work closely with your attorney to be sure your Agreement clearly states what payments are considered to be maintenance, for example: a periodic payment, rent or mortgage, insurance, taxes, utilities, or other expenditures.

PART VII - in Chapter 26: "Options And Their Consequences"

ADVANTAGES TO WORKING TOGETHER

Your filing status affects the amount of taxes you pay.

TAX RETURN STATUS

Your filing status is important in determining the amount of taxes you are required to pay. The tax rate, standard deduction, and eligibility for certain credits and itemized deductions are affected by the filing status you choose. In most cases, using the tax status of Married Filing Separately, while the divorce is pending, will noticeably increase your tax burden. Financially, it is generally best to file a joint return until the divorce or legal separation is final, especially if one spouse is in a high-income bracket. One of the disadvantages is that both you and your spouse are liable for the total tax liability and the accuracy of the data on the return. If you fear that a joint return might not be accurate or you will be unable to verify its accuracy, you might want to protect yourself from future liability by filing separately. The fact that on a joint return maintenance cannot be deducted may be a disadvantage in your situation.

As an unmarried person, you might qualify for Head-of-Household status if you provide more than one-half of the household expenses for at least one relative, parent, or child. As a married person, you might qualify for this tax status if your spouse did not live in the residence for the last six months of the year and you provided over half of the costs for at least one dependent child. Head-of-Household is a more favorable tax status than Single or Married Filing Separately, because the tax rate usually is lower and the standard deduction higher. If you and your ex-spouse have joint physical custody and more than one minor child, you may each qualify for Head-of-Household tax status by having a dependent child live in each of your homes for more than half of the year. Consult your tax advisor.

APPENDIX – Customizing Guide

EXEMPTIONS AND CREDITS

The parent with whom the children live can take tax exemptions for such dependents unless she/he signs a waiver, Internal Revenue Service Form 8332, Release of Claim to Exemption for Child of Divorced or Separated Parents, giving the exemption to the other parent. These exemptions might be valuable to one spouse and offer little financial advantage to the other. If you agree to give up the exemption to the other parent, do so for only one year at a time. If you and your ex-spouse have joint physical custody, you can alternate who claims the children as dependents from year to year. If you have more than one child, you can each claim one or more each year. Do some planning and negotiate what is best for you and share any tax savings.

To qualify for education tax credits, the parent paying the education costs must also claim the child as a dependent. The Child Tax Credit, the Hope Scholarship Credit, and the Lifetime Learning Credit are available to parents. Tax laws change frequently; obtain the latest information from your tax preparer. The IRS Web site, *www.irs.gov*, can help keep you informed.

PROFESSIONAL HELP

If your attorney is not extremely knowledgeable regarding tax law and you have complex tax issues, find a financial specialist. If you signed joint tax returns in the past and you now fear your spouse may have been under reporting income, the Innocent Spouse Exception Law might protect you from being unfairly penalized for your spouse's actions. Meet with a tax professional to learn about the requirements of the law. This law has been modified to better protect innocent spouses. Consider seeking ongoing professional help to keep up with changes in tax laws affecting your situation.

OPTIONS WITH TAX CONSEQUENCES

Know which options benefit you.

Maintenance payments continue to tie you to your spouse financially and, possibly, emotionally. Negotiating a lump sum property settlement, instead of extended maintenance, may help bring closure to the relationship. The disadvantage is that property settlement payments are not tax deductible for the payer, so there would be no opportunity to take advantage of a tax savings. It might be an advantage for the recipient, however, because a lump sum property payment is not taxable as income. Also, there may be greater security for the recipient to accept a one-time property settlement, instead of gambling on prolonged periodic maintenance. If, however, you are the recipient and fear the payer may declare bankruptcy, maintenance would probably be a more secure choice. Support payments cannot be canceled due to bankruptcy, whereas property settlement payments can be reduced or eliminated. Do what is most secure, especially if you have concerns that you and your ex-spouse may not be able to work constructively together.

PART V - in Chapter 18: "Bankruptcy Alert"

The payer of support may offer to pay more maintenance and less child support, because maintenance payments create a tax deduction. Keep in mind:

- ◆ Maintenance payments that are deductible for the payer are taxable income for the recipient.
- ◆ Child support is easier to modify, usually to increase.
- ◆ Child support is not as difficult to collect as is maintenance from a delinquent payer.
- ◆ The Internal Revenue Service has precise definitions for maintenance and child support and rules regarding the declaration of each.

18

ESSENTIAL PRACTICAL CONCERNS

MAINTENANCE

IS MAINTENANCE A POSSIBILITY?

To determine the need for maintenance and its amount and duration, the Court considers:

- ◆ Income, property, and liabilities of each spouse.
- ◆ Present and future capacity to be self-supporting.
- ◆ Length of the marriage.
- ◆ Age, physical, and emotional health of each spouse.
- ◆ Time necessary to acquire the training or education to become financially self-sufficient.
- ◆ Standard of living established during the marriage.
- ◆ Wasteful dissipation of assets.

Presently, in New York, short-term maintenance from three to five years may be awarded for retraining with the expectation that the recipient will become self-supporting. Lifetime maintenance is generally reserved for older spouses of long-term marriages who gave up earning potential to stay home with children. Spousal support is non-gender; it is awarded to both men and women.

If obtaining temporary maintenance is an issue while the matrimonial lawsuit is pending, your lawyer can file a pendente lite motion to request relief. If no action for divorce has been commenced, and your spouse has deserted the household, and you need support, you can petition the Family Court to request the necessary relief.

PART IV - *Chapter 9: Family Court*
in Chapter 11: "Pleading Stage: Pendente Lite Motions"
APPENDIX – *Customizing Guide*
Exhibits: Order To Show Cause (for pendente lite relief)

SPECIAL CONSIDERATIONS

Try to negotiate a provision in your Agreement that the payer is to have disability and life insurance to secure maintenance payments. If you are to receive long-term maintenance, try to protect against inflation with a periodic cost of living adjustment

(COLA), based on changes in an agreed upon index of inflation. It is not uncommon for an Agreement to include the circumstances under which maintenance is to be modified or terminated, such as the cohabitation or gainful employment of the recipient or the commencement of Social Security or pension benefits.

Anticipate the future and evaluate your options. The payer may refuse to keep up with the payments or withhold them for some reason. Being overburdened financially with remarriage and a new family can seriously limit a payer's resources, and he or she may request a modification. Negotiating to receive a lump sum distributive award, instead of relying on an extended payment schedule, might be suitable for your situation. This transfer of property paid to a spouse as part of the distribution of marital property is not taxable. This financial obligation, however, could be canceled if the payer were to declare bankruptcy. To evaluate whether a lump sum distributive award would be wise in your situation, you might want to work with a certified financial planner (CFP) who has experience with divorce issues and options or a certified divorce planner (CDP).

PART V - in Chapter 15: "Pension: Plan Carefully"
in Chapter 17: "Options With Tax Consequences"
in Chapter 18: "Bankruptcy Alert"
PART VII - in Chapter 25: "Spousal Maintenance"
in Chapter 26: "Spousal Maintenance"

HEALTH CARE

Keep health insurance in effect. The working parent with health benefits generally keeps the children on his or her policy. A Qualified Medical Child Support Order (QMCSO) provides the assurance that medical coverage for dependent children is to continue under a parent's health insurance plan. Having a QMCSO also guarantees the parent paying the child's medical expenses the right to deal directly with the child's health care provider and be directly reimbursed.

The Consolidated Omnibus Budget Reconciliation Act (COBRA) is a federal law stipulating that the nonemployee ex-spouse can continue with the company's group health plan for up to three years at his or her own expense. A company with more than twenty employees is obligated to provide health insurance under COBRA. Determine in your Agreement whose responsibility it is to pay for this insurance. To continue with this group insurance, you are required to apply and provide proof of divorce or legal separation.

PART III - in Chapter 6: "Proposed Budget"
APPENDIX – Customizing Guide
Money Matters: Monthly Budget

COUNSEL FEES

According to New York state law, a Judge "may" award legal fees to the financially dependent spouse by requiring the moneyed spouse pay an amount equal to his or her own legal fees. The law, however, does not require the Judge to make the award unless there is a willful violation of a court order. If you are the financially dependent spouse, ask your lawyer at the outset to make a motion to the Judge to order the moneyed spouse to pay legal fees for the nonmoneyed spouse. Request that the funds be made available during the course of litigation, not at the conclusion of the case, so you can secure appropriate legal representation.

If you fear the funds available for legal representation will be exhausted before there is a settlement, try to draw up a written agreement with your lawyer, whereby he or she agrees to wait until the end of the divorce proceedings to be paid what is still due. This is referred to as a "charging lien" and gives your lawyer the right to be paid from your part of the settlement proceeds.

PART IV - in Chapter 12: "Awarding Legal Fees"
PART VI - in Chapter 22: "Billing"
APPENDIX – Customizing Guide

FINANCIAL PLANNING

Secure the assistance you need from professional experts, not only to locate hidden assets and value property, but also to help with financial planning and tax issues. Certified divorce planners (CDP) are trained to analyze how your present decisions will affect your lifestyle in years ahead. There are many factors to consider including income, expenses, support, investments, and retirement. Plan for those big purchase items following divorce such as buying health insurance and paying for college. Understand the long-term effect of inflation; it is especially important in planning for the children's college costs and for your retirement. If your child is a toddler now and will be in college in eighteen years, the cost of that education will be twice its present cost with four percent inflation during that period. If you are forty-eight now and plan to retire by sixty, the cost of living will double if the inflation averages six percent during those twelve years.

If there are substantial assets, negotiate and include in your Agreement a provision requiring a specified amount of money be placed in a trust to guarantee support payments. If that is not a possibility, try to negotiate that disability and life insurance of sufficient amount are to be in effect to secure financial obligations.

PART V - Chapter 14: Let's Look At The Tax Bite
Chapter 17: Remember The IRS
PART VII - in Chapter 26: "Support Payment Assurance"

BANKRUPTCY ALERT

Federal laws governing bankruptcy have precedence over state divorce orders. Some debts owed by a spouse who files for bankruptcy can be canceled. Financial obligations included in your Agreement regarding the payment of debts or buy outs of the home or a small business may be canceled. Support obligations, however, are exceptions; child support and maintenance cannot be canceled.

If you fear your spouse may declare bankruptcy, plan and negotiate a settlement that provides the best protection. Consider trading extended property settlement payments for a greater amount of child or spousal support. Agree to pay the marital debt in exchange for more of the marital property. If your spouse were to agree to pay marital debt and then declares bankruptcy, the creditors can come after you, the non-filing ex-spouse, for what is owed. Work closely with your legal counsel on the wording of your Agreement to specify which payments are the support payments. Check the phrasing to be sure it is comprehensive and accurate. Be sure your lawyer completes and submits for approval a Qualified Domestic Relations Order (QDRO) as soon as possible to try to protect your portion of your ex-spouse's pension. Consult an expert on bankruptcy regarding your specific circumstances in an effort to protect your financial future.

APPENDIX – Exhibits: Qualified Domestic Relations Order

19

NEGOTIATE LIKE AN EXPERT

Please note: Trying to negotiate directly with an abusive, violent, or addicted party is often impossible and, perhaps, dangerous. Use the information to become informed, but secure the specialized professional assistance your circumstance may demand.

PREPARATION

You may not get what you deserve, but you can get much of what you negotiate.

During your divorce proceedings, negotiations are going on at some level and you are involved, quietly or actively, to some degree. The more aware of this you are, the more successful you will be in helping to create a satisfactory settlement. You may not get what you deserve, but you can get much of what you negotiate.

INNER WORK

Take a critical look at what is going on within you. Recognize anger and resentment about what is happening, anxiety about loss, fears about the future, and the unremitting pain. Try to release what is not useful and get the reins on the rest. Holding on to painful, negative feelings can cause you to argue over meaningless things and can lead to bad decisions. Do not allow yourself to be drawn into a struggle to find the truth. Your past relationship does not have one agreed upon truth; it has, and will always have, two or more interpretations. While honoring your pain as natural and necessary, accept the facts and focus on planning for your future. Your feelings can help you clarify what you want, need, and deserve. Use them inwardly to bolster your determination and to keep you goal focused. If you reveal your emotions during negotiations, try only to do so under control as a strategic move.

BASICS FOR SUCCESS

➥ Be informed. Knowing the facts empowers you to determine what is possible and to negotiate from strength.
➥ Make the facts work for you.
  PART III – What Is There And Where Is It?
➥ Decide what you want and need, and what you will give up for what you really want and need. Be sure you can afford to maintain the family residence if that is

what you feel you need. Calculate your future financial needs in order to realistically negotiate adequate support. Be realistic about your children's needs and what is best for them.

PART V – Areas Of Concern
PART VII – Legal Agreements

→ Behave agreeably but do not expect the opposition to be agreeable or fair.

→ Prepare for the possibility of less than honest representation of the facts and psychological attacks by the opposition.

→ Realize you know something about your spouse that can help you succeed. For example, possibly, he or she does not like details, or making decisions, or having certain information revealed, or taking responsibility. Subtly use this knowledge to your advantage.

→ Have reasonable expectations.

→ Remain open to finding creative solutions.

→ Design an agreement that works for you, not one to fit others' views of what is acceptable.

LISTENING

Effective listening is a powerful tool. Listening acknowledges another's right of expression. It helps to reduce resistance and induce willingness. Listening can allow for changes to evolve without solutions being imposed, and thereby end impasses.

INEQUALITY

If you are preparing to negotiate with a spouse you feel is more powerful than you are, develop a strategy to overcome your fears and balance the power. By recognizing and modifying self-defeating reactions you have to your spouse and marital issues, you can begin to build strategic leverage. The opposition will be thrown off by failing to get you to react predictably in a familiar manner. This will be a tremendous psychological advantage to you in negotiating, because your spouse will no longer know how to control you. If you have a low tolerance for uncertainty and risk, and the opposition decides to use this to his or her advantage, you will be at a noticeable disadvantage. Become aware of how uncertainty affects you. Practice techniques to modify the appearance of any behavior that diminishes your strength to negotiate effectively.

PART II - Chapter 4: Caring For Yourself

TECHNIQUES

*Be like ever-powerful water in motion
with flexible determination, flowing toward your goal.*

Your comfort level and relationship with your spouse will determine whether negotiations are to be one to one or with others present such as lawyers, a mediator, or another third party.

→ Meet at a neutral location with a quiet, businesslike atmosphere.

→ Bring the necessary documents.

→ Have a planned agenda and notes with you.

→ Listen attentively and intentionally. It will help reduce resistance, keep you open to new information, and create solutions.

→ Take notes.

→ Sit confidently and maintain a professional attitude.

→ Keep your emotions behind the scene; focus on the business being conducted.

→ Avoid reacting defensively when opposed.

→ Use language intended to defuse anger: *I understand how you might feel that way.*

→ Phrase your opinions and objections in a positive manner.
I am having difficulty with that. Let me show you where.
A more just way to handle that might be….

→ Learn to recognize when power and control become the issue, instead of the issue being negotiated.

→ Pace yourself. Know there will be times to stand firm and times to back off some in order to move ahead.
We have accomplished a lot so far, maybe we should move to another issue.

→ Keep a lid on pride; indulging it will impede progress.

→ Avoid confrontation; it can poison the proceedings.

→ Paraphrase what has been said to help replace a reactive response.
My understanding of what you are saying is…. Is that correct?

→ Ask questions to have the opposition clarify his or her position.

→ Answer questions to support the worthiness of your reasoning.

→ Focus on the issues to be resolved, not on the personalities involved.

→ Be as firm as needed on issues and as respectful as possible toward the people.

→ Remain open to possibilities; almost everything is negotiable.

→ Use your insight and knowledge in a positive manner. You know more about your spouse than anyone else. You know the sensitive areas to touch to stimulate his or her interest in compromising, as well as the areas to avoid. Use this in a positive manner to help create and maintain momentum and leverage.

→ Avoid being pressured into responding if you are uncertain. Say: *I will have to think about that.*

→ Manage stress by keeping your goals in focus as a beacon toward which you are moving.

→ Release your body's tension periodically with slow, deep breathing.

Become like ever-powerful water in motion, moving around obstacles, wearing them down with flexible determination, flowing toward your goal.

PART IV - in Chapter 11: "Your Approach To The Legal Process"
"Basically There Are Two Ways To Attain Your Divorce"
Chapter 12: Problems With The Legal System

The work will teach you how to do it.
Estonian Proverb

I find that the harder I work, the more luck I seem to have.
Thomas Jefferson

PART VI – SELECTING AND WORKING WITH LEGAL COUNSEL

Daily proceedings of the matrimonial legal system are not monitored by any independent authority. You must learn how to protect yourself.

20 SELECTING A LAWYER
    Get Down To Business
    Where To Start
    Is Pro Se A Possibility?
    Attributes To Consider
    First Meeting
      Preparation
      Questions
        Basic
        Child Issues
        Financial Issues
        Spouse's Attorney
        Professional Qualities
        Pension
        Fees And Work To Be Done
        Payment Of Legal Fees
        Strategy
        Include In The Retainer Agreement

21 LEGAL PROTECTION
    Your Rights
    Retainer Agreement
      Introduction
      General Format
      Negotiate Changes And Additions

22 WORKING WITH YOUR LAWYER
    Be Prepared And Alert
    Save Time, Confusion, Money
      Be An Efficiency Expert
      Billing
      Beware
    Firing Your Attorney

23 DIVORCE MEDIATION
    How Divorce Mediation Works
    Selecting A Mediator
      Attributes To Consider
      Interviewing
        Qualifications
        Sessions
        Your Case
        Expenses
    Pros And Cons Of Divorce Mediation
      Appropriate
      Not Appropriate
      Advantages
      Disadvantages
    A Workable Alternative

It is best to act with confidence, no
matter how little right you have to it.
Lillian Hellman

Skill to do comes of doing.
Ralph Waldo Emerson

20

SELECTING A LAWYER

GET DOWN TO BUSINESS

Your relationship with your lawyer is a business one.

Having realistic expectations is crucial for maintaining a productive working relationship with your lawyer. Feeling your grief and sadness is an integral part of the healing process. Set aside time for it. Sharing your emotions, however, with your attorney will be costly and can effect how you are perceived. You hire a lawyer to provide a needed legal service. To be most productive and cost-effective, your relationship with your lawyer needs to be a business one. The legal aspects of your case require the expertise of your lawyer. Whoever you see for emotional support is likely to be less expensive.

Choosing the right lawyer to help you reach your goals will take time and effort. The wrong choice can lead to the loss of marital assets, rightfully yours, and possibly, the custody of your children. Know the facts of your case and how the legal system works, so you are in the position to positively effect the quality of the service for which you are paying. You are a vital partner in the client-attorney team. Keep decision-making power in your hands. You know your spouse and the psychology of the situation. Set the goals and the boundaries; you do not want your case to be needlessly expanded.

PART III – What Is There And Where Is It?
PART IV – Legal Process And Terms
PART V – Areas Of Concern

WHERE TO START

Visit the courthouse and watch lawyers in action.

It is difficult to distinguish a good attorney from one who is incompetent, and possibly, unethical. Guides such as *The Martindale Hubbell Law Directory* are not very useful, because they do not list complaints against attorneys and have no information regarding satisfied clients. Local bar associations are similarly limited in screening referrals. Even if there are numerous complaints filed against an attorney, bar associations recommend a colleague to be in good standing, unless he or she has been disbarred, suspended, or censured. Legal awareness groups can be a starting point, but beware; they generally refer the lawyers who are connected with them, some of whom may not be very competent. Divorce decrees are public records. You might want to use the County Clerk's journal of courtroom proceedings, the "minute books," to review several cases similar to yours to get a sense of how they were handled. The minute books contain case summaries, names of litigants, and their attorneys.

One way to learn about lawyers in your area is to visit the courthouse and watch them in action. Get names or ask for business cards of those with whom you are impressed. The Clerk's Office has a list of the dates of hearings. Also attend lectures where lawyers speak about matrimonial issues. Take notes and ask questions about the information presented. Speak with members of the audience to learn about their legal experiences and to evaluate the presenting lawyers. Your local mental health professionals, neighbors, friends, and colleagues may have referrals. You could try using the Internet to check electronic bulletin boards or chat groups for up-to-date information.

Ask others about their experiences.

➡ *Why did you select your attorney?*
➡ *What do you feel were your lawyer's strengths? Weaknesses?*
➡ *Were you kept informed? Were your calls returned in a timely fashion?*
➡ *Was the work done efficiently and the cost kept to what was originally estimated?*
➡ *Were you satisfied with how your case was handled?*
➡ *Would you use the same attorney again?*

Use the phone to screen possibilities. To get a feeling about an attorney, ask some key questions specific to your case. Also ask if there is a charge for a consultation; some lawyers do not charge for an initial consultation. Trust your reactions to this first impression. Personally interview a minimum of three attorneys.

IS PRO SE A POSSIBILITY?

Representing yourself in a divorce action is generally not wise.

"Pro se" (for yourself) means you represent yourself in a legal action without the help of an attorney. Most divorces are complicated with property transfers, tax issues, child custody, and support issues. If your case involves any of these issues, do not attempt pro se, unless you are highly skilled and organized or have no other choice. Moreover, you can hurt your case by not being familiar with Court procedures, such as certain deadlines for filing papers and the complexities of the discovery process.

Representing yourself without legal counsel might be a possibility if your divorce is uncontested, no children are involved, there is agreement regarding grounds and property distribution, and each spouse is capable of being self-supporting. Furthermore, you must have the mental and emotional stamina to handle the details of this difficult, time-consuming process. Even if you do most of the work yourself, it is in your best interest to hire an attorney to go over your agreement before signing it. In reality, representing yourself in a divorce action is generally not wise. The process is complicated and the paperwork is demanding.

ATTRIBUTES TO CONSIDER
Be prepared and use your instinct.

It is vital that you expend the time and effort to find a lawyer who understands the components of your case and will help you attain realistic goals. Do not blindly trust recommendations. You need an attorney who practices family law and has enough experience and competence to successfully handle the aspects of your case, such as custody, business valuation, tax issues, and other concerns. It may be best to retain a skilled negotiator who is also an experienced litigator in the event negotiations break down. Remember, the legal process is adversarial and competitive. Most of the work, however, can be accomplished through negotiations. An attorney committed to the negotiating process may be more realistic in helping you reach your goals timely, with less cost and trouble.

Depending on the complexity of your case, you may either prefer to work with a sole practitioner or need to retain a larger firm with a support staff. Working with a sole practitioner may allow for a closer personal connection regarding what is being done and how. It may, however, be more efficient to retain a firm whose support staff can do some of the work at a lower hourly fee. A firm often has professionals specializing in tax and bankruptcy law.

You hire a lawyer to provide a legal service, not to be your friend. Retain an attorney who:
→ Maintains a businesslike, professional manner.
→ Is willing to handle the case according to an agreed upon strategy.
→ Agrees to be candid with you about the strengths and weaknesses of your case and of your spouse's case.
→ Grasps and appreciates the facts of your case.
→ Remains focused, not preoccupied or distracted.
→ Can be firm and assertive when necessary.
→ Has no negative personal or professional issues to work out with your spouse's attorney.
→ Is reasonable, knowledgeable, organized, and well prepared.
→ Provides references.

Acknowledge to yourself how you really feel about each attorney you interview; you are likely to have a working relationship of a year or longer. Exam and trust your feelings. How do you feel when a professional:
→ Responds impatiently to your inquires for clarification? Does it intimidate you? Do you fear your suggestions or wishes will not be respected?

➥ Appears inattentive to what you say or abruptly or inappropriately responds? Do you question whether your case is understood and your needs are being considered?

➥ Is condescending? Do you feel controlled and unable to participate as you wish? Do you have concerns about how the negotiation process and, possibly, litigation may be affected?

➥ Stalls when responding to factual questions regarding your case? Is this an indication of lack of knowledge or an inability to think clearly under pressure?

➥ Evades answering direct questions? Do you feel the person is trustworthy? Do you worry about legal fees and being unable to verify the time spent on various tasks?

➥ Is impersonal and remote? Do you anticipate being uncomfortable with sharing and disclosing information pertinent to your case?

Make your decision based on being informed and courageous enough to ask tough questions to see how a lawyer reacts. Whatever you experience at the first encounter that does not feel right is apt to become more evident in a long-term working relationship. Measure your initial reactions with your head and with your instincts. A lawyer may have been recommended, but if you are not comfortable with him or her, it will be a stressful working relationship or worse.

There are also practical issues to consider when choosing a lawyer; one of the most obvious is the cost. How much of a retainer fee is required and what are the hourly fees of the lawyer, associates, and support staff? Being a reasonable distance from your lawyer's office may be important if you have to consult often or over an extended period of time. Keep in mind, a lawyer who has to travel a long distance to the Court is going to charge for traveling time. Also, will the gender of your attorney have an impact on your spouse, the opposing attorney, or the Judge?

FIRST MEETING

Decide what you want to learn; prepare thoroughly; stay focused.

PREPARATION

Prepare thoroughly for each consultation with an attorney and stay focused on your goals. You want to get the most out of the time allowed. Have basic personal and financial information with you and a clear, well-organized copy for the attorney.

First Meeting Data Organizer:

❑ Names, addresses, phone numbers of both spouses.
❑ Date and place of marriage, number of years married.
❑ Length of time as a resident of the state.
❑ Present county of residence.
❑ Social Security numbers of both spouses and the children.
❑ Names, dates of birth, addresses and special needs of the children.
❑ Previous marriages: certified copies of divorce decrees.
❑ Custodial arrangement and support of children of prior marriages.
❑ Prenuptial Agreement, if one exists.

☐ Income of each spouse, its source, business addresses.
☐ Previous year's income tax return.
☐ Estimate of annual expenses.
☐ Summary of assets and liabilities.
☐ Education, training, degrees, licenses, dates obtained.
☐ Grounds for dissolution of the marriage.
☐ Objectives and strategy.
☐ Name and address of spouse's attorney.
☐ Copies of any Court documents concerning pending matters.
APPENDIX – Money Matters: Monthly Budget and Financial Puzzle Pieces

Become informed about the basics of your state's matrimonial law before interviewing any lawyer. Be realistic and knowledgeable about how the legal process works. Know the grounds for divorce. Have an understanding of the legal steps involved so you can clarify your approach. Evaluate the psychology of your situation to determine whether to anticipate a contested or uncontested divorce. Be informed about the Summons and Verified Complaint and understand the impact of serving them. Is there a less inflammatory or more advantageous time and method of serving the Summons and Complaint? Know the methods and legal devices used with formal discovery and how likely they are to produce sufficient results for your situation in view of the cost associated with employing them.
PART IV – Legal Process And Terms
APPENDIX – Customizing Guide
Exhibits: Summons With Notice and Verified Complaint

Be aware of the limitations of the matrimonial legal system. It is an adversarial system whose procedures intensify discord. The regulation of the conduct of lawyers and judges is under their own control. Judicial discretion gives judges the power to decide cases as they, in good faith, deem to be appropriate. This adds to the lack of predictability in how your case may be decided. Subtle bias involving gender, money, power, image, and certain problems is not uncommon in family law litigation. Perjury is rarely punished. Also, a law guardian may lack the training, experience, or natural skills to protect the interests of children within an emotionally charged atmosphere.
PART IV - Chapter 12: Problems With The Legal System

Understand your rights so you know what you can expect. Limit questions to aspects that are not entirely clear. Asking a lawyer to explain your rights can waste interview time and money if there is a fee for the initial consultation. Some lawyers can be, needlessly, wordy. Understand the purpose and format of a Retainer Agreement. Know what it is likely to contain and what you need to add for adequate protection. Do not sign the Retainer Agreement in the office during the first consultation. Take a copy with you; go over it thoroughly. After understanding all parts of the Agreement and successfully negotiating necessary changes and additions, sign it.
PART VI - Chapter 21: Legal Protection
APPENDIX – Customizing Guide
Mind Matters: Statement Of Client's Rights And Responsibilities

Your goal is to learn about the lawyer you are interviewing. Use your time efficiently.
↪ Introduce yourself in a businesslike manner.
↪ Briefly explain the reason for being there.
↪ Summarize the financial data.
PART III - Chapter 6: Financial And Personal Documents

➥ Summarize how you have contributed to the financial value of the marriage.
  PART III - in Chapter 7: "Compiling Your Marital History"
➥ Hand the attorney a copy of the *First Meeting Data* Organizer. After giving him or her a moment to look it over, continue.
➥ Share your personal objectives for the case and how you would like it handled.
➥ Share any major concerns.
  PART V – Areas Of Concern
➥ Before starting to ask some selective questions, inquire whether there is any other factual information the attorney needs at that time.

QUESTIONS

Design questions that not only help you evaluate attorneys but also teach you more about how divorce cases are handled, especially ones like yours. Your questions need to be specific, not open-ended. To get the most out of a consultation, be organized and be prepared to take charge. You do not want a lawyer to go on at length about something you already know or is not relevant to your case. The questions you decide to ask will depend on the circumstances of your case, the qualities you want in an attorney, and whether the lawyer is a sole practitioner or part of a firm. Be familiar enough with what you are asking so you appear knowledgeable and self-assured.

Some of the following sample questions may be pertinent. The order in which they are presented is not intended to be an order to necessarily follow; organize your questions in a fashion to best reach your goals.

Be focused and clear about what you need to learn, and be selective about what you ask. Some questions are more powerful than others, reflecting forethought and insight. Be an informed, astute consumer. Your goal is to be able to make a discerning decision about retaining a valuable and expensive service.

BASIC

➥ *Presently, how much of your practice is in the area of matrimonial law?*
➥ *How long have you practiced family law?*
➥ *How do you feel about clients being present at court conferences?*
➥ *Do you feel your strength is in negotiating or litigating?*
➥ *During the past three years, how many divorce trials have you had?*
➥ *What motivated you to choose to practice matrimonial law, instead of another area of law?*

CHILD ISSUES

➥ *Do you handle cases where child custody is contested?*
➥ *How many contested child custody cases have you handled in the last three years? What percentage of those cases did you win for your clients?*
➥ *Are you handling any contested custody cases presently?*
➥ Ask as many questions as necessary for you to anticipate the problems your children may face. Examples: *Under what circumstances are siblings separated? What is the procedure for determining who would be the most suitable parent? Will children be asked to express their preferences?*

FINANCIAL ISSUES

→ *In your opinion, what are the limitations to formal discovery in determining the true monetary value of the marriage?*
→ *What is the best way to find hidden assets?*
→ *Who are the professionals you use for accounting, appraisals, small business valuation, and tax advice? What is the approximate cost for each?*
→ *What is the most realistic way to value a professional degree, license, or goodwill?*
→ *When may I meet the accountant and tax expert?*
→ *What departments are available within your firm for consultation on other aspects of the law such as bankruptcy and tax law?*
→ *What percentage of your cases, during the last three years, has been large asset or financially complex cases?*

SPOUSE'S ATTORNEY

Name your spouse's attorney and ask:
→ *How would you characterize this lawyer?*
→ *Have you worked opposite him or her previously?*
→ *Did he or she have a definite strategy?*
→ *What was the outcome for your client?*
→ *Can you tell me the name of that case? I would like to review it.*

PROFESSIONAL QUALITIES

→ *Do you have malpractice insurance? How much?* (Minimum professional liability insurance is about $100,000/$300,000.)
→ *Do you accept any pro bono cases? How many per year?* ("Pro bono" means a lawyer takes a case without compensation for the public good.)

PENSION

→ *Have you ever had a Qualified Domestic Relations Order (QDRO) you have prepared rejected by a pension plan administrator? If so, for what reasons?*
→ *Would you prepare and submit a QDRO to the pension plan administrator previous to the divorce for approval, to be sure it conforms to the pension plan's rules?*
APPENDIX – Exhibits: Qualified Domestic Relations Order

FEES AND WORK TO BE DONE

→ *What is your hourly fee?*
→ *How much would the retainer fee be for my case?*
→ *If I were to retain you, will you be doing 100% of the work on my case, or will other lawyers in the firm be involved?* If the answer is other lawyers will be involved, ask: *How much and what type of work will you be doing? What areas of the work will other lawyers be doing? When can I meet the other attorneys? What is each lawyer's expertise? What are their hourly fees?*
→ *Will some work be assigned to staff? What type of work? What is the hourly cost?*
→ *What is your practice in returning phone calls? How are phone calls charged?*
→ *Can you provide me with a minimum/maximum estimate of the total legal expenditures, based on the best- and worst-case scenarios?*
→ *Would you be willing to provide me with references from former clients?*

PAYMENT OF LEGAL FEES

➥ *Has your experience been that legal fees for the nonmoneyed spouse are generally ordered to be made available as the case progresses, or that the Court postpones the decision until the end of litigation?*

➥ *If the request that the moneyed spouse pay the legal fees for the nonmoneyed spouse is denied, or if insufficient funds are awarded, would you wait until the end of litigation for the remainder of your payment to be taken out of the settlement?*

PART IV - in Chapter 12: "Awarding Legal Fees"
PART V - in Chapter 18: "Counselor Fees"
APPENDIX – Customizing Guide

STRATEGY

➥ *Have you had any cases similar to mine? What was the outcome?*

➥ *What would your basic strategy be for my case?*

➥ *What is the best strategy to follow when the opposition is not forthcoming with documents and information during formal discovery?*

➥ *What do you foresee will be the outcome of my case?*

➥ *How would you characterize each of the matrimonial judges?*

➥ *Would your strategy change depending upon which judge is assigned to my case?*

➥ *What is your strategy in dealing with an opposing attorney who is delaying and excessively litigating?*

INCLUDE IN THE RETAINER AGREEMENT

Would you consider including the following in the Retainer Agreement?

❑ A "good faith" statement of a minimum/maximum estimate of the total legal expenditures, based on the best- and worst-case scenarios.

❑ The hourly fee of the Attorney, <u>name</u>, is to remain constant for the duration of the legal representation.

❑ The Attorney is to send to the Client copies of all case-related correspondence and court documents within forty-eight hours of releasing or receiving them.

❑ With the signing of the Retainer Agreement, the Attorney is to provide the Client with a copy of initials and codes used on bills, designating staff and tasks with the matching names, positions, hourly rates, and task descriptions.

❑ The Attorney is to return calls to the Client within twenty-four hours, unless there are unusual, justifiable reasons for not doing so.

PART VI - in Chapter 21: "Retainer Agreement"
APPENDIX – Customizing Guide

21

LEGAL PROTECTION

This chapter uses New York State to create an informative legal model.
The principles presented apply to all states. See the *Customizing Guide*.

YOUR RIGHTS

*Know what you have a right to, and what your
lawyer is required to do and prohibited from doing.*

In an effort to protect consumers of legal services, some new rules were put into effect in New York State in 1993. Lawyers are required by New York state law to give prospective clients a copy of the *Statement Of Client's Rights And Responsibilities*. It is a standard form stating what clients have a right to, and what lawyers are required to do and forbidden from doing.

APPENDIX – Mind Matters: Statement Of Client's Rights And Responsibilities

Highlights of the *Statement Of Client's Rights And Responsibilities*:

♦ What you share with your lawyer is to be kept confidential.
♦ "You are entitled to a written retainer agreement" from your lawyer. Before signing it, you can negotiate to add provisions that further protect you.
♦ Lawyers are not allowed to accept contingency fees, which are fees based on the settlement of the client's case. It is illegal for a lawyer to get more money based on the results of the case.
♦ If either you or your attorney terminate the working relationship, the balance of the retainer fee is to be returned to you.
♦ "You are entitled to receive a written, itemized bill...at least every 60 days."
♦ You are not to be charged for time spent discussing, clarifying, or correcting bills.
♦ You have the right to be present at conferences.
♦ You have the right "to make the final decision regarding the settlement of your case." Your lawyer does not have the right to force you to settle.
♦ Your attorney does not have the right to abandon your case without the consent of the Court. It must be specified in the Retainer Agreement under what circumstances your attorney would seek to withdraw. Nonpayment of fees is a valid reason. Other reasons are a client's lack of honesty or inability to follow the attorney's instructions, thereby making a working relationship impossible. The Judge must approve the action by determining if there is just cause. The Judge can grant your lawyer a "charging lien," which entitles him or her to be paid from the proceeds of the final settlement.

◆ "You are under no legal obligation to sign a confession of judgment or promissory note or to agree to a lien or mortgage on your home to cover legal fees." If you do agree to sign a confession of judgment, it means you admit to owing a debt and voluntarily submit the matter to the jurisdiction of the Court. A promissory note is an agreement in which one party promises to pay a specific amount at an agreed upon time to another party. Your attorney must have the approval of the Court to obtain a security lien on your property. The document you sign is filed by your attorney with the Court and, with the permission of the Judge, becomes a lien on your property.

◆ You have the right to fee arbitration in the event there is a dispute regarding legal fees. This helps to minimize the need for you to hire a second attorney to protect your interests.

A proposed reform to prohibit "retaining liens" was opposed and did not go into effect. This means that if the relationship with your lawyer terminates, he or she can hold your file until you pay the legal fees you owe. It is almost impossible for you to proceed with your case if you do not have access to the documents in your file. Take precautions; make copies of everything; keep originals. Include in your Retainer Agreement that you are to receive copies of all case-related correspondence and documents within forty-eight hours of your attorney releasing or receiving them.

PART VI - in Chapter 21: "Retainer Agreement"
in Chapter 22: "Save Time, Confusion, Money"
APPENDIX – Customizing Guide

RETAINER AGREEMENT

Clarify, negotiate changes, and add provisions.

INTRODUCTION

Your lawyer must provide you with a written Retainer Agreement, which is a legally binding contract, specifying what your attorney agrees to do for you, what is expected of you in return, and the payment terms. Read the Retainer Agreement and analyze how well it protects your interests. Be sure your rights as specified in the *Statement Of Client's Rights And Responsibilities* are covered by the agreement's terms, so there is no possibility later of someone claiming you waived a specific right. You have the right to negotiate changes and necessary additions to provisions about which you have concern. You might have a lengthy working relationship with this lawyer. Slow progress can be frustrating; attitudes can change. While the relationship is fresh and hopeful, design a contract that is precise, inclusive, and protective.

PART VI - in Chapter 21: "Your Rights" and "Negotiate Changes And Additions"
APPENDIX – Customizing Guide

GENERAL FORMAT

A basic Retainer Agreement is to include:
◆ Names and addresses of the parties entering into the agreement.
◆ Nature of the services to be provided.
◆ Amount of the retainer fee.
◆ Circumstances under which the unused portion of the retainer fee is to be refunded.

◆ Client's right to terminate the Retainer Agreement and how the fee for the work done up to that time is to be determined.

◆ Hourly rates of the lawyer, associates, and staff working on the case; method of charging for telephone calls and letters; and other anticipated expenses.

◆ Acknowledgment that an itemized bill is to be provided at least every sixty days, and that the client is not to be charged for time spent discussing and clarifying bills.

◆ Method of making payments due beyond the initial retainer fee.

◆ Circumstances under which the lawyer might seek a security interest in the client's property.

◆ Client's right to receive copies of correspondence and documents relating to his or her case.

◆ Circumstances under which the lawyer can withdraw from the case because of nonpayment of the legal fees and the lawyer's right to seek a charging lien.

◆ Disputes over the fee can be decided by arbitration, binding on both parties.

PART VI - in Chapter 21: "Your Rights"
APPENDIX – Customizing Guide

NEGOTIATE CHANGES AND ADDITIONS

The following are some concerns to consider as you clarify, change, and add to the original version of your Retainer Agreement.

➡ Some words and phrases, included in the original Retainer Agreement presented to you, may not be in your best interest. For example: "This Retainer Agreement confirms <u>client's name</u> has retained the firm of <u>firm's name</u>." You may have been interviewed by a high-profile attorney of a firm, but if your Retainer Agreement does not specify that person as the attorney to handle your case, any lawyer in the firm may be assigned your case. If you are retaining a law firm, clearly state the name of the lawyer to handle the case. Your lawyer must have your permission and specifically state the reasons for bringing in another lawyer to help with the work or for retaining experts to make evaluations.

➡ To maintain control over the selection of professionals hired to assist with the case, include words to the effect, "The final decision regarding the hiring of experts to value property and to assist on other matters remains with the client."

➡ You might want to clarify who is to draft the Qualified Domestic Relations Order, the attorney or a pension specialist (at what fee).

➡ Try to negotiate that the hourly fee is not to be increased for the duration of the legal representation or for a specific period of time, and that any change would be made only by mutual consent. Be sure a provision stating the client can go to fee arbitration is included, even though it is one of your stated rights. By doing so, you give the impression you are serious about business and go over your bills thoroughly.

➡ Carefully review the list of anticipated expenses, referred to as "disbursements," that are not covered by the attorney's hourly fee. You want to know the extra costs for which you will be responsible, including court fees, faxes, long distance calls, and travel.

➡ Be sure the provision covering the circumstances under which the unused portion of the retainer fee is to be returned is clear.

➡ Remember, your lawyer does not have the right to a bonus. Be sure there are no provisions suggesting otherwise. Be watchful for phrases such as "based on results obtained" or "the complexity of the case may result in an additional charge." New York State does not allow any form of contingency fees in matrimonial cases.

➡ Make it clear in your Retainer Agreement that you want to see and approve correspondence before it is forwarded to the opposing attorney or to the Court.

➡ Include that copies of all case-related correspondence, legal motions, and orders are to be sent to the client within forty-eight hours of sending or receiving them, unless there is a legitimate reason for not doing so. It is essential that you keep your own working file up to date.
PART VI - in Chapter 21: "Your Rights" for more on "retaining liens"
in Chapter 22: "Save Time, Confusion, Money"

➡ Specify that the attorney is to return calls to the client within twenty-four hours, unless there are justifiable reasons preventing such.

➡ Include a provision stating that the attorney is to provide the client with a copy of designated task codes and the initials of those who might work on the case. Each task is to be described and each staff member is to be identified by name, position, and hourly rate. Updated versions are to be provided as necessary. This can be valuable in monitoring bills.

➡ If you are the nonmoneyed spouse, include a provision requiring that with the commencement of the lawsuit, the lawyer is to make a motion to the Court ordering the moneyed spouse to pay the legal fees. Having this in writing helps to highlight its importance.

➡ Try to include that once the attorney has accepted the case, he or she will not abandon it because of the client's inability to keep up with the fee payments. Instead, he or she will exercise the legal right to obtain a charging lien and collect fees owed from the client's portion of the settlement.

➡ A minimum fee clause should clearly explain under what circumstances the fee is to be refunded. If you feel that your case may be resolved quickly with very little legal work, or that you and your spouse may reconcile, a minimum fee clause could work to your disadvantage. Either negotiate to revise it or delete it.

➡ Be sure it is clearly stated that the client is to be notified by the lawyer of all Court appearances and conferences, and that the attorney must have the client's prior consent to enter into agreements at any conference.

➡ Include the method to be used to discharge the attorney, if the need were to arise.
PART VI - in Chapter 22: "Firing Your Attorney"

Any words or phrases in the Retainer Agreement that are unclear in their intent or make you uncomfortable need to be clarified with the attorney until their intent is clear and agreeable to you. These clarifications and explanations can be included in the text of the agreement. If something is important to you, put it in writing so it is not forgotten or reinterpreted, as can happen with oral clarifications over time.
APPENDIX - Customizing Guide

22

WORKING WITH YOUR LAWYER

BE PREPARED AND ALERT

Take part in planning strategy and negotiating issues.

Your business relationship with your attorney starts once you have signed a Retainer Agreement and paid the retainer fee. This fee is a lump sum payment made in advance for services to be performed in your case. Usually, it is just a deposit against which hourly fees and other expenses are charged and may be exhausted quickly because of the high cost of legal services. Once your retainer fee is spent, you are required to either pay another lump sum or pay periodically as the work is performed. The method of payment is to be specified in your Retainer Agreement. To help you maintain control over your case and track its progress, arrange to pay a reasonable retainer fee to begin the work and then pay subsequent fees as they occur.

After selecting an attorney and agreeing on the terms of your Retainer Agreement, prepare for subsequent meetings. Be sure your attorney has a copy of the *First Meeting Data* Organizer you used to introduce your case at the initial consultation. It is your responsibility to educate your attorney. Be ready to tell your lawyer the truth; the opposition is likely to bring up a version of it. What is shared with your legal counsel is to be kept confidential. Be prepared with accurate, complete information for all meetings and telephone exchanges. The more equipped you are with the essential data and documentation, the less costly the procedure will be. Know what there is and what you want, as well as how and when to compromise.

PART VI - in Chapter 20: "First Meeting"

Flesh out the data you have collected so the monetary value of the marriage becomes clear. Determine the fair market value of your property through formal or informal appraisals. By knowing the market value and subtracting the loan balance and anticipated taxes due, you can make reasonable estimates of property values. For example, to determine the fair market value of the principal residence, either pay for a formal appraisal or have a real estate agent do a price comparison. To estimate the home's equity, subtract the remainder due on any mortgages and the fees connected with its sale. List each real estate holding by address along with the name and address of the lending institution, mortgage number, remaining balance, appraised market value, and estimated net equity. Consult your tax advisor, so you know the tax liability and the real value of each property.

PART V - in Chapter 17: "Real Value Of Property"
*   Chapter 14: Let's Look At The Tax Bite*

Try to have a complete, organized list of your assets and liabilities and a copy for your lawyer. You can work with reasonable estimates of the assets at the beginning and refine the figures as the divorce progresses. Special collections may need an expert appraisal. Privately held businesses, closely held corporations, professional practices, licenses, degrees, and high-profile reputations are difficult to value and need special attention. Other assets such as vehicles are easier to value. To find out the market value of each vehicle, either call your insurance agent or use the Kelly Blue Book online at *www.kbb.com*; then subtract the remainder due on each loan. List the make and year of each vehicle, market value, net equity, lending institution, loan number, and balance due.

List each checking and savings account by number, including type of account, current balance, name of the institution, and address. List investments and loan obligations similarly. Individual assets and liabilities need to be identified clearly. This information will eventually be written into your Agreement. Some accounts are easier to value than others. For example, the Statement of Account for a defined contribution retirement account shows the latest balance, whereas a defined benefit plan will probably need to be analyzed by an actuary to determine its value.

PART III – What Is There And Where Is It?
PART V – Areas Of Concern
PART VI - in Chapter 22: "Save Time, Confusion, Money"

Your personal involvement in keeping your attorney informed, planning strategy, and negotiating the issues can greatly increase your chances of attaining a satisfactory settlement. Unlike anyone else, you know the unique dynamics of your situation. Have realistic goals and be sure you and your attorney are in agreement regarding the strategy to follow. Remain mindful of the fact that the client-attorney relationship is a business arrangement. Keep your long-term goals foremost in your mind, continue to become informed, and keep your emotions in the background.

You need to be attentive to be certain your lawyer is adequately focusing on the demands of your case. Seek clarification about legal issues when necessary. Discuss any differences of opinion in order to resolve them, so you can continue to work together productively. Do not relinquish control of your case or assume things will be done as you expect. Be sure your attorney:

➥ Knows the facts of your case and uses them effectively.
➥ Is following the agreed upon strategy.
➥ Has your input on decisions to be made and your approval for actions to be taken.
➥ Does not unreasonably pressure you.
➥ Keeps you satisfactorily informed.
➥ Has reasonable explanations for delays.

SAVE TIME, CONFUSION, MONEY

The longer an attorney works on a case, the more money he or she makes on that case.

BE AN EFFICIENCY EXPERT

Using formal tools of discovery to accomplish financial disclosure is time consuming, costly, and often inadequate. Gathering the information and documentation yourself, if possible, can save money and lead to more satisfactory results. Make copies of documents such as real estate closing statements, deeds, bank statements, and tax returns to submit to your lawyer; keep the originals. Also make two copies of all documents for yourself. Store one copy and the originals, if available, in a safe place. Keep the other copy in your own personal working file.
PART III – What Is There And Where Is It?
PART IV - in Chapter 11: "Discovery Stage"

Be sure you receive copies from your attorney of all correspondence, motions, orders, and other documents connected with your case as they are generated. You must keep your personal file up to date. If the relationship with your lawyer ends, he or she can hold your file until you pay the legal fees owed. If you are unable to do so, it will be impossible for you to proceed with your case unless you have copies of all the necessary documents.
PART VI - in Chapter 21: "Your Rights" (for more on retaining liens) and *"Retainer Agreement"*
APPENDIX – Customizing Guide

Be prepared for each meeting and phone contact. Have a written list of questions and concerns, organized in a manner to efficiently keep you and your attorney focused. Always take your own set of copies with you to client-attorney meetings, so you have ready access to needed documents and will not waste time looking for them. Keep a dated record of the precise time spent and what is covered during each meeting and telephone conversation. Your phone calls with your attorney are billed at his or her hourly rate. Keep up-to-date lists of tasks you and your lawyer must complete. Consider either faxing or e-mailing periodically with clear, concise, bulleted lists of what needs attention. It may be a cost-effective way to stay in touch, make your needs known, and stay on top of your case. It also provides a written record.

BILLING

It is difficult to calculate how long it takes an attorney to complete individual tasks. Often you cannot determine the exact cost of a legal service, but you can closely examine and evaluate your bills.

- ◆ New York state law requires that your bill be itemized, showing subject matter, the initials of the professionals who did the work, and their billing rates. Include a provision in your Retainer Agreement that you are to be provided with a list of the full names of the staff, their positions, hourly rates, and codes used to identify different tasks, so you will be able to monitor your bills.
  PART VI - in Chapter 21: "Retainer Agreement"
- ◆ Be sure you are not charged an attorney's hourly rate for work done by office staff.

- Examine the explanations of the work done. Question vagueness; the tasks should be specifically described.
- A second attorney's initials should not show up on the bill unless you had authorized that he or she work on your case.
- Compare your records of time spent at meetings and on the phone to see if they agree with the bill.
- Check listed phone calls carefully. Do the phone numbers and length of time for each seem reasonable? Which were made by your lawyer and which by office staff? Were they charged appropriately?

APPENDIX – Customizing Guide

BEWARE

In an adversarial system, truth is not necessarily the goal; winning is. Laws against perjury are not usually enforced in civil cases, and perjury, unfortunately, is not an uncommon practice in divorce proceedings. The opposing attorney may use tactics to wear you down, such as attacking your credibility or complicating the process with unnecessary motions. This strategy of delaying agreement and, possibly, outspending you is designed to force you to give in. Develop a strategy with your lawyer to cope with less than ethical tactics if they are used against you. Respond to legitimate requests and try to keep the case moving in a positive direction. Progress may be slower than you wish, but if your case is on the court calendar, there are deadlines to be met by both sides.

PART IV - in Chapter 11: "Three Phases Of The Legal Process"
in Chapter 12: "Adversarial System" and "Perjury"

If you agree to the bifurcation of your case, it could lessen your leverage in negotiating a settlement. "Bifurcation" allows for deciding a divorce case in two parts. First, the divorce is granted based on legal grounds and then the custody, support, and property issues are to be resolved. The danger is that once a spouse who wants a divorce has been granted it, he or she has less incentive to compromise on the other issues.

FIRING YOUR ATTORNEY

Keep your attorney on target.

There are some warning signs when a client-attorney relationship is not working. Possibly, your lawyer is unable to get the work done on time or your phone calls are not being returned. Have a clear understanding at the outset about your expectations of having your calls returned in a timely fashion. If your lawyer files motions when a more efficient approach would be to make phone calls, there may be reason to be concerned. He or she might be dragging out the case needlessly with "motion churning." Set the boundaries; do not allow your legal counsel to drag out or escalate the case if it does not fit your needs. You have hired your attorney to provide needed legal services. It is your responsibility to keep him or her appropriately on target. Keep power in your hands by being informed and involved.

You have the right to discharge an attorney with whom you are dissatisfied. Your Retainer Agreement should include the method to be used, for example, "written notification." If litigation has started and the attorney has indicated to the Court he or she is your legal representation, you must have the Court's approval to discharge the lawyer. The reason for this is to help prevent unwarranted delays. You are required to pay for the legal services performed by the attorney you are releasing, unless he or she was discharged "for cause," such as malpractice or unethical behavior. Be aware, in New York, the attorney discharged "without cause" has the right, unless otherwise stated in the Retainer Agreement, to keep the client's file until the bill has been paid, or until a Court has awarded a charging lien.

PART VI - Chapter 21: Legal Protection
APPENDIX – Customizing Guide

One of the best ways to persuade others
is with your ears—by listening to them.

Dean Rusk

Trust your hunches. They're usually based on
facts filed away just below the conscious level.

Dr. Joyce Brothers

23

DIVORCE MEDIATION

HOW DIVORCE MEDIATION WORKS
Divorce mediation may be a reasonable alternative.

Divorce mediation is a process in which a separating or divorcing couple works with an impartial third party to negotiate an agreement regarding child support, maintenance, and the division of assets and debts. The mediator is a facilitator, not a representative or advocate for either spouse. During negotiations the mediator's role is to keep the emphasis on the issues to be resolved, clarify options, suggest alternatives, overcome impasses, and restate the ground rules regarding conduct if either party becomes overly agitated. Often the mediator is a lawyer or a mental health professional.

For some couples, divorce mediation is a reasonable alternative to the more adversarial approach of working through opposing attorneys. The focus in mediation is on cooperation and on what you and your spouse have in common. This helps to tone down the urge to win at the expense of the other. The goal is to design an agreement that satisfactorily addresses the needs of each of you and of your family. You maintain the control to represent yourself. You speak for yourself, not through a lawyer. Your lawyer's role is as a behind-the-scenes advisor. Usually, you and your spouse attend the meetings together. Occasionally, however, there may be a situation that requires each of you to meet with the mediator separately to get past a stalemate. Children are rarely involved directly in the meetings but, sometimes, if all involved feel it would be beneficial, older children might attend a session regarding issues concerning them.

The initial meeting enables the mediator to become familiar with your situation, needs, and manner of communicating. You learn about what to expect from the mediation process and fees involved. Usually, you are asked to fill out a questionnaire regarding personal information such as names, addresses, phone numbers, employment, and the date and place of marriage. A schedule for meetings is set up. You are expected to follow basic ground rules: no interrupting, no degrading remarks or abusive language, no yelling, and so on.

Financial documentation and information you are typically asked to provide:

☐ Tax returns – most recent two to three years.

☐ Bank and credit card statements.

☐ Investments – stocks, bonds, mutual funds.

☐ Insurance policies – health, life, disability.

☐ Deeds, titles, closing statements.

☐ Pension – defined benefit plan statement, defined contribution statements (401(k), 403(b), profit sharing), IRA accounts.

☐ Statement of Net Worth.

☐ Monthly budget – current household and child-related expenses, current income, source of income.

You and the mediator review the documents and information together and decide whether there is a need to consult financial or other experts.

PART III - Chapter 6: Financial And Personal Documents
APPENDIX – Money Matters: Monthly Budget and Financial Puzzle Pieces
        Exhibits: Statement Of Net Worth

You and your spouse each need your own lawyer to consult regarding specific legal issues and to review the agreement. Either the mediator, if legally qualified, or one of the lawyers will write up the Agreement, draft the necessary legal papers to accompany it, and file all necessary forms with the Court. Depending upon your circumstances, you might want to consider commencing an action and obtaining an index number when you start mediation, so your case can be placed on the court calendar. Then, if mediation does not work and you have to litigate the divorce, the case will not be delayed.

PART IV - in Chapter 8: "Court Calendar"
APPENDIX – Customizing Guide

SELECTING A MEDIATOR

There is no state or national licensing for divorce mediators.

ATTRIBUTES TO CONSIDER

Since there is no state or national licensing for divorce mediators, it is not easy to determine their qualifications. The New York State Council on Divorce Mediation attempts to qualify mediators by requiring sixty hours of training, one hundred hours of experience, ten hours per year of continuing education, as well as instruction about domestic violence. You want a balanced, focused mediator who comes highly recommended and also has training, experience, and a good working knowledge of family law, psychology, and negotiation techniques. Getting a personal referral from someone who has had a successful experience with a particular divorce mediator could be the surest way to find a qualified professional. Some mediators work as a team, one woman and one man. The advantage of this female/male model is it offers a gender balance for clients.

Professional organizations can give you some information about requirements and, possibly, furnish referrals. Accredited members' qualifications are likely to be superior to those of unaffiliated mediators.

- New York State Council on Divorce Mediation (*www.nysmediate.org*) (800) 894-2646 or (516) 227-2595
- New Jersey Association of Professional Mediators (*www.njapm.org*) (800) 981-4800

INTERVIEWING

When interviewing mediators, consider asking some questions similar to the following.

QUALIFICATIONS

- ➥ *Describe your training.*
- ➥ *How long have you worked as a divorce mediator?*
- ➥ *Are you affiliated with any professional organizations? Which ones?*
- ➥ *What degrees or licenses do you have?*
- ➥ *How many mediations are you presently doing?*
- ➥ *What percentage of your mediations in the past three years ended with a successfully negotiated agreement?*
- ➥ *What have been some of the reasons for the failure to successfully negotiate a settlement?*
- ➥ *Could you provide us with the names of past clients with whom we could speak?*
- ➥ *What type of written contract do you provide clients?*
- ➥ *How do you handle valuation issues?*

SESSIONS

- ➥ *Describe a typical mediation session.*
- ➥ *Do you ever meet with the spouses individually? Under what circumstances?*
- ➥ *When, if ever, are children actively involved in the process and present at meetings?*

YOUR CASE

- ➥ *Have you mediated any cases like ours?*
- ➥ *Do you think other experts will be needed for our situation? If so, what type?*
- ➥ *Whom do you generally use for expert evaluations for accounting, appraisals, valuing businesses, and tax issues? What is the approximate cost for each?*

EXPENSES

- ➥ *What is your hourly fee?*
- ➥ *Do you require a retainer fee? If so, how much?*
- ➥ *Are there any other costs about which we should be aware?*
- ➥ *How do you bill for your services?*
- ➥ *How many sessions do you anticipate it will take to resolve the issues in our situation?*

PROS AND CONS OF DIVORCE MEDIATION
You might cooperate in designing an unfair settlement.

APPROPRIATE

Mediation is appropriate when each spouse:

- Puts emotions aside long enough to seek fair, equitable solutions to issues.
- Has equal knowledge, power, and understanding of the financial value of the marriage.
- Expresses needs and justifies viewpoints clearly.
- Negotiates in good faith.
- Focuses on how best to provide for the needs of the family.
- Knows and understands his or her legal rights.
- Wants to avoid an adversarial court proceeding.

If you are poorly informed, you will, probably, cooperate in designing an unfair agreement. To maximize your chances of getting a fair settlement, you must know and understand:

☐ The financial issues involved and the true financial value of your marriage.
   PART V - Chapters 13 through 18

☐ What is marital and nonmarital property.
   PART V - in Chapter 13: "Marital And Nonmarital Property"

☐ How your state laws determine the division of assets and debts. New York uses equitable distribution.
   PART V - Chapter 13: Division Of Property

☐ How taxes affect the apparent value of assets.
   PART V - Chapter 14: Let's Look At The Tax Bite
   Chapter 17: Remember The IRS

☐ Your legal rights.
   PART VI - in Chapter 21: "Your Rights"

NOT APPROPRIATE

Divorce mediation is not appropriate when:

- Either spouse is unwilling to provide full disclosure of assets, debts, or income.
- Abuse or violence exists in the marriage.
- One spouse is inadequately informed about the financial value of the marriage.
- Emotions of both or either spouse are too strong.
- One spouse feels afraid of or is controlled by the other.
- One or both spouses want revenge.
- Trust is lacking.
- Vastly different views of what constitutes a fair settlement separate the parties.

There are some situations where immediate legal action is necessary, for example, when a spouse might sell or hide marital assets or is not paying adequate support.
PART IV - in Chapter 11: "Situations In Which It Is Important To Commence Legal Action"

ADVANTAGES

Mediation does not encourage polarization. It focuses on what you and your spouse have in common, instead of presuming you are in conflict. With a less adversarial atmosphere, negotiations usually move faster than with a litigated settlement, and as a result, you save time and money. With greater control over and responsibility for the outcome, you have more opportunity to design an agreement that engenders greater compliance with less resentment. If you anticipate an ongoing relationship as parents, mediation may help you plan for the family and move into the future with a workable parenting relationship.

DISADVANTAGES

The mediator's goal is to reach a settlement, not to protect individual interests. An agreement may be achieved but may not be fair. If one spouse is more demanding and less compromising, the more reasonable spouse may be subtly pressured by the mediator to compromise so issues can be resolved. Some power imbalances are not noticeable or are difficult to recognize. An unidentified power imbalance is likely to lead to an unfair settlement.

If your spouse is not acting in good faith, and you are unaware of it, you will negotiate an unfair agreement. No legal tools are available in mediation to force full disclosure of assets and debts. Your spouse may use the mediation process as a "flushing out" tactic to obtain information regarding your psychological needs and what you really want. Never intending to follow through with mediation, he or she may then turn to the traditional adversarial approach with information to which he or she would not otherwise have had access. This can greatly increase his or her leverage in negotiating, because you have already "played your hand."

A WORKABLE ALTERNATIVE

*Choose an alternative to mediation with
many of its benefits, plus protection.*

An alternative to mediation that gives you many of its benefits, plus the protection you may need, is to direct negotiations from behind the scenes with the help of attorneys. This can be very successful:

- if both you and your spouse are willing to negotiate in good faith and fully disclose assets and debts,
- and you both know and understand the financial and legal aspects involved,
- and each of you selects an attorney who is willing to emphasize negotiation.

This method is preferable if you are not emotionally prepared to negotiate face to face with your spouse or fear the dynamics of your situation do not lend themselves to successful mediation. Legal discovery tools of interrogatories and depositions, not available in mediation, would be available to use, if necessary. As with mediation, you must be informed and involved to instruct your lawyers.

You got to be careful if you don't know where
you're going, because you might not get there.
Yogi Berra

Obstacles are those frightful things you
see when you take your eyes off the goal.
Hannah More

PART VII – LEGAL AGREEMENTS

24 PREPARE FOR SUCCESS
  Introduction
  Continue To Develop Your Strategy
  Know The Issues And Your Concerns
    Division Of Assets And Liabilities
    Immediate And Future Financial Needs
    What Is Best For The Children
  Psychology Of The Situation
  Your Lawyer's Responsibility
  Goals
  Not Sure You Want To Divorce?

25 GENERAL FORMAT
  Introduction
  Articles
    Separate Residences
    Property Division
      Marital Residence
      Other Real Property
      Other Property
    Custody And Access Rights
    Visitation / Access
    Child Support
    Spousal Maintenance
    Responsibility For Debts
    Income Taxes
    Life And Disability Insurance
    Waiver Of Claims To Pension Plans
    Mutual Release And Discharge Of Claims In Estates
    Mutual Release Of General Claims
    Legal Representation
    Full Disclosure
    General Provisions
  Reminders

26 DESIGN AN AGREEMENT THAT PROTECTS YOU
  Introduction
  General Considerations
    Deadlock Provision / Arbitration Clause
    Connecting Factors
  Specific Issues
    Property
      Leases
      Liens
      Pension
      Money Awards Or Damages
      Trusts
      Bankruptcy – Be Aware

Custody And Visitation / Access
  Parental Decision Making
  Children's Assets
  Parental Involvement
  Parents Keeping Each Other Informed
  Relocation
  Death Of A Parent
  Visitation / Access Schedule
Child Support
  Annual Modification
  Consider And Resolve
  Emancipation
  Health Insurance
  Special Needs
  Method Of Payment
  Life Insurance
  Disability Insurance
  New Will
  Deadlock Provision
Spousal Maintenance
  Existence
  Method Of Payment
  Modification
  Tax Consequences
  Medical
  Deadlock Provision
Debts And Liabilities
Income Taxes
  Filing Status
  Deadlock Clause
  Hold Harmless Clause
  Exemptions And Credits
Support Payment Assurance
  Life Insurance
  Disability Insurance
  Annuity
Options And Their Consequences
  Possibility Of Bankruptcy
  Accepting A Property Settlement As A Trade For Maintenance
  Accepting Maintenance Payments As A Trade For Child Support
  Wording Your Agreement
Conclusion

24

PREPARE FOR SUCCESS

INTRODUCTION

Your Agreement may determine the quality of the remainder of your life.

Settlement and Separation Agreements are legally binding contracts that set forth the specific terms of a divorce or legal separation. Asset and liability distribution, custody, visitation/access rights, and support issues are covered. In New York State, grounds accompany a Settlement Agreement or Stipulation of Settlement, and there is no waiting period required to be divorced. A Separation Agreement is usually entered into with the intent of putting the legal aspects of an impending divorce in order without specifying "fault" or finalizing the divorce. After living apart for at least one year, according to the terms of the Separation Agreement, either spouse can commence a divorce action based on the ground of living apart pursuant to the terms of the Agreement. It is a more gentle approach to ending a marriage than using fault grounds, and some spouses prefer to have the time to adjust. Since the articles and provisions found in a Settlement Agreement or Stipulation of Settlement are similar to those in a Separation Agreement, the term "Agreement" will be used hereafter for ease and consistency. The quality of the remainder of your life may depend on how well your Agreement protects you. You are the key player in helping to structure a favorable settlement.

PART IV - in Chapter 10: "Separation Agreement"
PART V – Areas Of Concern
PART VII - Chapter 26: Design An Agreement That Protects You
APPENDIX – Customizing Guide
         Agreement Matters: Pathfinder

CONTINUE TO DEVELOP YOUR STRATEGY

Remain quiet and reveal very little, especially if your spouse is uncooperative.

Plan and monitor how you behave with your spouse while your settlement is being negotiated. If your spouse is not working in good faith with you, remain quiet and reveal very little until you are actively involved in formal negotiations. Listen and absorb information, possibly uncovering your spouse's intentions. Keep everyday informal discussions on the issues with your spouse tentative; do not agree to anything. Do not discuss specific money amounts or share anything in writing. Keep focused on your goals without disclosing them. If you are planning on joint custody, however, it would probably be in the best interests of all involved to have an earnest exchange regarding some of the basics. For example, try to clarify the major decisions you plan to make jointly for the children. It might be best to avoid discussing specific money issues until formal negotiations.

PART I - in Chapter 2: "Framework For Your Strategy"
PART II - Chapter 3: First Things First
*   in Chapter 4: "Starting To Build Strategic Muscle"*

KNOW THE ISSUES AND YOUR CONCERNS
Be informed about assets, liabilities, and financial needs.

DIVISION OF ASSETS AND LIABILITIES

❏ How the Equitable Distribution Law is likely to be applied to your case.

PART V - Chapter 13: Division Of Property
APPENDIX – Customizing Guide

❏ What constitutes marital property and separate property.

PART V - in Chapter 13: "Marital And Nonmarital Property"
APPENDIX – Customizing Guide

❏ Value of your assets and amount of your debts.

PART V - Chapter 13: Division Of Property
*   Chapter 14: Let's Look At The Tax Bite*
*   Chapter 15: Who Gets What?*
*   Chapter 17: Remember The IRS*

❏ Tax options and consequences.

PART V - Chapter 17: Remember The IRS

IMMEDIATE AND FUTURE FINANCIAL NEEDS

❏ Monthly household costs.

PART III - in Chapter 6: "Proposed Budget"
APPENDIX – Money Matters: Monthly Budget

❏ Children's present and anticipated future financial needs.

PART IV - in Chapter 8: "Laws Change"
PART V - in Chapter 16: "Child Support"
PART VII - in Chapter 26: "Child Support"
APPENDIX – Customizing Guide
*   Money Matters: Monthly Budget*

❏ Earning potential.

PART V - Chapter 18: Essential Practical Concerns

❏ Health considerations for yourself and your children.

PART V - in Chapter 18: "Health Care"
APPENDIX – Customizing Guide

❏ Children's special needs.

PART V - in Chapter 16: "New York's Child Support Standards Act (CSSA)"
PART VII - in Chapter 26: "Child Support"
APPENDIX – Customizing Guide

❏ Necessary expenses over and above the basic child support guidelines.
PART V - in Chapter 16: "Child Support"
PART VII - in Chapter 26: "Child Support"
APPENDIX – Customizing Guide

❏ Retirement needs.
PART V - in Chapter 15: "Pension"
      Chapter 18: Essential Practical Concerns
APPENDIX – Customizing Guide

❏ Tax consequences concerning filing status, maintenance, child support, and credits.
PART V - Chapter 17: Remember The IRS
PART VII - in Chapter 26: "Options And Their Consequences"

❏ Will and health, disability, and life insurance.
PART V - in Chapter 15: "Your Will"
      in Chapter 16: "New York's Child Support Standards Act (CSSA)"
PART VII - in Chapter 26: "Support Payment Assurance"
PART IX - in Chapter 30: "Estate Planning"
APPENDIX – Customizing Guide

WHAT IS BEST FOR THE CHILDREN

Clarify issues affecting your family such as what type of custody arrangement is best for your children, their primary residence, and a visitation/access schedule.
PART V - Chapter 16: Child Custody / Support / Visitation
PART VII - in Chapter 26: "Custody And Visitation / Access"
APPENDIX – Customizing Guide

PSYCHOLOGY OF THE SITUATION

Improve your negotiating leverage.

Analyze the psychology of the situation in an attempt to gauge your success with negotiations. Anticipate the opposition's general mode of operation, such as his or her demands, methods, and reactions to your proposals. Keep in mind what is most dear to your spouse. Know what you intend to demand, what you really want, and what you need. Become empowered by understanding your own behavioral patterns. To prevent yourself from being controlled, recognize and modify how you react to your spouse and marital issues. You know the situation better than others do. Plan how to appropriately motivate the opposition to keep negotiations moving in a positive direction, possibly by touching upon areas sensitive to your spouse and then strategically backing off. By getting his or her attention, you may inspire a greater willingness on his or her part to compromise. How you present yourself can increase your negotiating leverage and help you design an Agreement to satisfactorily protect your well-being.
PART II - in Chapter 4: "Starting To Build Strategic Muscle "
PART V - Chapter 19: Negotiate Like An Expert

YOUR LAWYER'S RESPONSIBILITY

Your attorney is the legal technician.

Your lawyer's responsibility is to:
◆ Provide you with necessary legal advice.
◆ Help you attain an Agreement that is best for you.
◆ Ensure that your Agreement is not contrary to federal and state laws.
◆ Protect your rights.
◆ Be sure you understand and agree to what is included in your Agreement.
◆ Write the Agreement in legal language.
Once the Agreement is incorporated into a divorce decree, it will become enforceable as a court order and will be the terms by which you and your spouse live.

PART VI - in Chapter 20: "Get Down To Business"
in Chapter 22: "Be Prepared And Alert"

GOALS

Emerge with as much of your lifestyle intact as possible.

Design an Agreement that works for you, not one to fit others' views of what is acceptable. Address present and future financial needs and try to emerge with as much of your lifestyle intact as possible. Agree to a custody arrangement that best fits the children's needs and enhances positive parenting. Make an effort to avoid ongoing entanglements with your spouse that may interfere with your moving on with your life.

NOT SURE YOU WANT TO DIVORCE?

With a Separation Agreement you can remain married.

If you and your spouse are living apart and are not sure you want to divorce, it might be in your best interests to have a Separation Agreement to decide and define the legal aspects of your relationship. Once the Separation Agreement is signed, it will be the contract by which you and your spouse live, whether you remain married or decide to divorce. It is intended to legally determine the division of property, custody, support, and responsibility for past debt. Do not sign the Agreement, however, thinking some part of it is temporary. Consult your attorney regarding your concerns. You might want a court order for purposes of enforcement or modification of the terms of the Agreement. If so, you can bring a lawsuit for a legal separation, which culminates in a Judgment of Separation. This converts the Agreement from a contract to a court order without having to be divorced from your spouse.

APPENDIX – Customizing Guide

25

GENERAL FORMAT

INTRODUCTION

Each Article deals with a specific issue.

A Settlement or Separation Agreement follows a basic format; much of it is written in standard wording called "boilerplate." Most of an Agreement is divided into parts, usually called "Articles," each dealing with a specific issue to be resolved, such as child support, income taxes, property division, and so on. The general format and order of the Articles may vary depending on the style of the attorney compiling the contents. Two informational sections precede the Articles. The first is a paragraph including the names of the parties, their addresses, and a place for the date on which the Agreement is signed. The next section is referred to as the "Recitals." It includes the date and place of the marriage, children's names and dates of birth, reason for the legal action, and a statement that the parties desire the Agreement to settle the financial and property rights, provide for the children, and settle other rights and obligations. The following is a basic summary of what an Agreement commonly contains; it is only a brief summary. Your Agreement should contain many details, to be as precise as reasonably possible, to adequately protect you.

PART VII - Chapter 26: Design An Agreement That Protects You
APPENDIX – Customizing Guide
        Agreement Matters: Pathfinder

ARTICLES

Know what a typical Agreement normally contains.

SEPARATE RESIDENCES

Each shall live separately in a place of his or her choice, free from interference, harassment, and control by the other.

PROPERTY DIVISION

Part of this Article is boilerplate legalese stating that, regarding marital property, the parties have not agreed to anything other than what is stated in the Agreement.

MARITAL RESIDENCE

☐ Address and tax map number.

☐ Mortgage information: amount, payments current or delinquent, name of bank, and loan number.

☐ Ownership status:
  → Co-owned, with one spouse and the children residing in the house until a specific contingency, such as the emancipation of the children. The payment of expenses, taxes, and mortgage is determined, as is the allocation of income tax deductions. There may be a clause stating under what circumstances the house is to be sold prior to the specified contingency, for example, remarriage, cohabitation, or death of the resident spouse.
  → Sold, including details pertaining to how to proceed with the sale and the division of the profit.
  → Transferred to one spouse, including the terms of continuing to hold the mortgage jointly or of refinancing to remove the name of the nonowner.

PART V - in Chapter 15: "Principal Residence"

OTHER REAL PROPERTY

Vacation, Business, and Leased Property:

☐ Determine who is entitled to possession or to the income (specify amounts), who is liable for payments (identify expenses), and how any security deposits are to be apportioned.

☐ This Article is likely to have a format similar to that describing "Marital Residence" but may include greater detail regarding the terms of the transfer or sale of business property.

PART V - Chapter 13: Division Of Property
*   Chapter 14: Let's Look At The Tax Bite*
*   Chapter 15: Who Gets What?*

OTHER PROPERTY

☐ Each of the following is described in detail, including value, account numbers, and other necessary data. The terms of division are clearly set forth.
  → Bank accounts: savings, checking, CDs.
  → Vehicles: cars, boats, other.
  → Professional licenses, degrees, goodwill.
  → Royalties, copyrights, patents.
  → Defined benefit pension plans, IRA accounts, profit sharing, 401(k), other defined contribution plans, stocks, bonds.
  → Personal property: furniture, tools, equipment, jewelry, club memberships, art collections, frequent flyer miles, other.
  → Private businesses.
  → Custodial accounts.

☐ Separate property may also be described with a waiver indicating the nonowning spouse relinquishes any claim.

PART V - Chapter 14: Let's Look At The Tax Bite
*   Chapter 15: Who Gets What?*
PART VII - in Chapter 26: "Property"

CUSTODY AND ACCESS RIGHTS

The custody arrangement is described. The parent, if not both, with whom the children are to live is named. Visitation and access rights of the other parent are set forth, and a schedule may be included here or in a separate Article. With sole legal custody, one parent has full responsibility for the major decisions and for the everyday needs of the children. With joint legal and physical custody this Article is likely to be more detailed. It may include a descriptive list of "major decisions" to be made jointly, the specific time each parent is to have physical custodial care, and the manner to be used to consult with each other (phone, e-mail, fax, certified mail). It may also describe how to break impasses when there is disagreement.

PART V - Chapter 16: Child Custody / Support / Visitation
PART VII - in Chapter 26: "Custody And Visitation / Access"

VISITATION / ACCESS

Some Agreements are designed with a separate Article entitled "Visitation And Access Rights" and are very detailed in setting forth the schedule.

❏ Weekends: for example, "alternating," including the beginning and ending time of visits.

❏ Special days: such as children's and parents' birthdays, Thanksgiving, Christmas and religious holidays, Monday holidays, spring and other school vacations. Include with whom the days are to be spent and specific time of commencing and ending the visits.

❏ Extended period during summer vacations: usually to be agreed upon two to three months in advance.

PART V - in Chapter 16: "Visitation"
PART VII - in Chapter 26: "Custody And Visitation / Access"

CHILD SUPPORT

❏ It is acknowledged that the State's Child Support Guidelines are fully understood, and if the Agreement deviates from the state guidelines, the parties waive application of those guidelines and agree the child support obligation be governed by the Agreement.

PART V - in Chapter 16: "New York's Child Support Standards Act (CSSA)"
PART VII - in Chapter 26: "Child Support"

❏ Basic child support paid by the noncustodial parent is detailed including:
↪ How much is paid each month or week.
↪ When paid (1st and 15th of the month, other).
↪ How paid (check, money order, direct bank deposit, wage or salary deduction).
↪ Where paid (address).

❏ It is determined whether the support is to be increased or decreased periodically according to some agreed to financial measurement such as change in income. If so, each parent's income may be reviewed.

PART VII - in Chapter 26: "Child Support: Annual Modification"

❏ The parents' understanding of what constitutes emancipation for each child is included in the Agreement, as well as the percent child support payments decrease as each child reaches emancipation.

PART V - in Chapter 16: "Child Support"
PART VII - in Chapter 26: "Child Support"

❏ The parent who is to assume responsibility for health insurance coverage is identified. The specified coverage may terminate with emancipation, as defined previously in the Agreement or as defined in this clause. Type of coverage is specified, for example, medical, dental, psychiatric, and prescription drugs. Documents regarding the medical plan are to be made available upon request. Parents are to cooperate in filling out forms and exchanging information regarding reimbursement of expenses. Proof that the agreed upon coverage is in effect is to be made available at periodic intervals or upon request.

SPOUSAL MAINTENANCE

If maintenance is not an issue, there will be some standard wording to indicate: "Each party declares that his or her assets and income provide sufficient support and waives all spousal support."

PART V - in Chapter 18: "Maintenance"
PART VII - in Chapter 26: "Spousal Maintenance"

If maintenance is an issue, the Agreement may include most or all of the following.

❏ Basics about payments:
  ↪ Lump sum or periodic.
  ↪ Amount to be paid and duration.
  ↪ Payment intervals (monthly, weekly).
  ↪ Penalties for late payments.
  ↪ Name of recipient and location where payments are to be made.
  ↪ Type of payment (money order, check, automatic bank deposit).
  ↪ Social Security number of recipient.

❏ Modification of amount or termination in the event of:
  ↪ Death of either party.
  ↪ Disability of either party.
  ↪ Retirement of payer.
  ↪ Commencement of Social Security payments to recipient.
  ↪ Beginning of a pension for recipient.
  ↪ Remarriage of recipient.
  ↪ Cohabitation of recipient.
  ↪ Gainful employment of recipient.
  ↪ Change in financial condition of either party: loss of job, increase in income, inheritances.

  PART VII - in Chapter 26: "Spousal Maintenance"

❏ Schedule for automatic increases or decreases is to be based on an agreed upon cost of living index or other agreed upon factors.

❏ Tax consequences: Payments are considered to be taxable income to the recipient and tax deductible to the payer, unless another arrangement has been agreed upon and is acceptable according to the present tax law. Consult your tax advisor to verify what payments qualify as maintenance.

  PART V - in Chapter 17: "Support Payments" and "Options With Tax Consequences"
  PART VII - in Chapter 26: "Options And Their Consequences"

☐ Medical coverage:
- ➥ Identification of insurance policy.
- ➥ Coverage included: medical, dental, psychiatric, prescription drugs, other.
- ➥ Responsibility for the cost of the policy.
- ➥ Duration of the medical coverage.
- ➥ The parties are to cooperate regarding the application of forms and exchange of information relating to the reimbursement of expenses.
- ➥ Proof that the agreed upon coverage is in effect (to be made available at periodic intervals or upon request).
  PART V - in Chapter 18: "Health Care"
  PART VII - in Chapter 26: "Spousal Maintenance"

☐ Life and disability insurance are to be maintained on the payer with the recipient as beneficiary of the life insurance policy.
  PART VII - in Chapter 25: "Life And Disability Insurance"
  in Chapter 26: "Support Payment Assurance"

☐ Reimbursement for expenses and legal fees: A clause is usually included that states if the payer is delinquent in making maintenance payments and still has not compiled with the obligations of the Agreement after receiving a written notice delivered by certified mail, he or she agrees to reimburse the recipient for expenses and legal fees, resulting from trying to recover the money.

RESPONSIBILITY FOR DEBTS

☐ Identifies the creditors and specifies balance due to each.

☐ Names the party responsible for paying each debt and states commencement dates.

☐ Hereafter, any debts or obligations incurred by either party are his or her sole responsibility for which the other party is not liable.

☐ If existing debts are revealed after the signing of the Agreement or future debts arise, the party who incurred those debts is responsible for their payment.

☐ Each party shall "indemnify" (compensate for loss) and "hold harmless" the other for debts he or she is responsible.
  PART VII - in Chapter 26: "Debts And Liabilities"

INCOME TAXES

☐ Specifies filing status to be used until the legal Agreement is finalized, and:
- ➥ If it is to be a joint return, how the tax deficiency is to be paid or the refund distributed.
- ➥ If there are to be separate returns, which parent is to claim the children as dependents and take the mortgage interest, real estate taxes, and child care credit as deductions.

☐ Specifies past filing status and affirms each party represents to the best of his or her knowledge that all income taxes due have been paid, and:
- ➥ If any deficiency on past joint returns arises, who is responsible for paying that deficiency and any interest or penalties.
- ➥ If there is an audit, each party is to provide necessary records and documents.
  PART V - in Chapter 17: "Advantages To Working Together"
  PART VII - in Chapter 26: "Income Taxes"

LIFE AND DISABILITY INSURANCE

❐ Insurance policies of each party are to be identified, including the amount of insurance, duration of policy, name of the beneficiary, individual responsible for paying the premium, and the name of the company providing the insurance.

❐ When insurance policies are in effect to secure child support, the Agreement may specify:
➥ Beneficiary status is to terminate with the emancipation of the children.
➥ Amount of reduction in insurance payable to the recipient with the emancipation of each child.

❐ When insurance policies are in effect to secure spousal support, the Agreement may specify under what circumstances maintaining the recipient as beneficiary is no longer an obligation, for example, remarriage.
PART VII - in Chapter 25: "Spousal Maintenance"
in Chapter 26: "Support Payment Assurance"

WAIVER OF CLAIMS TO PENSION PLANS

This Article will appear only if the parties agree not to divide and distribute their pensions. It is standard wording, stating each party is informed regarding the retirement plans of the other, and each waives claims with respect to any pension or retirement plan of the other party.

MUTUAL RELEASE AND DISCHARGE OF CLAIMS IN ESTATES

Each party relinquishes and waives any claims or rights, as a surviving spouse, to property which the other party owns at death. This is necessary to have in the Agreement to cover the period of time between signing the document and finalizing the divorce, which could be more than one year with a Separation Agreement.

MUTUAL RELEASE OF GENERAL CLAIMS

❐ All claims and causes for action each party has regarding the other party are set forth in the Agreement.

❐ Each party waives and releases all other claims and causes for action against the other party that occurred prior to the signing of the Agreement of which he or she is aware or might become aware.

❐ Nothing in this Article is to prevent either party from taking the necessary action against the other party to dissolve the marriage and to enforce the terms of the Agreement.

LEGAL REPRESENTATION

❐ States each party has had the benefit of legal counsel or has represented himself or herself.

❐ Names each attorney or firm.

❐ Acknowledges that each party understands the terms, waivers, and other provisions contained in the Agreement and is entering into the Agreement voluntarily and that the Agreement is binding.

❐ Specifies responsibility for payment of legal fees.

FULL DISCLOSURE
- ☐ States annual salary of each party.
- ☐ Lists Social Security number of each.
- ☐ Acknowledges each party is fully informed regarding income and marital and separate property.
- ☐ Each party is satisfied that full disclosure has been made or knowingly waives his or her right to full disclosure.

Sometimes, the Statement of Net Worth is annexed to the Agreement, so each party is clear about the information relied upon to negotiate the settlement.

GENERAL PROVISIONS
- ☐ The Agreement is complete and contains all the agreements between the parties; no oral or previously written understanding shall have legal effect.
- ☐ The Agreement will be interpreted according to the laws of the state.
- ☐ If any provision of the Agreement is held to be invalid according to state law, the remainder of the Agreement will continue to be valid and in effect.
- ☐ The Agreement can only be changed by a written statement, signed by both parties, and filed according to the laws of the state.
- ☐ "Reconciliation" of the parties or the resumption of "marital relations" does not terminate the Agreement, unless the parties sign a statement and file it with the state, acknowledging they are canceling the Agreement.
- ☐ The parties agree to cooperate in the implementation of the provisions of the Agreement, without further cost to each other.
- ☐ If either party fails to hold the other to a strict adherence to a provision of the Agreement on one or more occasions, the provision is still in effect.
- ☐ Addresses of each party to where written notices are to be sent are included, and each party is to notify the other, by certified or registered mail, of a change of address or telephone number within a specific period of time.

REMINDERS
Protect yourself now and in the future.

Be vigilant as you work with your legal and financial advisors. You want an Agreement detailed and complete enough to protect you in your present circumstances, as well as in the future. The format of Agreements can vary depending upon preferences; for example, your attorney may add Articles to further protect you. Do not assume the first draft will be complete or detailed enough. Go over drafts thoroughly and have the necessary changes and additions made. Your Agreement is a contract by which you will be required to live for the remainder of your life. It can have a great impact on the quality of that life.

PART VII - Chapter 26: Design An Agreement That Protects You

Luck is a matter of preparation meeting opportunity.
Oprah Winfrey

By perseverance the snail reached the ark.
Charles Haddon Spurgeon

26

DESIGN AN AGREEMENT THAT PROTECTS YOU

Analyze your situation for all possibilities.

Once you are familiar with the general format of an Agreement, you can fashion and include provisions specific to your circumstances. Analyze your situation for all possibilities and design an Agreement that best protects you. Suggestions, ideas, reminders, and warnings are offered to inspire and guide you. The following information builds upon the previous two chapters. To fully benefit from this information, it is advisable to first read and use the cross-references cited in *Chapter 24: Prepare For Success* and *Chapter 25: General Format.* Use the *Agreement Matters* Organizer in the Appendix entitled *Pathfinder* to help stay focused and organized.

INTRODUCTION
Know what to include and advise your attorney.

Knowing what you want and need and what you can include in your Agreement will empower you to structure a settlement to fit your needs. Do not trust that your lawyer will include all that you need, especially if you have not informed him or her. Your attorney's role is to advise you on the legal aspects, negotiate skillfully to help you attain your goals, and write the document in the acceptable legal form required by your state. To help you see the economic effects of the choices available, you might want to work with a certified divorce planner (CDP). If you plan to change your name, it would be efficient and less costly to do so as part of the Agreement, giving you the added benefit of being able to insert your new name on deeds, titles, and policies.
APPENDIX – Agreement Matters: Pathfinder

GENERAL CONSIDERATIONS
Many Agreements are "living documents."

DEADLOCK PROVISION / ARBITRATION CLAUSE
Many Agreements are "living documents" in which modifications are anticipated in the future due to a change of circumstances. The need to increase or decrease child or spousal support is not uncommon. You want to be able to respond to improved or declining health or economic well-being of either party. Adjustments to the visitation

schedule may be necessary if a parent relocates to another area. Instead of returning to Court to modify your Agreement, include a "deadlock provision," which sets forth how to resolve those issues about which you and your ex-spouse cannot agree. Specify that you and your ex-spouse will go in good faith to a third party to break deadlocks. The third party can be named or agreed to as needed.

Your working relationship with your former spouse will influence whether your method of dispute resolution is to be more informal or formal. For a less formal approach, you can decide upon a familiar, trusted party who has the appropriate skills, such as a spiritual leader or health professional. A more formal approach would be to agree to "binding arbitration," and use the services of a professional arbitrator such as a retired judge. One source for arbitrators is the American Arbitration Association. To find a local office near you, call (800) 778-7879 or survey their Web site at *www.adr.org*. To help guide an arbitrator, include your intent and philosophy in the relevant Articles. You have the right to go to Court to resolve disputes, but you do not have to relinquish the power to make decisions when you may be able to resolve issues yourself with the help of an unbiased third party.

CONNECTING FACTORS

Co-parenting and other factors can continue to connect you to your ex-spouse. To help prevent misunderstandings and ensure an orderly routine, make visitation schedules as specific as reasonably possible. Be prepared for your former spouse to exert his or her right to look over your tax returns, if spousal support is based on your income being below a specified amount. Since child support is based on parents' incomes, there might be a periodic review of earnings. It can feel invasive to have your financial records examined. In addition, it may be upsetting as you view your ex-spouse's financial well-being or you may not want to disclose your new spouse's income.

PART VII - in Chapter 26: "Child Support: Annual Modification"

SPECIFIC ISSUES

Suggestions, ideas, reminders, and warnings may inspire and guide you.

PROPERTY

PART VII - in Chapter 25: "Property Division"

LEASES

☐ Have your name removed from property to which you are no longer a leaseholder.

☐ Determine the distribution of any security deposits.

LIENS

Allowing your name to remain on any lien on property deeded to your spouse continues to connect you to your ex-spouse and makes you liable for the debts. Your credit rating can be jeopardized if your ex-spouse does not make scheduled payments.

☐ Have your name removed from any lien on property you no longer own. When you transfer real property to your spouse, state specifically in your Agreement that your name is to be removed from the mortgage or loan contract.

☐ Including an Indemnification and Hold Harmless Clause in your Agreement regarding any debt is prudent, but it will not protect your credit rating if the other party fails to make timely payments, and it will not release you from being liable for the debt. The bank, which is not a party in the Agreement, will hold both ex-spouses responsible for the debt until it is paid. The only sure way to protect your monetary well-being is to have your name removed from any liens on property deeded to the other.

Be financially prepared. If you are the party to whom property with a lien is being transferred, your spouse is likely to insist upon having his or her name removed from the contract regarding that lien. The bank may "call the loan," such as the mortgage on the principal residence, and insist upon your refinancing, based upon your sole financial ability to do so.

APPENDIX – Customizing Guide

PENSION
PART V – in Chapter 15: "Pension"
APPENDIX – Exhibits: Qualified Domestic Relations Order

A pension legally belongs to the spouse enrolled in the pension plan, hereafter referred to as the "Participant." To divide a pension, a Qualified Domestic Relations Order (QDRO) must be drafted by your attorney or a pension specialist and filed with the Court, as well as qualified by the administrator of the pension plan, making sure it conforms to requirements. Without a QDRO, the retirement plan is not authorized to pay the nonemployee ex-spouse, hereafter referred to as the "Alternate Payee." Be specific in your Agreement detailing the division of the pension, because the QDRO distributes the pension according to the written terms of your Agreement.

Include:

☐ Amount or portion the Alternate Payee is to receive.

☐ Method of calculating payments.

☐ Time period of payments: periodic payments in the future at the employee's retirement, or when benefits would normally start, or a lump sum at divorce if the plan allows.

☐ Type of payment the Alternate Payee is to receive if the Participant dies prior to retirement.

☐ Rights of the Alternate Payee as the death beneficiary and any specific death benefit options the Participant is required to choose.

Be precise:

☐ Consider including that the Participant is not allowed to borrow against the Alternate Payee's portion during the time it takes the plan administrator to qualify the domestic relations order.

☐ State that the Alternate Payee is to be allowed to take money from the plan at the earliest retirement age, usually fifty-five years, even if the Participant does not retire at that age. The Alternate Payee cannot take money from the plan until the Participant is eligible to do so. If the Participant is eligible at fifty-five years of age but chooses to continue working, it may be interpreted that the Alternate Payee must wait for the Participant's actual retirement before drawing a pension. Leave nothing to interpretation; be specific.

☐ Include wording to cover the event of early retirement, often accompanied by a monetary incentive, so the Alternate Payee can share in this enhanced benefit.

☐ If the Participant is allowed to borrow from the plan, be sure your Agreement states that the Alternate Payee is to be assured the same right.

☐ Include wording to assure that the Alternate Payee is to receive "death benefits" if the Participant dies before the earliest retirement age. A standard QDRO form might not include a "death benefits provision," so be alert and include it.

☐ If the company does not provide death benefits, or if the Participant does not want to choose an option that allows for a death benefit, specify in your Agreement that a life insurance policy on the Participant is to guarantee the Alternate Payee's portion of the pension in the event of early death of the Participant.

Follow Up:
The more specific your Agreement is regarding the distribution of the pension, the more detailed the QDRO document will be in protecting this asset. Be certain the QDRO is filed with the Court and submitted to the pension plan administrator for qualification as early as is appropriate. If this court order has not been drafted and submitted for approval by the time the Separation Agreement is signed or the final papers for the divorce are filed, be certain it is done at that time. Insist upon going over the document to be sure it includes all the necessary provisions and wording.

MONEY AWARDS OR DAMAGES
If there is any other litigation in which either you or your spouse is a plaintiff or defendant and might receive a money award or be liable for paying damages, include how the award or payment is to be distributed.

TRUSTS
Set forth the necessary changes for any trust, regarding the beneficiary and trustee.

BANKRUPTCY – BE AWARE
Federal laws governing bankruptcy have precedence over state divorce orders. Some debts owed by a spouse who files for bankruptcy can be canceled. Financial obligations included in your Agreement regarding buy outs of the home, or a business, or the payment of debts may be canceled. Complete and submit for approval a Qualified Domestic Relations Order (QDRO) as soon as possible to try to protect your portion of your ex-spouse's pension.
PART VII - in Chapter 26: "Options And Their Consequences"

CUSTODY AND VISITATION / ACCESS
PART V - Chapter 16: Child Custody / Support / Visitation
PART VII - in Chapter 25: "Custody And Access Rights" and "Visitation / Access"
PARENTAL DECISION MAKING
Clarify which parent, if not both, has the right to make important decisions regarding the children. With joint decision making, specifically list the decisions.

☐ Choice of doctors, dentists, and other health professionals.

☐ Type of health care, such as counseling, orthodontia.

☐ Religious training.

❏ Participation in enrichment programs, such as music, dance, lessons, sports.

❏ Schools attended, especially for higher education.

❏ Summer camps.

❏ Vacation and school trips.

❏ Frequency and timing of telephone contact with noncustodial parent and with custodial parent, when children are visiting the noncustodial parent.

❏ Setting time limits for the completion of parentally financed college or professional training.

CHILDREN'S ASSETS

Determine whether one or both parents have the responsibility for the management of the children's careers, incomes, and investments.

PARENTAL INVOLVEMENT

Resolve whether one parent or both are to be kept informed and involved on a regular basis by medical professionals, school personnel, and others connected with the children's activities. Cover medical treatments and reports, school conferences, back-to-school activities, interim reports, report cards, recitals, and sporting events. Be prepared to take appropriate action. You might have to insist that two addresses be put into the computer database.

If there is to be joint custody and each parent wants full access to school communications and records, clearly state that both parents have the right to contact all third parties involved with the children and receive information. This means both parents can attend school conferences and events in which the children are involved, even when it is not their "access day."

If you have sole custody and the noncustodial parent is abusive or dangerous, make it clear to the school administration and to those supervising your children's activities that you are the only parent to be contacted and involved. You may have to show the school authorities a copy of the court order granting custody.

PARENTS KEEPING EACH OTHER INFORMED

Set forth your plan to keep each other informed regarding:

❏ Injury to or serious illness of a child. In the event of an emergency directly involving the welfare of the child, either parent retains the right to act unilaterally.

❏ General health and well-being of a child, especially when there is a prolonged illness.

❏ Location of the children.

❏ Notices regarding events and activities in which the children are participating.

❏ Information, records, and reports from schools or other professionals, if they are not sent directly to both parents.

RELOCATION

Permanent relocation of either parent is a sensitive issue, especially if the custodial parent wants to move with the children. If relocation is not a financial necessity, but just for financial betterment, and the move is opposed by the other parent, it is unlikely that the Court will allow the custodial parent to move with the children out of the geographical area where both parents live. Being aware of the Court's view on this matter emphasizes the importance of trying to resolve the issue in your Agreement. You may have to trade away some of your legal rights to marital property or financial support to be free from being restricted to living in a specific locality.

PART V - in Chapter 16: "Relocation Disputes"

❑ Establish the terms whereby a parent can permanently relocate such as:
  ➻ What are acceptable reasons.
  ➻ Whether written notice is required, and if so, how much notice.
  ➻ How to modify the visitation schedule to allow the noncustodial parent longer visits to compensate for less frequent visits.
  ➻ How the children's visitation travel and telephone costs are to be distributed.
  ➻ How the children's preferences are to be considered after a certain age.

❑ If you are unable to clarify this issue at the time of designing your Agreement, consider including a deadlock provision, stating that you agree to submit any possible dissension in the future to arbitration.

PART VII - in Chapter 26: "Deadlock Provision / Arbitration Clause"

DEATH OF A PARENT

Specify a custody arrangement in the event of the death or incapacitation of one or both of the parents, for example, solely with the surviving parent or with a third party such as grandparents, an aunt, or a friend.

VISITATION / ACCESS SCHEDULE

As you and your spouse design a visitation/access schedule, keep foremost in your minds what is best for the children. Idealistically, having access to two responsible, loving parents is most beneficial for youngsters.

❑ A detailed schedule helps to establish a stable routine and minimize confusion. Accepting an Agreement with a clause simply referring to "reasonable visitation and access," without specific details, can lead to unnecessary misunderstanding.

❑ Include a schedule for other people important in your child's life, such as grandparents, relatives, and friends. Your intention is to keep the child's world as intact as possible, regarding loving support and nurturing contacts.

❑ Visitation and access with the noncustodial parent and third parties is to include reasonable, unobstructed mail, e-mail, and telephone contact.

❑ Including a clause allowing access to the child during a period of serious illness seems to be in the best interests for all involved.

❑ Address items such as:
  ➻ Who provides the transportation for visits.
  ➻ How to arrange for temporary variations in the schedule.
  ➻ How makeup visits will be arranged in the event of illness of the child or parent.

❑ When there are children involved, your Agreement is a living document that may need to be modified in the future. Be wise and cautious; insert a deadlock provision for any issues about which you have concern.

PART VII - in Chapter 26: "Deadlock Provision / Arbitration Clause"

CHILD SUPPORT

PART V - in Chapter 16: "Child Support"
PART VII - in Chapter 25: "Child Support"
APPENDIX – Customizing Guide

ANNUAL MODIFICATION

Arrange for child support to be increased at regular intervals. If you agree to base the periodic increase on income, you may be forced to agree to reductions if the payer's income were to decrease. Also, sharing tax returns can be an emotional strain and keeps you tied to your ex-spouse in one more way. Agreeing to an annual increase of a specific percentage avoids the problems associated with exchanging tax returns and ensures an increase, regardless of whether the payer received a raise or not.

CONSIDER AND RESOLVE

How to pay:

- ❏ Children's extended visits with the noncustodial parent.
- ❏ Telephone costs for child-parent communication.
- ❏ Long-distance travel expenses for visitation.
- ❏ Increased transportation and auto insurance costs when a child receives a driver's license.
- ❏ Higher education including tuition, room and board, and transportation.
- ❏ Extras during the younger years, including tutoring, sports equipment, camp, fees for programs, lessons, and school trips.
- ❏ Medical expenses not covered by insurance, such as deductible premiums, nonprescription drugs, orthodontist, optometrist, ophthalmologist, eye glasses, mental health, and nonessential elective procedures.
- ❏ Increasingly expensive needs as children grow older.

EMANCIPATION

Clearly set forth your interpretation of emancipation. For example, state in your Agreement "when the child completes college," if you feel that event will occur after the child reaches twenty-one years of age. Be precise to avoid the possibility of misunderstandings in the future.

HEALTH INSURANCE

Signed insurance cards, claim forms, and policy numbers are to be provided annually or as needed. If insurance is not maintained in full force, the recipient parent may acquire a policy for the children, and the cost is to be reimbursed by the payer.

SPECIAL NEEDS

It is your responsibility to document special needs and bring them to the attention of your attorney, so each can be addressed in the Agreement. Set forth the emotional or physical limitations of the child and the special education, emotional support, and medical attention needed.

METHOD OF PAYMENT

- ☐ Personal check or money order to be delivered or mailed to an agreed upon address.
- ☐ Voluntary account deduction in which the payment is automatically deducted from the payer's bank account and deposited into the custodial parent's account.
- ☐ Wage deduction through the payer's employer with the payment automatically deposited into the custodial parent's bank account.

LIFE INSURANCE

Each parent is to take out a life insurance policy on his or her life for the benefit of the children in an amount commensurate with their support obligations.

DISABILITY INSURANCE

Each parent is to have disability insurance.

NEW WILL

If you die without a will, your property will be distributed according to the laws of your state. Write a new will to adequately provide for your children. Try to include a provision in the Agreement stating that each parent is to leave a portion of his or her estate to the children, or at least to the younger ones. This can help to provide for your children in the event your ex-spouse remarries and has another family.

PART V - in Chapter 15: "Your Will"
PART IX - in Chapter 30: "Estate Planning"

DEADLOCK PROVISION

Include a deadlock provision, detailing how to resolve any future disagreements involving the interpretation or modification of issues related to child support. As long as you meet the state's guidelines and your requests are reasonable, you can work out necessary changes and submit them to the Court for approval.

PART VII - in Chapter 26: "Deadlock Provision / Arbitration Clause"

SPOUSAL MAINTENANCE

PART V - in Chapter 18: "Maintenance"
PART VII - in Chapter 25: "Spousal Maintenance"

EXISTENCE

If spousal support is not an issue now, an option to waiving your right to it is to include a clause providing for a minimal amount, perhaps twenty dollars per year. This will allow you to go to Court at a later date if the quality of your life changes substantially and attempt to modify the amount.

METHOD OF PAYMENT

Spousal support payments continue to connect you to your former spouse. Some forethought about how those payments are to be made can prevent potential financial and emotional hardship. Consider either of the following.

- ☐ Voluntary account deduction in which the payment is automatically deducted from the payer's bank account and deposited into the recipient's account.
- ☐ Wage deduction through the payer's employer with the payment automatically deposited into the recipient's bank account.

MODIFICATION

To keep the value of maintenance payments up with inflation, agree to some measure for increases, such as a cost of living adjustment (COLA) tied to the change in the consumer price index (CPI). Carefully go over "Spousal Maintenance" in *Chapter 25: General Format* to be aware of the life-changing circumstances that can result in a modification of the amount or duration of support payments.
APPENDIX – Customizing Guide

TAX CONSEQUENCES

Maintenance payments are often treated as taxable to the recipient and deductible to the payer. This helps many divorcing couples, because usually the payer is in a higher income tax bracket than the recipient and can benefit from taking a deduction. An overall tax savings occurs, which can be divided. To qualify as maintenance, the payments must meet requirements established by the Internal Revenue Service. If it fits your needs, however, you and your spouse can choose to file your taxes with maintenance being neither tax deductible nor taxable.
PART V - in Chapter 17: "Support Payments"

If you are offered a lump sum or accelerated payments, such as receiving four years of maintenance in two years, carefully consider the option. Receiving a greater amount within one tax year could put you into a higher income bracket with more taxes to pay. If this is the case, factor the added expense into your support calculations, so you truly benefit from an overall tax savings. The advantage of receiving the money without having the uncertainty of extended payments may outweigh the tax consequences.
PART V - in Chapter 17: "Options With Tax Consequences"
PART VII - in Chapter 26: "Options And Their Consequences"

MEDICAL

❑ Specify who is responsible for maintaining health insurance and paying the deductible amounts.

❑ If the party providing the health insurance were to change jobs, he or she is to make the benefits of any insurance plan offered by the new employer available to the ex-spouse, or obtain substantially equivalent insurance through other sources.

❑ If insurance is not maintained in full force, the recipient may acquire a policy and the cost is to be reimbursed by the payer.

To continue to be covered by your spouse's company plan after the legal separation or divorce, you are required within a certain period of time to apply for coverage under COBRA (Consolidated Omnibus Budget Reconciliation Act). You will have to provide proof of divorce or legal separation with an applicable section of the Separation Agreement or divorce decree.
PART V - in Chapter 18: "Health Care"

DEADLOCK PROVISION

Include a deadlock provision detailing how to resolve any future disagreements involving the interpretation or modification of any issues relating to maintenance.
PART VII - in Chapter 26: "Deadlock Provision / Arbitration Clause"

DEBTS AND LIABILITIES

PART VII - in Chapter 25: "Responsibility For Debts"

If you allow your name to remain on any documents relating to liabilities for which your spouse is responsible, you will be liable for the debt until it has been paid. You will be tied to your ex-spouse for years. If he or she fails to make timely payments, your credit rating will be jeopardized. If he or she defaults, the creditors can come to you for payment, and your credit rating could be seriously damaged.

❏ Specify whatever is required to have your name removed from any lien on property transferred to your spouse.

❏ Try to agree to pay off credit card debt and other large bills before the legal separation or divorce is finalized. It might be necessary to sell some jointly held property, or for you to assume the responsibility for paying the debt, in exchange for a greater share of the marital property.
APPENDIX - Customizing Guide

❏ It is common practice and wise to include an Indemnification and Hold Harmless Clause in an Agreement regarding debts for which one party assumes responsibility, but such a clause will not protect you enough. The terms of your Agreement are not binding on creditors who are not parties in the divorce lawsuit. To a creditor, if your name is on a loan agreement, you are liable for the debt.
PART VII - in Chapter 26: "Property"

INCOME TAXES

FILING STATUS

You and your spouse can file joint tax returns while legally separated before the divorce is finalized. If you decide to do so, remember that you cannot use maintenance payments as a tax deduction. Financially, the joint filing status is usually the most beneficial, especially if one spouse is in a high-income bracket. In addition, filing a joint return might allow you to view financial information to which you might not otherwise have access. You may be at a disadvantage, however, if you do not have some control over compiling the returns and are not able to verify their accuracy.

For your protection, you might want to state in your Agreement that you reserve the right to file separately until the divorce is final. This will help to prevent your being pressured into cooperating with a joint return over which you have little control or fear will not be complete and correct. As the cosigner, you are liable for any inaccuracies, interest, and penalties. Check with an accountant to see if your situation qualifies you for Head-of-Household status, which would provide you with a lower tax rate than the Single status.
PART V - in Chapter 17: "Tax Return Status"

DEADLOCK CLAUSE

After the marriage is dissolved, you and your spouse will be legally and financially connected for some years. Your joint tax returns are subject to a tax audit for a minimum of three years from the date of filing and longer in the case of fraud. Issues can arise, such as the payment of deficiencies, interest and penalties, the distribution of refunds, or the possibility of amending past returns. You might want to include a deadlock clause in this Article, stating disagreements regarding the above matters are to be decided by arbitration.

PART VII - in Chapter 26: "Deadlock Provision / Arbitration Clause"

HOLD HARMLESS CLAUSE

If you have signed past returns and now wonder whether the information was represented correctly by your spouse, take some precautions to try to protect yourself. An audit could reveal deficiencies. Specify how any deficiency, interest, and penalties are to be paid. Agree to abide by and include an Indemnification and Hold Harmless Clause.

PART V - in Chapter 17: "Professional Help"

EXEMPTIONS AND CREDITS

Generally, the parent with whom the children live can take the dependency deduction unless he or she signs an Internal Revenue Service release Form 8332, allowing the other parent to take the deduction.

❏ If you agree to give up the exemption to the other parent to generate a shared tax savings, do so for only one year at a time. Clearly state in your Agreement that the transfer of this exemption is to be reviewed on an annual basis and will be in effect for only one year in duration, if not renewed. You may also want to include that your consent to waive the tax exemption is contingent on the payer being current with all support obligations.

❏ If it is appropriate for your situation, you may also want to clarify which parent is to be eligible for credits, such as the Child Tax Credit, the Hope Scholarship, and the Lifetime Learning Credit, or for the day care deduction. Confer with your tax preparer to learn how to qualify.

Tax laws change frequently; consult a tax professional for up-to-date information to help design your Agreement.

SUPPORT PAYMENT ASSURANCE

PART VII - in Chapter 25: "Life And Disability Insurance"

LIFE INSURANCE

Spousal support payments end with the death of the payer. With divorce or a signed Agreement, each spouse's right to the other's estate ends.

❏ Write into the Agreement that life insurance is to be carried on the payer in an amount sufficient to cover the support obligations. It is in your best interests to determine insurability before the agreement is finalized. Agree upon an alternate plan to provide for such support, if the payer is denied life insurance.

❏ To be eligible to have up-to-date information regarding the life insurance policy, the recipient spouse must either own the policy or be an "irrevocable beneficiary." You want to be sure the premiums are being paid. To avoid the estate tax on life insurance proceeds, it is preferable for the recipient spouse to be the owner of the policy. In addition, life insurance premiums paid as a result of a divorce settlement qualify as maintenance and are tax deductible to the payer, as long as the recipient is the owner of the policy. Arrange that the total amount of spousal support is to include the cost of the insurance premiums, and that the recipient is to make the payments.

❏ Set forth the details regarding the life insurance policy, such as whose life is being insured, who is responsible for paying the premiums, and whether the recipient of the support is to be the irrevocable beneficiary or the owner of the policy.

❏ If your spouse will not agree to your being the owner or the irrevocable beneficiary of the policy, include in the Agreement that you are to periodically receive proof that the premiums are being paid and that the insurance is in effect. Specify what evidence you need, and state that you have the right to pay the premiums yourself if there is a lapse in payment. Make lapsed premium payments "a charge and lien" against your ex-spouse's estate. This is a less secure approach than being the owner or the irrevocable beneficiary of the policy, and it continues to tie you to your spouse in a watchdog position, but it is better than no protection.

DISABILITY INSURANCE

You cannot be the owner of a disability insurance policy on your former spouse. To be sure the coverage continues to be in effect, however, you can arrange to be the one making the payments. This will also empower you to be notified of any changes made in the policy.

ANNUITY

For those with sufficient resources, purchasing an annuity that generates enough in interest to pay the monthly support is a financially secure and tax-wise solution. Work with your accountant or tax advisor on this approach.

OPTIONS AND THEIR CONSEQUENCES

POSSIBILITY OF BANKRUPTCY

If bankruptcy is declared, financial obligations included in your Agreement, regarding buyouts of real estate and business property and the payment of debts, may be canceled. Support obligations, however, are exceptions; child support and maintenance are to be paid. If you fear your spouse may file for bankruptcy in the future, consult an expert on bankruptcy and take precautions.

❏ Have a greater amount of child or spousal support paid in exchange for extended property settlement payments. Be sure your Agreement clearly states what payments are designated as maintenance, for example, a periodic payment, rent or mortgage, insurance, taxes, utilities.

❏ Pay the marital debt yourself in exchange for more of the jointly held property. If your spouse is responsible for some of the marital debt and declares bankruptcy, the creditors can hold you responsible for what is owed.

ACCEPTING A PROPERTY SETTLEMENT AS A TRADE FOR MAINTENANCE

Property settlement payments are neither deductible for the payer nor taxable as income to the recipient. There is no opportunity to take advantage of and share a tax savings. However, there may be greater financial security and peace of mind in accepting a lump sum property settlement, instead of gambling on an extended schedule of periodic maintenance payments.

❏ Be sure the wording of your Agreement clearly defines the type of payment you are to receive, especially if a property settlement is to be made in several payments over time.

❏ If the recipient has the slightest fear that the payer will declare bankruptcy, maintenance could be a more secure choice. Maintenance payments cannot be canceled due to bankruptcy, whereas property settlement payments can be reduced or eliminated.

If you are the recipient, do what is most secure for you, especially if you do not have a good working relationship with your spouse, or you fear your ability to work positively together will deteriorate over time.

ACCEPTING MAINTENANCE PAYMENTS AS A TRADE FOR CHILD SUPPORT

Since maintenance payments can qualify as a deduction on his or her tax return, the payer may offer to pay more spousal support and less child support. Keep in mind:

❏ Maintenance payments that are deductible for the payer are taxable income for the recipient.

❏ Child support is easier to modify; usually to increase.

❏ Child support is not as difficult to collect from a delinquent payer as is maintenance.

❏ The Internal Revenue Service has definitions of what constitutes "maintenance" and "child support" and rules regarding the declaration of each.

If it is child support you need, it might be best to call it "child support."

WORDING YOUR AGREEMENT

Precise wording of your Agreement regarding tax consequences is important. Remember, receiving a lump sum maintenance payment is taxable, whereas receiving a lump sum payment intended as part of the distribution of marital property is not considered income and is not taxed.

CONCLUSION

Take nothing for granted; you cannot afford any mistakes or omissions.

◆ Be informed and courageous.

◆ Stay focused on what is best for you and your family.

◆ Refuse to be pressured into arrangements that sound good but may complicate your life too much or are too risky.

◆ Work closely with your attorney regarding the completeness, wording, and intention of your Agreement.

◆ Consult a tax expert to clarify options and tax ramifications.

◆ Use the *Agreement Matters* Organizer entitled *Pathfinder*, located in the Appendix, to be sure what needs to be included is, indeed, included.

◆ Take nothing for granted. Lawyers have many cases; they make mistakes and omissions. You have one case and cannot afford to have any mistakes or omissions.

Turn your stumbling blocks into stepping stones.

Anonymous

If you want others to be happy, practice compassion.
If you want to be happy, practice compassion.

Dalai Lama

PART VIII – ADJUSTING AND HEALING

Seek help to heal. Work with skilled mental health professionals.

27   BASIC ADJUSTING AND PLANNING
    Divorce Frazzle
    Reminder – Take Care Of Yourself
        Physical, Emotional, And Spiritual Well-Being
        Stay Connected
    Moving Toward Your Future

28   YOUR HEALING
    Time To Heal
        Mourning
        Telling Your Story
        Recognizing And Facing Common Emotions
            Anger And Fear
            Depression
            Resentment And Guilt
            Shame-Based Guilt
    Releasing Negative Emotions
        Acknowledge Your Feelings
        Take Responsibility For Your Part
    Healing Thoughts
        You Have The Power
        Select Affirmations
            Self-Worth
            Security
            Releasing Pain And The Past
            Forgiveness
    Healing Ceremonies
        Life Mural Ceremony
        Life Mural Themes
            Ways You Benefited From Your Marriage
            Aspects Of Your Marriage From Which You Are Thankful To Be Free
            Positive Characteristics And Talents You Possess

29   FAMILY HEALING AND CO-PARENTING
    Transition And Co-Parenting
    Co-Parents' Relationship
    Co-Parenting Your Children
    Communication
        Child Focused
            Reassurance And Reaction
            Child Connected
            Personalized Tape Recordings
        Productive Communication Styles
            Businesslike Communication
            From-The-Heart Communication

Holding on to anger is like grasping a hot coal with the intent of throwing it at someone else; you are the one who gets burned.

Buddha

What we choose to exercise becomes stronger.

27

BASIC ADJUSTING AND PLANNING

DIVORCE FRAZZLE

*About eighty-five percent of divorced women report
being happier than they were while married.*

In addition to pain and anger, divorce can trigger memories of past losses and fear about the future. Unresolved issues can burst to the surface and demand attention. Mourning the end of a marriage varies in degree and duration. Some determining factors are depth of denial about the health of the relationship, cause of the breakup, amount of notice, and the presence of abuse or addiction. A common reaction initially is disbelief about what is happening, followed by depression, anger, and eventually, acceptance. It is also common to be unable to define exactly what you are feeling. Anger, depression, shame, fear, resentment, and guilt can mask one another. Any of these feelings can take up so much of your energy, they block other healthy, healing emotions.

For most people divorce is life shattering. The experience, however, can help you find previously unknown strengths and abilities that enable you to survive and, eventually, to grow. Women initially have a harder time than men financially, emotionally, and socially. It has been reported, however, that about eighty-five percent of divorced women say they are happier after divorce than they were while married. Less than sixty percent of divorced men report being happier.

REMINDER – TAKE CARE OF YOURSELF

Your thoughts help to create your reality.

PHYSICAL, EMOTIONAL, AND SPIRITUAL WELL-BEING

Your physical well-being is the foundation for your mental strength and emotional balance. If you do not get adequate rest and maintain a nourishing diet, it will be harder for you to do all that you must. Consider taking vitamins and other supplements to help your overstressed body. Treat yourself as if you are in training for a high-stakes contest that you must win.

PART II - Chapter 4: Caring For Yourself

To help conserve your physical and emotional energy, stay away from "energy vampires" who will deplete you for their own needs. You know who they are; some may be family or friends. They exhaust you quickly and never seem to nourish you. It is necessary to put yourself first. Plan to tactfully avoid these people or keep your interaction with them brief, excusing yourself politely. Along with helping you conserve your energy, this small intentional action may give you an increased sense of empowerment and encourage you to take more control over other matters.

Each of your thoughts helps to create your reality and your future. Your head may be filled with a lot of negative chatter, heightening fear about your ability to take care of yourself or doubts about your worthiness. If so, now is the time to begin to replace some of those negative thoughts with positive ones. Say something like: *I am capable of taking care of myself and providing all that I need*. Every time you are aware of the negative thoughts stirring up your fear, say your heartening affirmation several times. Do battle; beat back the negative chatter. With determination and practice, you can take control of any present moment. At the same time, you are planting the seeds for an abundant future. What you put your attention on is often what you get.

Create variations of your affirmation.
- ♥ *Life is changing and I am changing and walking into a rewarding future.*
- ♥ *I choose to create abundance.*
- ♥ *I am willing to learn and change and enjoy a rich future.*
- ♥ *I have the power to create the future I want.*

As you think and speak differently, your perception of your world will change, and positive experiences will begin to be reflected back to you.
PART VIII - in Chapter 28: "Healing Thoughts"

STAY CONNECTED

Stay in touch with the needs of your body, heart, and soul, so you are able to release stress and are open to being comforted and validated. Divorce-related stress arises from excessive demands regarding legal matters, and especially from intense pain and feelings of anger, fear, resentment, shame, and guilt. This stress is likely to be held in your body's cells until released. Trapped stress can cause physical imbalance and disease, as well as negatively affect the openness of your heart and interfere with the energy nourishing your soul.

Actively and consciously, release stress in a manner that suits you. Physical movement and the mental/emotional techniques of meditation, visualization, and prayer are beneficial. Laughter is a highly effective stress reducer. Deep breathing can be done anywhere, anytime. Deeply breathe in calmness and strength; breathe out confusion and pain. To enhance the healing effects of deep breathing, visualize and feel the Divine Energy (the healing energy of a Higher Power) surrounding you; draw it in with each breath. As you exhale, allow the Divine Energy to carry away some of the pain and negative emotions from within. This healing energy is here for you to use and you can choose to do so. Nature is a great teacher and healer. It gives assurance of renewal and evidence that there is a grander plan where everything has a place and value and arrives when it is meant to appear.

Social interaction at work and with friends helps to reduce loneliness and anxiety. A work schedule has great value in offering structure and routine when much of your familiar structure and routine has disappeared. It can help prevent you from becoming too isolated in a world of worry. Work performance can provide a sense of self-worth at a time when self-esteem is low. Sharing your story with a confidant, support group, or health professional can help to ease the wrenching feeling of aloneness and what might feel like a bit of craziness.

PART II - in Chapter 4: "Mental And Emotional Well-Being"

MOVING TOWARD YOUR FUTURE

Rebuild your life in a fashion better suited for you.

Divorce can motivate you to rebuild your life and live in a manner better suited for you. Possibly, the surest way to walk into a future suitable for you is to take small steps. There is no need for a grand plan; you may be debilitated emotionally and struggling financially. Taking small steps allows you to try out a variety of new ideas and styles. You will develop with your experiences and accomplishments and become more aware of your skills, needs, and desires. Include your children; they are also in transition. Involvement in school, religious, social, and family activities can help you stay connected to a familiar foundation as you move into an unknown future.

Weed out relationships that are not supportive. Surround yourself with positive people who have compassion and respect your determination. New friends you meet in divorce groups can be a great source of support and may become lasting companions. Many are going in the same direction as you. There seems to be a consensus that it is best to work on your adjustment and healing for a minimum of two years before serious dating.

There is no one right way to move into your future. There are many things to try. Some can be very simple. Your goal is to learn more about yourself and what you want. Each action helps you clarify your preferences, refine the larger picture, and promote your healing.

Start with little changes, projects, or adventures that would give you satisfaction or are out of character with how you have previously acted. A few suggestions might be:

Projects
→ Redecorate your home.
→ Start a garden.
→ Refinish a piece of furniture.
→ Clean out clutter.
→ Paint a picture.
→ Plan and carry out a repair.

Adventures
→ Horseback ride for an afternoon.
→ Take a glider ride.
→ Walk the beach with camera in hand.
→ Travel to somewhere you have always wanted to go.

Out of character
- Sing in the church choir.
- Change your hair style.
- Bicycle to work.
- Train in martial arts.

Take a class
- Improve your practical skills.
- Enhance your career opportunities.
- Explore your artistic talents.
- Develop greater self-understanding.
- Have fun and laugh.

There are many imposed changes with divorce, so try to avoid making unnecessary major transitions, such as switching to a different career, until you have had some time to adjust.

Actions you choose to help you move ahead may have unique, personal value. For example, you might be determined to do the house repairs that your spouse had said were impossible. By referring to manuals and getting advice from your local hardware store, you would be amazed at how easy some home repairs are to do. By successfully completing each, you will be empowered and enriched, especially if your spouse had not been able to do the repair. Your handiwork and accomplishments will reflect back to you your determination and new skills. They will be a constant, joyful reminder of how far you have come and a permanent nurturing force in your new life. You can reap the same benefits by losing the weight you were never able to lose, getting the education you never allowed yourself, painting the picture you never had time to compose, and becoming the "you" you never gave yourself permission to be.

The steps you take to move to your future will be many and varied. Some will test your courage and fortitude. Select actions that will give you feedback about your fears and your ability to conquer those fears, and about your desires and your ability to fulfill those desires. Each step, challenge, experience, and accomplishment will strengthen and heal you and refine who it is you are becoming.

28.

YOUR HEALING

TIME TO HEAL

There may always be some sadness, but the misery will end.

MOURNING

Taking the time you need to release your marriage, your spouse, and your married identity is essential to healing. Speak about your pain and other emotions to those who will understand and have compassion. Your distress will begin to subside, opening the way for healing. Expressing your grief, verbally and emotionally, can help to loosen its hold. The misery you feel during the mourning process will eventually cease. There may always be some sadness, but the misery will end. The amount of time to mourn the loss of a marriage varies depending on the circumstances and personalities. Grieving sufficiently is vital for your mental and physical health.

TELLING YOUR STORY

Telling your story is fundamental to your healing. Talk about your sadness and any feelings of anger, fear, resentment, guilt, or depression. Describe techniques that are working for you. Clarify your immediate and long-term goals and ask for the assistance you need.

Sharing your story:
- ♥ Gives meaning to your experience, struggle, and resolve.
- ♥ Helps you gain perspective about where you have been, where you are, and where you want to be.
- ♥ Provides an emotional release.
- ♥ Connects you with a supportive, nonjudgmental community.
- ♥ Awakens hope and encouragement as you work and listen to others who might be further along in the process and are doing well.
- ♥ Sparks the motivation to continue to grow.

To help guide you through divorce recovery, consider working with a support group or mental health professionals. Some groups are free, or reasonably priced, and can provide ongoing support from people having similar experiences. If your divorce has triggered and brought to the surface unresolved issues, individual counseling may be advisable. Experiencing depression and not moving ahead with your life are warning signs to take seriously. You deserve help identifying and working positively with negative emotions that need to be released.

RECOGNIZING AND FACING COMMON EMOTIONS

While you are going through the mechanics of the divorce, you want to try to make your emotions work for you in a positive manner. You have unfamiliar tasks to complete, goals to reach, and your balance to maintain. Using negative emotions in a positive way can energize and inspire you and help keep you focused. Be watchful and alert, however. When negative emotions are no longer serving you in some beneficial manner, it is time to begin to dismantle and release them.

Recognizing and facing painful, damaging emotions is part of healing. It is common for divorcing people to experience anger, fear, shame, resentment, guilt, and depression but sometimes it is difficult to recognize or get in touch with these feelings. They are tied together and trigger one another; they can overlap and disguise one another. For example, anger and fear seem to be the most obvious to identify but often they camouflage each other.

ANGER AND FEAR

Anger is a potent tool during divorce. It can help you get things accomplished and break the emotional connection to your marriage and partner. There will come a time, however, when your anger will no longer serve you, and you need to honor it for the protection and motivation it has provided and let it go. If you do not, this emotion will begin to limit you. Anger turned inward and not expressed can become depression.

Anger seems especially intertwined with fear. For many, anger is easy to identify. For others, it is too threatening or unacceptable to acknowledge or to express. Unconsciously, some prefer to just feel fear, which is a less volatile emotion and more socially acceptable. Fear, resentment and/or guilt are often the source of anger but are covered up by it. By releasing anger, you begin to free up and, eventually, recognize and release harder to reach, more deeply rooted emotions like resentment and shame. Freeing yourself of anger needs to be done in a fashion that will cause no harm to you or anyone else.

DEPRESSION

Be especially alert if you feel hopelessly or mildly depressed or seem to have no feelings. Your natural anger may have been suppressed and turned in on yourself, possibly out of fear it would get out of control in some way. Now, instead of doing its natural job of helping to protect you in time of crisis so you can survive, it is attacking you. Do not let this go untreated. Depression can be a serious condition; take it seriously. With help, it will become clear to you that your anger is not meant to be directed at yourself and you will find a healthy way to release it.

RESENTMENT AND GUILT

Resentment can be difficult to release. It can be very deep-rooted. You might have resentment over lost years, wasted best years, unrealized career opportunities, unsuccessful efforts to make the relationship work, unfulfilled love, and other unrealized hopes and opportunities.

You might feel guilty for having ended the relationship, or for having hurt and disappointed your spouse during the marriage, or both. Some guilt feelings, however, have nothing to do with a recognizable cause. A sense of guilt can be connected, instead, to an intense sense of inadequacy, to shame.

Even though resentment and guilt are distinct emotions, they have some similar characteristics. Both are difficult to release, sometimes hard to recognize, and toxic to living a life filled with love, freedom, and joy. Bringing to the surface and "feeling" resentment or guilt is not enough to release either of them. Forgiving yourself and others seems to be the key to freeing yourself of these injurious emotions. Talking about your feelings of resentment or guilt in support groups, where nonjudgmental acceptance is available, might help you to recognize these emotions and to begin the forgiving process.

PART VIII - in Chapter 28: "Take Responsibility For Your Part"

SHAME-BASED GUILT

Feeling guilty as a result of your own questionable or hurtful actions is different from getting in touch with deep, long-standing guilt originating from a sense of shame or inadequacy. You might be burdened with a sense of guilt that goes back so far that you have never been free of it, always controlled by it, and unable to recognize it. If you have ignored, excused, rationalized, or blamed yourself for the irresponsible, inappropriate, or hurtful behavior and attitudes of others, you may have done so because of a deep sense of inadequacy. Feeling less than adequate might have motivated you to try harder to make things right or, possibly, to not try at all.

In your marriage, you may have been the one trying harder, doing more than your share, and taking care to say it the "right way." If so, you were probably easily manipulated and all of your efforts did not bring you a lasting, healthy sense of value. Possibly, a haunting or persistent, but unrecognizable, feeling became intensified within you, because you were unable to "do it better" and "make things all right." A sense of deep-seated guilt may have caused you to take on unrealistic responsibilities. Such guilt originates not from having made a mistake, but from a sense of inadequacy. Some marriages function with this "shame/try harder/increased guilt" energy pattern, which is very difficult to detect while you are in the situation. As you begin releasing negative emotions and healing, this deep sense of guilt may become apparent. If so, deal with it. You deserve to live free of being, unconsciously, controlled by the emotionally deadening effects of undeserved guilt feelings.

RELEASING NEGATIVE EMOTIONS

Own your part of the marriage's failure, as well as its success.

ACKNOWLEDGE YOUR FEELINGS

To reduce the damaging influence of negative energy on you and those you love, acknowledge what has happened to you and wrestle with what you are feeling. Divorce shakes loose potent emotions. Identify what you can and accept what you find. Some emotions such as anger and fear often have tidal wave power as they surface; their intensity can be frightening and exhausting. Getting in touch with your anger and fear can help you see some aspects of the marriage more clearly. Recognizing and facing your fears can help clarify what is important to you. Staying with powerful emotions until they subside or transform in a constructive manner takes courage and tenacity.

When it is time to release negative emotions, commit yourself to the work with positive intent. Envision cleansing every cell of your heart and body of damaging feelings. For your well-being, there is no way around it; allow your feelings to surface with the intention of freeing yourself of their negative energy. That is the work. You cannot move on with your life if you get stuck in your pain, anger, or fear. As you confront and release negative energy, it will diminish in strength and you will make more room for healing, nurturing energy.

TAKE RESPONSIBILITY FOR YOUR PART

Take a critical, truthful survey of the part you played in the relationship from its beginning to end. Were you attracted to your spouse because you had an unconscious need to complete yourself with the qualities he or she had? Did you have a hidden agenda: married second choice, wanted a good provider, was not really in love? Were you attracted to traits similar to those of your parents and maybe, unconsciously, felt you were, finally, going to get what you had not gotten during childhood? Were your expectations realized? If not, did you have the experience and wisdom to effectively communicate and work together with your spouse on your mutual growth? What were you ill-equipped to accomplish due to your limitations? What did you do successfully?

Owning your part of the failure, as well as the success of the marriage brings powerful, lasting insights. You have not failed; you were one player in a marriage with dynamics limiting its survival. You are responsible for the part you played, no less, no more. Accepting this completely, over and over, can help to put much of the emotional debris in order. Anger and resentment can be replaced by grief and sadness, which are healthier emotions for the circumstances.

Any feelings of guilt will lessen when you own your part and realize what you were able to do was limited, not only by the dynamics of the relationship, but also by who you were at that time. Forgiving begins to become possible as you accept the reality that both you and your spouse had a part in the breakup. Forgiving yourself helps release feelings of guilt; forgiving your spouse helps to release pain, anger, and resentment. Forgiveness usually happens gradually; a little bit at a time is fine. Just start. You may begin to understand the role you played in having been victimized or may realize you really were not a victim. Regardless of what your story is, be sure to recognize any presence of self-pity and rid yourself of it. Self-pity retards healing.

It can be extremely helpful to develop or recommit to the belief there may be the existence of powers far greater than yours, influencing your life. There may be a grander plan eternally at work that is designed to always have you where you are supposed to be, doing what you are capable of doing, in order for you to evolve into your essential self. Developing faith can go a long way in helping to unravel and release painful and confusing feelings. As difficult as it may be to accept at this time, the Divine Energy may have plans for your life, yet unknown to you. Your marriage may have been a time of growing and learning; now it is time to move on to the next phase of your life. Work at staying open to the possibilities. Your capacity to forgive yourself and others can increase as your faith deepens. Forgiveness is the key to releasing guilt, shame, resentment, and pain.

Think about it for a moment. If you were able to go back through time with your same strengths and limitations to your marriage with its same interpersonal dynamics, probably, there would be very little that would turn out differently. You evolve as you travel through life. Each experience is designed to refine you and bring forth your true essence.

HEALING THOUGHTS
You have the power to control any current thought.

YOU HAVE THE POWER
You have the power to control any current thought. Otherwise, your thoughts are controlled by memories of the past or fear of the future. Stay in the moment; practice controlling your current thoughts. Be aware; negative thoughts will retard your healing. Think nourishing thoughts that push aside any negative self-defeating chatter that is cluttering your thoughts. With practice, applying nurturing affirmations can, eventually, create a positive change in perception and accelerate healing. Awareness and perseverance are keys to healing. Enhance your self-worth and security by releasing the past, and the pain connected with it, and by forgiving yourself and others.

SELECT AFFIRMATIONS
SELF-WORTH
- ♥ *I am worthy of the best life has to offer.*
- ♥ *I have been created exactly as I am meant to be.*
- ♥ *I rejoice in the magnificence of my essence.*
- ♥ *I am discovering a treasure: me.*
- ♥ *I choose to recognize and value my qualities.*

SECURITY
- ♥ *I have the talent and determination to provide for all my needs.*
- ♥ *With each experience, I learn how to succeed.*
- ♥ *In each moment, I have the power to create my reality.*
- ♥ *I choose to be successful.*
- ♥ *I have the power to make wise, loving decisions.*

RELEASING PAIN AND THE PAST
- ♥ *I am willing to release the past.*
- ♥ *I release my spouse (my marriage) and am free.*
- ♥ *I release the past and make way for the future.*
- ♥ *I choose to live in the moment, open to its abundance.*
- ♥ *This moment is a fresh beginning in an ever-changing life.*
- ♥ *I release the pain from every cell of my body and know I am healing.*

FORGIVENESS
- ♥ *I forgive my spouse and release him or her from my life.*
- ♥ *I forgive myself for what I did not know how to do differently.*
- ♥ *I forgive myself for being in denial about my marriage.*
- ♥ *I choose to forgive....*
- ♥ *Forgiving frees me.*

HEALING CEREMONIES
Release pain and negative emotions.

At times it is hard to know or define what you are feeling. Participating in ceremony can be an effective healing tool, especially where there is emotional trauma. Some ways to participate in ceremony are praying, meditating, acting, dancing, singing, chanting, drumming, creating, making music, and being in nature. Your positive intent to release the pain and negative emotions that are diminishing the quality of your life contributes much to the healing benefits of ceremony.

LIFE MURAL CEREMONY
Life Mural Ceremonies are designed to allow you to work constructively with events and aspects of your life. Recognizing, honoring, and releasing the emotions connected with them can free you to heal and move into a healthy future. Being engaged in planning, assembling, and dismantling your Life Mural helps to focus your intent. You use your senses of vision, speech, hearing, touch, movement, and your imagination. The progression of the work helps you recognize, process, untangle, and release what may be causing you distress or holding you back.

Life Mural Ceremony lends itself to a variety of themes. Let's look at a few.
- ♥ *Ways You Benefited From Your Marriage.*
- ♥ *Aspects Of Your Marriage From Which You Are Thankful To Be Free.*
- ♥ *Positive Characteristics And Talents You Possess.*

    To prepare for the ceremony, select a place where you will be able to work without interruption or distraction. Working in a natural setting is preferable, but using a room in your home will do. Outline a circular area from three to six feet in diameter; use twine, ribbon, or draw a circle in the sand or dirt. This will be your work area; it is referred to as a "sacred space," a protected space set aside for the purpose of helping you heal. It is within this sacred space that you will create a mural representing aspects of you or your life. Doing this ceremony by using a timeline approach is also effective. To represent aspects or events related to your Life Mural theme, select personal items you are willing to part with, written phrases and drawings, or objects from nature such as stones, leaves, blossoms, seeds, shells, cones, feathers, thorns, twigs, and vines. The basic procedure for working with different themes is the same. What you honor, say, and release, and how you benefit, will vary depending upon the theme you choose.

LIFE MURAL THEMES
WAYS YOU BENEFITED FROM YOUR MARRIAGE
Possible benefits might be having and raising children and pets, growing, learning, developing skills, building a business, having fun, traveling, eating good meals, laughing, loving, and enjoying companionship.
- ♥ Select items to represent ways you benefited. As you place each item in the sacred space, honor what it represents and express thanks for having had that experience. It takes time to heal; work at a comfortable pace.
- ♥ When all of the items have been arranged in the sacred space and you have a visual representation of ways in which you benefited from the marriage, stay with it for a while. This can be difficult, because you may be experiencing much emotion and considerable pain. Honor your pain; let it surface and let it go.
- ♥ When you are ready, begin to dismantle your Life Mural, item by item. Your intent is to free yourself of painful, negative feelings. Pick up each object, individually, and again honor the gift it represents and express thanks for that gift. Listen to your words. Take the time you need to let the healing begin. When you are ready, either toss or carry the items back into nature or put them aside to bury or to burn in a ceremonial fire.
- ♥ With each action in dismantling your Life Mural, release the past and know that you helped to create what was beneficial in your marriage and have the power to create again as rich or richer experiences.
- ♥ Say good-bye to the memories, to the marriage, and to your former partner. Take with you your power to create the type of life you wish to live.

Doing this ceremony can be painful and exhausting but extremely freeing and healing. It helps you forgive yourself and your spouse, and thereby diminishes guilt, resentment, anger, and pain.

ASPECTS OF YOUR MARRIAGE FROM WHICH YOU ARE THANKFUL TO BE FREE

Use the same procedure for selecting representative items, placing them in the scared space, and dismantling the mural as described for the previous theme, but allow for a shift in focus and words used. Honor your pain and all other emotions and let them surface. Thank them for how they have served you up to this time and release whatever is possible.

As you compose this Life Mural and especially as you dismantle it:

♥ Honor each aspect of your marriage from which you are thankful to be free, expressing what you have learned from each or specifically how you are free.

♥ Honor your spouse's right (or limitation) to be as he or she is, expressing thanks for not having to experience it any longer, knowing you deserve better.

♥ Release the past, knowing you can create a future free of negative behavior and other limiting characteristics.

♥ Say good-bye to the marriage. Take with you your power and determination to create the type of life you deserve.

The benefits of doing this ceremony are that it helps you to:

♥ Restore some of your natural energy.

♥ Release feelings of victimization.

♥ Be more willing to leave the marriage behind.

♥ Feel the fertile opportunities your future has to offer.

POSITIVE CHARACTERISTICS AND TALENTS YOU POSSESS

Use the same procedure as described for the first theme, allowing for some different emphasis and use of language.

♥ As you place each item in the sacred space, acknowledge and express thanks for your talents and positive attributes, knowing you can create the type of future you desire.

♥ Once you have completed assembling your Life Mural, you will have a visual representation of your essential qualities. Stay with it for a while, absorb it, and celebrate yourself. Express thanks for your abundance and for being you. At this time, try to face any fears with which you may be struggling. Your essential qualities can be powerful tools in dismantling fear. Fear is probably at the root of all negative feelings; you want to be as free of it as possible.

♥ As you disassemble your Life Mural, honor each quality and recognize its power in confronting and overcoming fear and in helping to design a rich future.

Doing this ceremony helps to:

♥ Clarify strengths and abilities.

♥ Dismantle fear that may be holding you back.

♥ Repair self-esteem.

♥ Build confidence.

29

FAMILY HEALING AND CO-PARENTING

Please note: Content presented in this chapter is applicable to families that are able to work together. It does not address special problems where visitation is supervised, too much unresolved anger exists, or a parent is unfit, abusive, or misusing drugs or alcohol.

TRANSITION AND CO-PARENTING
Succeed as a family.

When your spousal role ends, you may still be a co-parent. If so, you may be emotionally stretched trying to give the additional attention and support your children need while dealing with your own issues. You will be learning to provide a healthy family environment as a co-parent while moving on with your own life. Your success in providing for the stability of your children will be a reflection of how you feel about yourself. Continue your own healing by mourning the end of the marriage, releasing negative emotions, and forgiving yourself and your spouse. This work will help release you from the pull of the past and help free you to co-parent effectively.
PART VIII - Chapter 28: Your Healing

Healthy child-focused goals include:

♥ Providing a stable environment, love, support, and safety so that your children grow and thrive emotionally, mentally, physically, and spiritually.

♥ Concentrating on the best interests of the children when making important decisions.

♥ Having two stable, caring parents actively involved in their children's lives.

If you envision having difficulty co-parenting with your former spouse, try to shift your perception. Try viewing your co-parenting roles as if you were business partners with the objective of raising healthy, well-adjusted, thriving children. The goal itself is not unfamiliar; the hard work is how you approach and respond to your former spouse. React with the same respect and support you would apply to any business relationship. Successful business partners often encourage each to contribute their unique skills and insights. Focus on future goals, not on the past; on respect, not on faults; on the importance of succeeding as a family.

Anticipate and prepare for adversity or irritating behavioral patterns. One ingredient for success is the ability to turn negatives into positives. Try planting helpful positive thoughts in your mind to counteract negative behavior. For example, if your ex-spouse often relates to you in a condescending manner, plant the thought that this behavior is due to his or her sense of inferiority. Then when you hear that patronizing tone, you will be alerted of his or her sense of inadequacy, knowing it has little to do with you. You will be less likely to react personally to the behavior; instead you may feel empowered and free. Substituting positive thoughts and mental suggestions for old, negative thought patterns can often make co-parenting less stressful.

CO-PARENTS' RELATIONSHIP

Focus on what each other is doing right.

Take extra care to avoid conflict as you move into this new co-parenting arrangement. Manage discord in a manner that avoids involving the children. Work to release any anger you have so it does not dominate communication. If it must be expressed, try to do so in a productive, goal-oriented manner. Co-parenting demands that information about the children's needs, emotional states, and preferences be shared. Communicate in the manner that best suits your emotions and lifestyle, such as verbally one to one, written notes, e-mail, or voice mail. It is not advisable to ask children to deliver verbal messages.

Mutual respect is necessary for the children's benefit. It may also help you feel better personally. Be alert to your feelings; separate any issues with your ex-spouse from issues regarding the children. Support the other parent's relationship with the children. Focus on what you are each doing right; it promotes success.

PART VIII - in Chapter 29: "Productive Communication Styles"

CO-PARENTING YOUR CHILDREN

Role model how to successfully deal with adversity.

Children have a fundamental need to love each parent and feel free to do so. Respect your children's relationships with the other parent and support their need to love and be loved by the other parent. Children do not want to have to take sides. Encourage members of the extended family to support this need. Keep open to your children's relationships with their grandparents, cousins, and aunts and uncles. Refrain from attempting to explain or make excuses for a co-parent's behavior. Avoid being pulled into contests about who is the better parent.

Try to handle the stressful transition generated by the divorce in a fashion that provides a positive example for your children on how to deal with adversity. Acknowledge their feelings, furnish guidance, and exhibit character. Spending individual time with each child helps him or her feel special. Accept that you cannot control the destiny of your children; do the most with the influence and time you have.

Organizing or reorganizing your household might be necessary. A sense of order can alleviate anxiety and contribute to an atmosphere of stability and security. Establish reasonable expectations and a routine so each child knows what to expect. Assigning age-appropriate household chores can help children feel appreciated and needed. Recognizing your children's contributions to the management of the household can help to build their confidence and self-esteem.

Review or establish safety rules. Go over and practice escape plans from the residence and where to meet. Minimize arousing unnecessary concerns about possible misfortune or emergency, especially with younger children. Say: *This is what family members do to take care of one another*. Be sure your children memorize their phone number and address. Have an available list of important phone numbers such as medical, emergency, neighbors, and friends.

To minimize the anxiety of living in two homes, think of special ways you can help your children feel comfortable in both homes. Keep everyday items such as clothing, toys, games, books, and personal hygiene items in each residence, so children are not burdened with having to remember to pack them. Provide bedrooms, dressers, and beds, so each child has a sense of his or her own personal space and a place to keep belongings. Keep an organized calendar in each home; it is a helpful organizing tool and conveys a feeling that the parents are working together.

COMMUNICATION
Healthy communication is the best love.

CHILD FOCUSED
REASSURANCE AND REACTION
Children, especially preteens and younger, may need to be repeatedly reminded and reassured verbally that they will be cared for and everything will be all right. Some youngsters ask for this reassurance; others may be quiet or act out their fears with inappropriate behavior. Children of divorce often feel a variety of confusing and conflicting emotions such as sadness, helplessness, anger, and guilt. Youngsters have little experience in expressing confusing, painful feelings so, frequently, they do not. For emotional well-being, children's feelings need to be expressed and validated.

CHILD CONNECTED
Frequent contact with your children gives concrete evidence that you are there and care. Phone conversations, e-mails, and faxes are reliable, effective ways to keep in everyday touch with your children. If you are a co-parent who is away for periods of time, you may want to send audio- or videotapes, photographs, letters, cards, or postcards. Provide younger children with stamped, addressed envelopes and paper so they can easily respond, possibly including examples of their schoolwork or artistic handiwork.

If you are a working custodial parent, have agreed upon expectations with your children about keeping each other informed.

- Where they (you) are.
- What they (you) are doing.
- When they (you) are expected home or will reach destination.
- Where and how they (you) can be reached.

Let your children know you are thinking about them and have expectations. This helps them know they are your top priority. Keep in touch in a variety of ways including written or taped messages, phone, answering machine, fax, cell phone, pager, and e-mail.

PERSONALIZED TAPE RECORDINGS

Openly expressing your love for your children can go a long way in helping them heal. Let your children know you understand this is a hard time for them and acknowledge their sadness and confusion. Reassure them that even though you may be sad for a while or cannot be with them as often, it does not lessen your love for them.

One effective way to communicate your love is to make a personalized tape recording for each of your children. A child can listen to it in privacy, hearing words he or she might be longing to hear, without any awkwardness in having to respond. This taped message, displaying your sensitivity and constant love, can be played as often as desired. It can help a child cope with insecurity and fear and be a powerful healing tool to promote self-worth, soothe pain, and alleviate loneliness. If you are the noncustodial parent, a personalized tape can be especially powerful as a communication and healing tool, helping to compensate for your absence from the home.

Focus on the source of joy your son or daughter is to you and how he or she fills you with love. Describe times you have enjoyed together, interests and events, celebrations and achievements, bedtime stories or books, and future experiences you anticipate having together. Describe how much the child's unique personal qualities (hugs, kisses, laughter, giggles, smiles, resourcefulness, alertness, flexibility, kindness, playfulness, fairness, bravery, honesty, generosity, humor, specific skills) connect you with the love you feel for him or her.

Taped messages add a reassuring connecting feature that written communications lack: the sound of a parent's voice and, possibly, laughter. This can enhance its healing effect. Make a copy for yourself; it will remind you of how deeply you love and your ability to share that love.

PRODUCTIVE COMMUNICATION STYLES

BUSINESSLIKE COMMUNICATION

With businesslike communication, you care deeply about reaching your goals, but you do not necessarily care deeply about the person with whom you are communicating. It can be a productive communication style to use with your ex-spouse in co-parenting.

- Recognize any emotional agenda and separate it from your business goals.
- Compliment your former spouse on what he or she is doing well as a parent.
- Focus on your business goals, not the personalities involved.

➥ Pace yourself; know when to keep quiet; listen with purpose.
➥ Phrase your objectives and needs in a positive, disarming manner.
   Another way to handle... might be... .
   Let's consider... .
   It might be helpful to... .
   What about trying... ?
➥ Recognize when a power play has taken over, instead of a meaningful exchange on the issues.
➥ Be prepared to back off if the dialogue is off course due to intense emotions, irreversible power play, or other problems. Say: *Let's talk about this again sometime in the future.*
   PART V - Chapter 19: Negotiate Like An Expert

FROM-THE-HEART COMMUNICATION

With from-the-heart communication, you care deeply about connecting with the person to share feelings or resolve an issue, and you also care deeply about the person. Interactions with children are often from the heart. Different emotional energy is invested with this communication style than with businesslike communication.

Feeling at ease communicating from your heart often depends on receiving responses you can handle. The other half of the dialogue, however, is not predictable. It can be unnerving if there is either not much of a response with which to work or too intense of a response. There is not a set script or reliable outcome. Hearts can open and shut quickly in dialogue.

If you lack experience with heart-based dialogue and feel inadequate or awkward, prime your mind and heart for success. Muster courage and focus on your positive intentions. Be dedicated; keep your children's well-being in your mind as a motivating force. Maintain reasonable expectations of the process, yourself, and your children. Talk with parents about what works for them and what does not work.

Be practical and flexible. Select appropriate settings where it is calm, private, and safe enough for meaningful exchange. Show that you have the time and that you care. This may be new for your child also; you are going to have to be the role model. Clear your emotional agenda so you can genuinely focus on the needs, concerns, and whimsy of your child.

Be willing to accept and work with what the dialogue brings forth, and be respectful of your youngster's right to choose not to express certain feelings. If you get stumped, or the exchange is not going in a positive direction, be prepared to back off with the intention of continuing at some other time. Use phrases that reassure your child of the value of his or her concerns and feelings. Be specific about what you want (for example, time to think) and about when and where you can talk again. For example: *I appreciate your sharing this with me. These are meaningful concerns and important feelings. I want to think about what we have shared. Let's talk again tomorrow afternoon on the way home from the baseball game if you feel like it.* The purpose of calling a "time out" is to give yourself a breather and the time to prepare to be more productive when you continue the dialogue at a later time.

Gary Neuman's *Helping Your Kids Cope with Divorce the Sandcastles Way* encourages parents to convey sensitive, divorce-related information to their children in a well thought-out manner. The goal is to clearly communicate a message while showing compassion and alleviating fear. Let's look at an adaptation of how to achieve this.

♥ Use plain, understandable language.
You will be spending part of each week with your mother in this house and part of your time in my new home.

♥ Express compassion for what your child might be feeling.
I know you will miss your friends here, but there are a lot of kids where my house is and a park nearby.

♥ Admit to how this will change your child's life.
It means you will have to pack some things, but you will have your own room to keep other things.

♥ Try to foresee concerns your child might have and add reassurance.
If you forget something, we can get it, and I will drive you to school, instead of your taking the bus.

♥ Encourage feedback and connection.
Tell me what kind of bedroom furniture you like. We can shop for it together.

Supportive communication is made up of the most powerful love you can give and is an expression of your love at its best. It is an ongoing process, not a one-time event to solve an immediate problem. Loving communication becomes a lifestyle, a way of sharing experiences and enjoying the journey together.

PART IX – MOVING INTO YOUR FUTURE

30 FOLLOWING MARITAL BREAKUP
Wrap Up Documents
Basic Financial Tasks
Insurance
Health / Disability
Support Assurance
Real Property / Vehicles
Estate Planning
Will
Life Insurance
Power Of Attorney / Durable Power Of Attorney
Healthcare Directive / Living Will
Record Keeping / Filing System
Ongoing Concerns
Periodic Evidence Of Payments
Co-Parenting – A Few Reminders
Child Support Payments
Be Prepared
Taking Action
Wage Withholding
Wage Garnishment
Garnishment of Personal Property
Income Tax Refunds
Qualified Domestic Relations Order (QDRO)
Credit Reports
Collecting From A Self-Employed Parent
Locating A Delinquent Payer
Contempt Of Court
Your Health

31 LOOKING FORWARD
Your Finances
Short-Term Planning
Long-Term Planning
Develop A Financial Psychology
Prenuptial Agreements
What A Prenuptial Agreement Is
Reasons For Prenuptials
What To Include
Assets And Liabilities Brought To The Marriage
Assets And Liabilities Acquired During The Marriage
Waiving Death Rights
Legal Considerations
Suggestions For Approaching The Topic
Some Protection Without A Prenuptial Agreement

32 GROWING INTO YOUR TOMORROW
    Know Yourself
      Loving Yourself
      Unresolved Needs
    Communication Is Key
      Gender Differences
        In Reality
        Stereotyped Model
        To Enhance Dialogue
      Communicate To Heal And To Stay Healthy
      Listening Is Loving
        Intentional Listening
        Conflict
        To Be An Effective Listener
    Life Demands Change
    Celebrate Yourself And Your Success

30

FOLLOWING MARITAL BREAKUP

To implement the terms of your Agreement, you must be certain that documents are transferred properly and that new documents are drafted. Use the *Wrap It Up Right* Organizer in the Appendix to help stay focused.

WRAP UP DOCUMENTS

Obtain properly processed documentation.

BASIC FINANCIAL TASKS

You may need assistance with postmarital, financial tasks. If you have not yet located and established working relationships with financial advisors who are not connected with your former spouse, consider doing so now.

→ Transfer retirement assets according to the Qualified Domestic Relations Order.

→ Be sure investment accounts (IRAs, stocks, bonds, mutual funds) are conveyed to you correctly in your name only.

→ Make sure all beneficiary designations and insurance policies are as you want them.

→ Verify that deposit accounts (savings, checking, money markets, certificates of deposit) are recorded correctly in your name.

→ Confirm that joint accounts no longer exist.

→ Determine whether you are required to pay quarterly, estimated income taxes.

→ Clarify your tax status. It will benefit you if you qualify for Head-of-Household filing status.

PART V - in Chapter 17: "Tax Return Status"

INSURANCE

HEALTH / DISABILITY

If you plan to continue your coverage with your spouse's health insurance provider under the provisions of COBRA (Consolidated Omnibus Budget Reconciliation Act), you must contact your ex-spouse's employer and submit the required information and documentation. If you have not already acquired disability insurance, look into it now.

PART V - in Chapter 18: "Health Care"

SUPPORT ASSURANCE

If your Agreement includes a provision that your ex-spouse is to have life and disability insurance to assure support payments, be sure to secure documentation proving the policies are in effect. You will be sent up-to-date information directly for the life insurance policy if you have arranged to be the irrevocable beneficiary or owner of the policy.

PART VII - in Chapter 26: "Support Payment Assurance"

REAL PROPERTY / VEHICLES

To transfer interests in real property (home, commercial, rental, land) you had previously owned with your spouse, deeds must be signed over to each other. These signed deeds are to be recorded with the County Clerk's Office as public records.

Remember, if you convey to your spouse an interest in property that has a lien in both your names, you will be held responsible for the debt by the creditors until your ex-spouse either pays it off or refinances it solely in his or her name. A document referred to as a "Satisfaction," verifying payment of the loan, will be issued by the creditor. Anything less than having your name removed from the lien will, at best, keep you tied to your ex-spouse, and at worst, force you to go back to Court to bring a lawsuit if he or she defaults on the loan.

To summarize:

- Exchange signed deeds for transferred property.
- Have the new deeds recorded with the County Clerk's Office as public records.
- Insist upon receiving copies of Satisfactions, verifying the payment of any liens for which you had been responsible.
- Obtain evidence that the Satisfactions have been recorded with the county as public records so it is officially on record that you are free of responsibility for those past liens.

PART VII - in Chapter 26: "Property"

Changing the title of any vehicle requires new registration with your state Department of Motor Vehicles. As with real estate transfers, have evidence that any loans for vehicles transferred to your former spouse have been either refinanced, and are in your ex-spouse's name only, or have been paid in full. Warranties and maintenance records connected with each vehicle should be included with the transfer of papers.

ESTATE PLANNING

Rewrite estate planning instruments such as your will, trusts, power of attorney, healthcare directive, and up-to-date life insurance. Be certain your children are provided for in the event you become unable to care for them. This is a more pressing matter if the children's other parent is unreliable or absent.

WILL

You want to plan for the care of your children and the management of their inherited property in the event you were to die. Unless there are extenuating circumstances, the children's other parent is likely to become the primary caretaker of the children. The other parent, however, does not automatically have legal authority to manage the children's inherited property.

To prepare for the eventuality of both parents dying before the children reach majority, you can name another adult, called a "personal guardian," to raise them. You and your ex-spouse need to agree and name the same individual in each of your wills. If the other parent is estranged from the children or does not take part in parenting, work with an attorney to determine your legal rights with regard to naming a personal guardian. Appoint someone to serve as a "property guardian" to manage the property the children inherit, in case they receive it while they are still minors and cannot wisely manage it by themselves. Keep the executor of the will informed about where you store the document.

PART VII - in Chapter 26: "Child Support"

LIFE INSURANCE

Life insurance may be a way to provide for your children. First, think about the sources of income your children would have, such as property you leave to them, Social Security survivor's benefits, and financial help from family members. If you are well enough off with a financially secure family who would take over, you may decide you do not need life insurance. On the other hand, if your budget is already strained, you may feel unable to divert present income to plan for something that is unlikely. A modestly priced term life policy might fit your needs.

POWER OF ATTORNEY / DURABLE POWER OF ATTORNEY

Consider drawing up a power of attorney, authorizing another adult, referred to as an "attorney-in-fact" or "agent," to legally act on your behalf. The agent's power can be general or limited to specific tasks. A durable power of attorney offers the advantage of remaining in effect if you were to become incapacitated.

HEALTHCARE DIRECTIVE / LIVING WILL

Consider preparing a healthcare directive, also known as a living will, to set forth your wishes and instructions regarding medical care to be provided or withheld. A durable power of attorney authorizes your agent to make medical decisions for you, but it does not necessarily detail the type of treatment you want. You can name a healthcare proxy in your living will to see that your wishes are carried out, but it is optional. The healthcare directive is a contract with the doctors; they are obliged to honor your instructions. Give a copy of your living will to your healthcare proxy, if you have appointed one, and to your doctor, attorney-in-fact, and a relative or friend. Let each of them know where the original is located; you want it to be available if needed.

RECORD KEEPING / FILING SYSTEM

Develop an efficient method of record keeping and a manageable filing system to help minimize some of the stress of this transition. Keeping accurate financial records, especially on the children's expenses, is a good practice. It is helpful evidence to have for your personal planning and for any future necessary modifications to child support. An easy, effective method of recording paid bills and organizing receipts is to divide a loose-leaf binder into sections with labeled categories.

- ◆ Children's Expenses.
- ◆ Mortgage or Rent.
- ◆ Interest.
- ◆ Property Taxes/Common Charges.

- Medical/Dental/Supplements.
- Insurance.
- Utilities/Fuel.
- Phone/Internet.
- Miscellaneous: Security System, Maintenance, Garbage Removal, Cable, Vet.
- Auto Expenses.

Paid bills and receipts can be inserted behind the list of paid expenses in each section. You will not only stay organized, you will also have a picture of your living expenses and easy-to-locate income tax data.

Store important documents and information in clearly labeled folders or large envelopes.

- Estate Planning Instruments: will, life insurance policy, power of attorney or durable power of attorney, healthcare directive.
- Other Legal Documents: deeds, titles, loan contracts, mortgage, lease, divorce decree and court orders, passports, birth certificates.
- Home: mortgage payment book, home or renter's insurance, personal property insurance, maintenance contracts, warranties on appliances and tools, other information.
- Vehicles: insurance policies and copy of card, information booklets, maintenance records, warranties.
- Health/Dental: records, insurance information, test results.
- Banking: statements, canceled checks.
- Investments: CDs, IRA, mutual funds, stocks, bonds, other. (Depending upon bulk, a separate binder might be more manageable for investments.)

APPENDIX – Money Matters: Wrap It Up Right

ONGOING CONCERNS

Action and determination are positive role model characteristics.

PERIODIC EVIDENCE OF PAYMENTS

If your Agreement states your former spouse is to pay for or maintain health, life, and disability insurance, be sure to get periodic evidence that the payments are up to date. Also get periodic evidence regarding the beneficiary of the life insurance policy. Contact creditors to be certain payments are being received for debts not paid off prior to divorce. If not, your credit rating will be negatively affected, and eventually the creditor will look to you for payment. If you can afford to pay the debt, you might opt to do so to save your credit rating, and then pursue legal action to be reimbursed by your ex-spouse.

PART VII - in Chapter 26: "Support Payment Assurance" and "Debts And Liabilities"

CO-PARENTING – A FEW REMINDERS

Successful co-parenting can test your fiber. Keep your focus on your goal: well-adjusted, successful, loving children. At times you may feel as if you are on stage playing a part for which you have had too little rehearsal and your children are watching. They may not often share affirmative feedback with you, especially if they

are young or are focusing on their own personal agendas. Try sharing with them without burdening them emotionally that you would, occasionally, welcome recognition for what you are doing right. This might help them to identify and verbalize their positive feelings. As they realize how hard you are working at being a caring parent under these circumstances, their appreciation is likely to mature.
PART VIII - Chapter 29: Family Healing And Co-Parenting

CHILD SUPPORT PAYMENTS

BE PREPARED

If you and your former spouse were not in the financial position or could not agree to secure child support payments with a bond or other assets, the scheduled payments themselves may be the sole source for child support. Custodial parents generally experience serious financial difficulties if for some reason support payments become sporadic or stop. Tragically, a considerable portion of child support payments go unpaid. According to the annual statistics of the National Child Support Enforcement Association in Washington, D.C., only fifty to sixty percent of court-ordered child support is collected each fiscal year. Be prepared if you are the custodial parent and need to take action. Role model positive characteristics, be courageous, and do what you must for the welfare of your children. Your actions will benefit them financially, socially, and ethically.

TAKING ACTION

If the payer defaults on child support, look for his or her income. It can be in the form of wages or in a less apparent form such as rental income and interest on investments. Income can be found in anything the payer owns that can be turned into earnings.

Your local Child Support Enforcement (CSE) Program may be able to assist you in collecting your court-ordered child support. The CSE Program was established in 1975 as Title IV-D of the Social Security Act. It functions in all states through the state or county Social Services Department or through an office that has a similar function, such as the Attorney General's Office or Department of Human Services. To obtain the phone number for your local office, look up Child Support Enforcement in the Government Listings of your phone book or call the state office for information. For example, New York: (518) 474-9081, Connecticut: (888) 233-7223, and New Jersey: (609) 588-5093, (877) 655-4371.

1. *Wage Withholding*

   With "wage withholding," also known as "payroll deduction," the defaulting parent's employer is served with a court order that requires money be deducted regularly from your ex-spouse's wages and sent to the custodial parent. Automatic wage withholding is permitted in situations where there is a child support order, and the payments are thirty days past due, or if three consecutive payments have not been made. Wage withholding is one of the easiest ways to collect child support and works well when there is a stable work history. Under federal law, the employer is compelled to obey the court order to deduct and forward the money to the custodial parent within ten days of its deduction. The employer is required to inform the custodial parent if his or her former spouse no longer works at the job.

To obtain an order for wage withholding, either call your state Child Support Enforcement (CSE) Program for assistance or file the petition yourself in Family Court. It might be to your advantage to do the paperwork yourself, instead of enduring the frustration and delays you may experience counting on an overburdened government bureaucracy. If, however, the employer is in another state, it can become a slow, frustrating experience, because two states are involved, and the procedure is more complicated. In that case, seriously consider letting the CSE handle the paperwork for you.

2. *Wage Garnishment*
   "Wage garnishment" is a bit different from wage withholding; however, the terms are commonly used interchangeably. Wage withholding results when a court order requires that the monthly child support payment be regularly deducted and sent to the custodial parent. Wage garnishment results when the purpose of the court order is to collect an arrearage (past due payments). Depending on the circumstances, the amount deducted may be either a lump sum payment or a percentage of the payer's check taken over time until the debt is paid. Know which you need, so you can ask the appropriate questions and use the proper forms.

3. *Garnishment of Personal Property*
   Personal property such as savings, checking accounts, and investments can be garnished and nonliquid assets can be seized and sold. More complicated legal procedures and greater costs are involved. Some of the procedures, however, are not too difficult and you may consider doing them yourself. For example, if you have information about a bank account of the defaulting payer, you can garnish it. Work with the Family Court to obtain a court order that requires the third party holding the assets to turn them over to the Court. In most states, your County Attorney or District Attorney can help.
   APPENDIX – *Customizing Guide*

4. *Income Tax Refunds*
   According to the Debt Collection Improvement Act of 1996 (DCIA), the Treasury Department can arrange to have unpaid, court-ordered child support deducted from a payer's federal tax refund and sent to the custodial parent. The Federal Income Tax Offset Program is administrated through the Child Support Enforcement (CSE) units, which can intercept tax refunds of parents who have been proven to owe substantial amounts of outstanding, court-ordered child support. Seek assistance from your local CSE unit. New York State income tax refunds can also be intercepted to pay delinquent child support.

5. *Qualified Domestic Relations Order (QDRO)*
   Under certain conditions a QDRO can be used to collect child support arrearages. This is most useful where the payer is self-employed but has rights to benefits through previous employment. The delinquent child support is sent directly to the recipient from the retirement funds. If the payer is retired and receiving benefits, the QDRO orders the money to be removed from his or her benefits check. Securing overdue child support through a QDRO can be used with private

employers' retirement plans but not with public employee or military plans. If there are few alternatives available to you, using a **QDRO** may be a viable option. It does, however, cost some money to have it drafted properly by an attorney. If the payer is still working, wage withholding is easier and less costly.

6. *Credit Reports*

A copy of the payer's credit report can be one of the most helpful tools in finding some assets. It also provides a current address and credit history. As a creditor, you have a right to this information, but the credit bureaus will not give it to you directly. The government lawyer with your state Child Support Enforcement can get the defaulting ex-spouse's credit report for you. However, it is likely to take a long time. If child support has been court ordered in New York State, a licensed private investigator can legally obtain a copy of the delinquent payer's credit report.

COLLECTING FROM A SELF-EMPLOYED PARENT

Getting child support payments from a defaulting, self-employed parent is especially difficult. In addition, the amount of self-employed income is frequently underreported, so even when child support is paid, it is often not proportionate to the payer's income. Wage withholding does not apply to the self-employed; usually, they are not W-2 wage earners. It is possible to execute an action to garnish liquid and nonliquid assets. Obtaining a copy of your ex-spouse's credit report may be a helpful tool for locating some of these assets.

PART IX - in Chapter 30: "Child Support Payments: Taking Action"

There are some ways to take money from a defaulting parent's business. If the business is a sole proprietorship or limited liability company (LLC), your ex-spouse's Social Security number is used as the identifying number on form Schedule C – Profit or Loss From Business of the income tax returns. This means, whatever the business owns, your ex-spouse owns. You can garnish business bank accounts. You also can garnish nonliquid business property and supplies that are seized and sold, but this can become complicated, costly, and possibly, dangerous.

Carefully evaluate the psychology of your situation; know what you are up against and make wise decisions. You do not want to take action that may endanger your safety or make the situation worse. Seek the professional advice and guidance you need to pursue a course of action that is designed to safely help you reach your goals.

LOCATING A DELINQUENT PAYER

If you cannot pay for assistance and need to locate a delinquent payer, try some things yourself. Start with the basics. Call directory assistance for the area where you think the payer might be living. Even a response that the number is unlisted narrows your search. Be resourceful. If your ex-spouse is a sportsman, call the state department that issues fishing and hunting licenses. Connecticut, Massachusetts and New Hampshire are among thirty states that will search their records at your request. Presently, New York does not release information about these licenses. Get creative with your computer. Sites such as *www.backgroundcheckgateway.com* offer tips and databases to help find people.

CONTEMPT OF COURT

Not receiving court-ordered child support creates financial hardship and cuts at the fiber of family life. Do whatever you can safely do emotionally, physically, and legally. Filing a contempt of court petition against the payer for nonpayment of child support will, at the very least, allow you to take a stand and have it on public record that what is happening is not acceptable. At best, you might receive some or all of the arrearage.

The person charged with contempt of court is required to appear before the Judge to explain why he or she has not made the child support payments. The Judge can order jail time for those who are willfully delinquent in their payments, but most judges rarely do this with the first contempt charge. Judges differ in their views and have judicial discretion with how they decide this matter. Gradually, judges are becoming more aware of the hardship nonpayment of child support causes and are not waiting for the defendant to be charged numerous times before ordering jail time. The law allows for the defendant to stay in jail until all back child support is paid, but usually is allowed out after a small amount of the support has been paid, with the remainder ordered to be paid over time.

PART IV - in Chapter 12: "Enforcement Of Orders"
APPENDIX – Customizing Guide

Even though filing petitions of contempt may not remedy your situation, often it is better to make this effort and take a stand in Court than not to do so. You can file a contempt of court petition yourself at minimal cost. Obtain the forms from the Family Court County Clerk. You will need a petition for an Order to Show Cause and an Affidavit to be filed together. Attach a copy of the child support court order, specifying the amount of support ordered with a detailed list of payments received and those missing. When you file these documents with the County Clerk, you will be given a court date and a certified copy of the Order to Show Cause to serve on the defendant.

Connecting with ACES (Association For Children For Enforcement Of Support) may offer you some support. ACES is the largest nonprofit child support group in the nation with chapters in various locations in forty-eight states; there may be a chapter near you. At their Web site (*www.childsupport-aces.org/*), turn to the Action Alert page for action you can take or call (800) 738-ACES (2237) for information.

YOUR HEALTH

The pervasive emotions divorce brings to the surface, combined with the unrelenting stress of dealing with the divorce process, can be very damaging to your body. It is time to consciously help your body regain a healthy balance so it can heal where it has been overstressed. Start with a physical exam to get medical feedback. Consider what you already know but may not have had the heart or time to do: exercise three to four times per week for thirty minutes. If you are unsure about which combination of foods would be best for your vitality and healing, work with someone knowledgeable in the field of nutrition and use of supplements. Borrow a juicer from a friend and see if juicing fresh vegetables and fruits is something you can do. Drinking these fresh juices is a very effective way to supply your body with health-enhancing nutrients and minerals, essential for renewal. Your body has kept going during this divorce ordeal; now is the time to return that kindness and give your body the attention it deserves and needs.

Along with focusing on your physical health, continue to allow emotions to surface so you can release them and be freer to move into a gratifying future. Try to stay in the present. Having regrets about what has happened will pull you into the past. Work at developing the belief that what has happened has brought you to where you are with purpose. If anxiety about the future arises, try to view it as a messenger bringing information about what needs attention.

PART VIII - Chapter 28: Your Healing

Each forward step we take we leave some phantom of ourselves behind.
John Lancaster Spalding

I've always wanted to be somebody, but I
see now I should have been more specific.
Lily Tomlin

31

LOOKING FORWARD

YOUR FINANCES
Become financially wise and independent.

Even though you may feel your finances are in a shambles, this is the time, if you have not already done so, to become well-informed about money matters and take control. You may be living with less income while being responsible for a greater proportion of the family's expenses.

SHORT-TERM PLANNING

Keep up-to-date records of income from all sources and regular monthly and periodic expenses. An organized system of recording bills as they are paid and filing the receipts may help alleviate some concern about your finances. Money often stirs up emotions; fear, helplessness, power, and envy are common. Be prepared for emotions connected with money to surface; accept and learn from them. As you keep comprehensive records of your income and expenses, your financial picture will become clearer to you.
PART IX - in Chapter 30: "Record Keeping / Filing System"

Critically evaluate your ability to afford to live as you are. If the residence in which you are living is straining your budget too much, where can you cut costs? Can you earn more income? If you own your home, be sure to calculate the tax benefit you will receive on your federal taxes. Your financial reality might be brighter than it, at first, appears. If your budget is not working, however, be decisive and cut what is not absolutely essential. This may be upsetting to your family, so reassure them that you are only taking temporary measures designed to move you through transition and into a comfortable, secure future.

You may be in financial survival mode for a while following your divorce so keep focused on your goals. Establish a plan to pay your debts. Make the payments on a specific day of the month, such as payday. Pay the agreed upon amount and do so on time. Be sure to establish credit in your own name but try to pay off any credit card balance each month, so you are not adding to your financial burden by paying high interest rates which are not tax deductible. It is best to have an emergency fund

available to cover living expenses for three to five months. To ease financial burdens and cope with emergencies, it is prudent to have a backup option, such as living with family for a while.
PART III - in Chapter 6: "Credit Cards"

LONG-TERM PLANNING

If you have little or no experience with investing, take some time before making any major decisions. Keep your assets safe and learn about your options. When you feel you have both emotional balance and enough knowledge, begin to make your decisions. Explore the retirement fund options available to you and, if it fits your needs and budget, contribute. Reevaluate your insurance needs for health, disability, home, auto, and if you have children, life insurance on yourself. You want to be sure you have enough of the right type of coverage.

As you work with your tax preparer, continue to learn. Do you qualify for Head-of-Household status and any of the child-related credits? What effect does owning a home have on your taxes? How does contributing to an IRA or 401(k) cut your present tax obligation? Find out if tax-free investments are appropriate in your situation.
PART V - in Chapter 17: "Tax Filing Status" and "Exemptions And Credits"

DEVELOP A FINANCIAL PSYCHOLOGY

Become as money-wise and independent as possible. Financial well-being is critical in determining quality of life. You want to live comfortably and securely, knowing your children have what they need and deserve. Do not allow yourself to be influenced by anyone saying: *Leave it to me. I'll take care of you.* In the real world, many well-intentioned promises are simply not kept. Be knowledgeable about and in control of your finances so you can survive any crisis and prosper.

PRENUPTIAL AGREEMENTS

Prenuptials are not for the wealthy only.

WHAT A PRENUPTIAL AGREEMENT IS

If you decide to marry again, consider drawing up a prenuptial agreement. Many considering a subsequent marriage are more realistic about the romance and economics of marital life and want to plan for any eventuality. A prenuptial agreement is a legally binding written contract designed and signed by a couple prior to marriage, detailing how their assets and liabilities are to be divided in the event of divorce or death.

REASONS FOR PRENUPTIALS

Prenuptial agreements provide a certain degree of legal, emotional, and financial protection and, as a result, can contribute to increased peace of mind and harmony. Prenuptials are not for the wealthy only; they are for those who want to take some judicious steps to protect their financial and emotional futures.

- Alleviate uncertainty about your financial future in the event of divorce and about the distribution of your estate upon death.
- Ease your children's suspicions about your pending marriage.

+ Keep separate the assets you bring to the marriage.
+ Insure the inheritance of certain assets to the children of a previous marriage.
+ Keep separate the income earned and the income-earning potential you develop (growing your business, advancing in your career, marketing your inventions and creations, building your professional reputation, or enhancing your celebrity status) during the marriage.
+ Specify how you are to be compensated for giving up career opportunities to stay home to raise the family.

WHAT TO INCLUDE

Generally, the more reasonably complete your Prenuptial Agreement is, the better it will protect you in the future. Include assets, liabilities, present circumstances, and future possibilities. Assets can include savings, investments, property, income earned, and income-earning potential. You can agree to divide your property in the way that best suits your needs.

ASSETS AND LIABILITIES BROUGHT TO THE MARRIAGE

Specifically identify assets and liabilities brought to the marriage and state how each is to be distributed in the event of the termination of the union. If you intend to keep these assets and liabilities separate, do not comingle them. Keep your accounts and investments separate and in your name only and your individual property in your own name. Be very clear about specific circumstances, such as you want your family home at Cape Cod to stay in your family, even though both you and your new spouse plan to work on refurbishing it.

PART V - in Chapter 13: "Conversion Of Separate Property Into Marital Property"

ASSETS AND LIABILITIES ACQUIRED DURING THE MARRIAGE

Determining the distribution of assets and liabilities to be acquired during the marriage is challenging; you are anticipating what is not yet evident. Consider real estate and other anticipated large items, as well as income derived from employment, businesses, degrees, licenses, celebrity status, professional reputation, and marketing inventions and creations. Pay considerable attention to the distribution of the increased value and income-generating capacity of separate property, resulting from the efforts of the other spouse. Be specific about distribution, for example, "separate," "proportional" such as fifty-fifty, or some other detailed plan, such as "separate with maintenance" for a specified period of time.

Do not comingle what you intend to keep separate. For example, if you plan to keep your income separate, be sure to set up an account for that purpose in your name only. Do not deposit your income into any account with your spouse or into any account holding marital funds.

If you plan to be the primary caregiver staying at home to raise the yet-to-be-born children, your state might not uphold your prenuptial provisions regarding custody and child support of those unborn children. If this is the case, consider including a provision allowing the primary caregiver to remain in the marital home if the marriage were to dissolve. It could have an impact on your children's quality of life and, possibly, be a factor in a custody decision.

WAIVING DEATH RIGHTS

By agreeing to waive death rights (right of inheritance to a spouse's estate), each spouse is allowed to draft a will leaving property to whom he or she chooses. Otherwise, state law requires a certain portion of an estate be left to the surviving spouse. A common concern when remarrying is to protect the inheritance of the children of a previous marriage. If you have very few assets, but you do have financial concerns about your future, you might want to negotiate to have your wealthier spouse take out a life insurance policy in exchange for waiving death rights. Arrange to be the owner or "irrevocable beneficiary." To avoid the estate tax on life insurance proceeds, it is preferable for you to be the owner.

LEGAL CONSIDERATIONS

Your Prenuptial Agreement must conform to the laws of your state, or to an accepted judicial interpretation, in order to be recognized by the Court as valid and enforceable. Some states have no specific statutes pertaining to premarital agreements but will recognize them as legally binding. To be sure the Court recognizes your Agreement as legal and enforceable, work with qualified legal professionals who are well-versed on your state's requirements. Each party to the Agreement needs to secure his or her own legal counsel.

Summary of common legal requirements:
- Your Prenuptial Agreement must be a written document signed by each party without coercion. The requirement that signatures be witnessed and notarized varies among the states. New York requires notarization.
- Design your Agreement leaving plenty of time to consider its terms and to seek the necessary legal advice before signing. There is the possibility the Court will not accept your Agreement if it appears to have been signed too close to the wedding date, possibly under duress.
- If you move to another state, retain an attorney experienced in prenuptials to review your Agreement to be sure it complies with the laws of your new home state. Changes must be made according to that state's legal standards. Be specific about what is to be amended or added and affirm that the reminder of the original document is to continue to be in effect.
- Concealing any assets or liabilities would be cause for the Court to invalidate the Agreement and might be viewed as fraud.

APPENDIX – Customizing Guide

SUGGESTIONS FOR APPROACHING THE TOPIC

Even though there are many practical and solid legal reasons for agreeing to a prenuptial agreement, it can be a delicate matter to approach. Highlighting concerns having nothing to do with the possibility of a future divorce might be one of the most effective approaches. Focus on your desire to insure that the assets you have accumulated be passed on to your children from a previous marriage or, if there are no children, to your nieces and nephews. Remember, death rights give your spouse legal rights to a large portion of your estate. Each of you can waive your death rights and be

free to write wills more suited to your personal needs. With this approach, you are being financially responsible for your family without saying anything about divorce. It is an approach that may very well satisfy the needs of your future spouse also, and is a realistic opener to widen the discussion into more sensitive areas.
PART V - in Chapter 15: "Your Will"

If you and your intended spouse each come to the marriage with accumulated assets or have previously experienced divorce, emphasize how agreeing to a prenuptial could benefit each of you. Stress that protecting the assets you have worked hard to accumulate is a practical matter, and you want to be free of the fear of ever again having to experience the financial uncertainty divorce can create. If your future spouse comes to the marriage with few assets, propose favorable terms to address the issue and alleviate his or her financial fears while protecting what is most dear to you. If any approach you try meets with resistance, working with a neutral party like a marriage counselor, therapist, mediator, or other respected person might break the impasse.

SOME PROTECTION WITHOUT A PRENUPTIAL AGREEMENT

If you are unable to get your future spouse to agree to a prenuptial or are unwilling to insist upon it, there are some ways you can protect the assets you bring to the marriage and the separate property you accumulate. About two-thirds of the states legally define separate property as assets brought to the marriage, as well as gifts, inheritances, and monetary awards from lawsuits and settlements received during the marriage. These states recognize with the dissolution of a marriage that the separate property goes with the spouse who owns it. Examples of states adhering to this interpretation are New York, Pennsylvania, and New Jersey. In the other one-third of the states, all property, including separate property, can be divided with the dissolution of a marriage. Examples of these states are Connecticut, New Hampshire, and Massachusetts. Become informed about your state's laws and application of judicial discretion regarding the distribution of property at the end of a marriage. What you find out may inspire you to try again to negotiate a premarital agreement.

To protect yourself financially, do not comingle your separate property with any marital property accumulated during the marriage. For example, do not deposit your paycheck or add savings acquired during the marriage into an account in which you have separate assets. Comingling this money with separate savings or investments may cause the Court to interpret that all the funds in these accounts are marital. Start new bank accounts for any income earned during the marriage. Keep your name alone on the assets; do not add your spouse's name.

In states recognizing separate property as solely belonging to the owner, you can protect your separate assets without a prenuptial agreement by keeping them truly separate and not comingling. Residents of other states might benefit by not comingling their separate property, because it might help to support claims to their separate property if the marriage were to end. Keep in mind laws and judicial interpretation change, so be prepared for the possibility. The issues of appreciation of separate property during marriage and spousal inheritance rights, however, cannot be addressed without a prenuptial agreement.

The best thing about the future is that it comes only one day at a time.
Abraham Lincoln

...and then the day came when the risk to remain tight in
a bud was more painful than the risk it took to blossom.
Anais Nin

32

GROWING INTO YOUR TOMORROW

There comes a time to celebrate you are not the same person you were before the dissolution of your marriage and never again will be. There is no need to rush into new relationships, but prepare to become the best "new you" possible.

KNOW YOURSELF

Divorce can leave you stripped bare of self-delusion.

LOVING YOURSELF

Divorce can leave you stripped bare of self-delusion. You can learn much about yourself when illusions no longer cover up the truth. Opening up to this opportunity takes resolve, but the reward can be life-expanding. Take time to experience single life and realize you can live alone. Your sense of independence can influence how you view yourself and relationships, as well as what you expect from each. Better understanding your personal needs and strengths can change your perceptions and enhance your ability to make choices – healthy ones.

You are likely to become more sure of what you have to contribute and less willing to settle for less than you deserve. Your relationships with others reflect back to you the strengths and weaknesses of your relationship with yourself. By loving yourself you are able to feel love for others and are open to their love. When you feel successful and valuable, you draw like-feeling people into your life who reflect back your worthiness.

UNRESOLVED NEEDS

Be careful you do not create illusions, instead of nurturing relationships. Instinctively, you may be drawn to others you feel will take care of you and fulfill your unresolved needs. This attraction may be stimulated by people who have characteristics similar to those of your parents or early caregivers. People having positive and negative traits with which you are familiar may, unconsciously, trigger within you a conditioned pattern of behavior. If you are not alert to changing your proactive and reactive behavior, you may re-create the type of personal interactions similar to those you have previously had. Examine the dynamics of past relationships, as far back as your early years. Become aware of the characteristics of the players, your expectations and longings, and the limitations of those involved.

Possibly, you are attracted to companions who have qualities you admire but are not well developed in yourself. For example, if you are a shy woman, you might find an outgoing man a comforting partner. If you are an unorganized man, you might find great comfort in matching up with a woman who is highly organized. If a partner's qualities complement yours, you have a good chance of developing a relationship rich in respect and appreciation for individual strengths. A relationship, however, in which you need, or allow, your perceived deficits to be compensated for by your partner's strengths is delicate and hard to keep in balance. Growth of either of you or a shift in awareness can upset the fragile balance and unhinge the relationship. It is not too difficult to recognize the trouble when it begins. The most obvious warning sign is those characteristics about your partner that once comforted you begin to irritate, embarrass, scare, or offend you.

Clarify what has influenced your past choices. Doing so can help to alter your perspective and refine your ability to make nurturing selections. Face whatever your personal issues are. You may feel unlovable, fearful, or shy. You may be uneducated or unorganized or lack direction, social skills, or confidence. Consider working with a professional to recognize and integrate desired qualities into your personality. You want to connect through your strengths, not through unresolved issues. Having needs is part of life and you want to be adept at getting your needs met and at selecting a healthy partner with whom to work.

COMMUNICATION IS KEY

Use connecting words such as "we, our, us."

Please note: Information in *Communication Is Key* applies to relationships where abuse, addiction, and violence are absent and partners demonstrate mutual respect.

GENDER DIFFERENCES

IN REALITY

Attentive communication can empower you to avoid needless misunderstanding and emotional distress. A stereotyped model about male-female communication is being presented for the purpose of highlighting gender-generated patterns in dialogue that you can encounter. In reality, vast individual differences exist among women and among men in how they participate in dialogue. There are many degrees along the continuum from being "very male" to "very female" in processing and responding.

STEREOTYPED MODEL

Women are often viewed as wanting to talk things out, to release their emotions by talking and having their feelings validated by "being heard." Men appear to resolve issues with less verbal expression. They are often viewed as unfeeling and "listen" by offering solutions to problems. A woman may interpret a man's communication style as emotionally repressed. She may further characterize him as an insensitive listener who just wants to end the communication with a quick solution, without any real understanding or support. A man may interpret a woman's communication style as excessively deliberating on issues, instead of resolving them and moving on. When he listens and tries to help solve the problem, he may feel his efforts are not appreciated.

A general stereotype might be that women tend to have an emotional orientation and are internally focused with a personal "house-cleaning-put-things-in-their-place" posture, feeling their way to resolution. Men seem more goal and action oriented, externally focused with a "fix-the-problem" attitude, thinking their way to resolution.

TO ENHANCE DIALOGUE

If you are the male half of a dialogue, try to remember your female partner may not be struggling to solve a problem; she may want to talk about how she feels regarding an issue. Practice listening without attempting to fix anything. Being heard may be what she is seeking. Attention focused on her emotional confusion, pain, or anger may be what she wants. See yourself not as a contractor trying to construct a solution, but maybe as a ski instructor, helping her navigate a tough trail. Select language that will help you reach your goal.

➥ *This sounds very painful for you. What do you feel is the best thing for you to do?*
➥ *This is a confusing situation. With time, it might become clearer. Is there anything else you want to share now?*
➥ *I can understand why you would be angry. Try to make that anger work for you in a positive way. Can you think of anything you could do or say now to help resolve this?*

Your intent is to communicate with her in a way that makes her feel you understand and care about her.

If you are the female half of a dialogue, try to remember some men do not dwell on their feelings when resolving issues. They often set their goals and decide upon a solution without much, or any, verbalization. Sharing some of their feelings might be of value and leaving other emotions unexplored or unexposed might be routine. Focusing on the process your partner goes through to arrive at a solution might be a useful approach in dialogue.

➥ *With which part of your decision are you most comfortable?*
➥ *What was the hardest aspect to resolve? How did you arrive at that decision? What factors did you have to consider?*
➥ *That was not one of the easiest choices to make. You must be stressed. What did you do to get through the confusion?*

Earnestly compliment his decisions where possible. Your intent is to communicate with him in a manner to create more openness for sharing.

Have appropriate expectations; consider communication as "work in progress." Being able to recognize signs of gender-style differences may help you to see beyond them and identify areas of true conflict needing attention.

COMMUNICATE TO HEAL AND TO STAY HEALTHY

To be fully prepared to do your part in keeping a loving partnership alive and healthy, learn communication skills that enable you to share and uncover what you and your partner need. As you evolve, more of your essential self is surfacing. You are becoming better equipped to recognize your needs and communicate them, ultimately helping a partner do the same. That which you have not yet resolved with earlier relationships is likely to be projected back onto the stage with new relationships. As you and a partner begin to recognize and work with each other's defenses and uncover needs and wounds, you can begin to help each other heal and build a nurturing union. Focus on developing the trust necessary to accept, respect, and benefit from sharing your pain with each other.

Both you and a new partner come to the relationship with pain that was created long before you met. Be compassionate, but remain vigilant, and know that you neither created each other's past heartache nor are responsible for it. You are each responsible for your own wounds and healing and, in doing so, can help each other. When one or both partners blame the other for pain left over from the past, there can be a terrible breakdown in the ability to communicate and support each other. If you are thinking about remarriage, keep in mind that you do not marry a cure; you marry a helpmate. Prepare yourself for the role and develop the awareness and self-worth needed to choose a functional helpmate.

One of the greatest challenges to staying open in a relationship is the management of your defenses; they are well-developed tools you have used for a lifetime. At one time, they served to protect you, but these defenses have probably outlived their initial usefulness. You may have one defensive trait that is dominant and, coincidentally, it may be just that mannerism that is most apt to upset your partner and trigger a negative response. Become increasingly conscious of your defensive behavior and learn to replace it with productive behavior. For example, if you tend to shut down when there is conflict or you feel unappreciated, try to verbalize some of what you are feeling, instead of going away in silence to be alone. Your major defense could be the behavior that will hurt your relationship most; learn to monitor it. Your goal, even when you are feeling vulnerable, is to stay connected with your partner, instead of being alienated and separate. This takes forethought, vigilance, courage, practice, and possibly, professional assistance.

What you are trying to accomplish with healthy communication is to let the other person know you have heard the message and care about what he or she is thinking and feeling. You do not necessarily have to be in agreement. When there is a serious issue to resolve, you need to work together toward creating a solution with which each of you can live. Most communication, however, requires no agreement in position or follow-up action. When speaking, use connecting words such as *we, our, us*. They will help keep you and your partner united as a team. Connecting words seem to circumvent the brain's defenses and go to the emotional core with positive effect.

Wholesome communication is enhanced by intentional listening and techniques, such as paraphrasing what was said to let the speaker know you:

- ♥ Heard the message and you understand his or her position. *I see what you mean.*
- ♥ Care about what he or she is thinking and feeling. *I can see why you would be upset.*

At this stage of your life, you know yourself better than you did in previous relationships. You know better what it is you are longing for and what is reasonable to expect. You know your pain is your responsibility, and you are learning how to be open to receiving help with your healing. You know more about your defenses and how to remain open. You are aware you need to practice patience and communication techniques, daily, to help keep yourself and relationships healthy and loving.

LISTENING IS LOVING

Positive communication benefits both parties and is like a dance where each knows when to enhance the steps of the other with his or her own movements. With communication, however, those steps and movements are being made up spontaneously. Intentionally trying to connect with each other reduces resistance and allows creativity to flow forth. You are transformed from dance partners into the dance.

INTENTIONAL LISTENING

Listening with respect, compassion, and the courage to respond in a productive manner is vital to meaningful communication. Attentive listening links the messenger and receiver in a joint journey of sharing, clarifying, and creating solutions. It requires that you have enough discipline to put aside your own agenda, receive your partner's message, and attend to his or her needs or confusion. Intentional listening has tremendous transformative power; both speaker and listener are changed and stay heart-connected.

Listening is key to loving; it makes others feel cared about. Listening gives birth to ideas, self-knowledge, trust, and the courage to share and love. It may be the most valuable tool in creating and maintaining a successful, loving relationship.

CONFLICT

Employ your listening skills to the fullest if you are in disagreement with the speaker. When you are in conflict with your partner, you may have a compelling urge to convince him or her of your reasoning or perspective. Remember, you and your partner have the same goal: a loving relationship. There is little chance for a quality future together if one partner has a driving need to be recognized as right, implying the other is wrong. This does not make for an enriching relationship; it stimulates competition and word-based power struggles. There are some issues about which you can quietly disagree and respect your partner's position. It can be an act of love to feel you are right and keep it to yourself.

When a serious issue needs a creative resolution, listening and courage are crucial. As you listen, you allow your partner to release frustration and emotion, freeing him or her to work toward a solution. It sets the stage for change, without forcing a specific direction. It defuses defensiveness, opening the way for a shift to creativity. You do not have to find an ideal solution; you just have to work together toward one. If you are lost as to how to positively resolve the matter, validate that you have heard and understand the message, and then let it be known that you need some time to think about an appropriate solution.

TO BE AN EFFECTIVE LISTENER

♥ Be attentive. Devote yourself fully to the task without distraction, judgment, or resistance. Attentive listening enables you and your partner to dissolve some of the emotional resistance built around an issue, so you can effectively work toward a resolution from your different perspectives.

♥ Show compassion. You do not have to agree with your partner's position but convey empathy for how strongly he or she may feel.

♥ Remember to validate. Regardless of your opinion or position on the issue, repeat what you have heard your partner say. Accurately reporting back what has been said conveys you have heard the message.

♥ Maintain positive intent. Receive the message with sensitivity and respect, thereby giving value to the speaker.

♥ Exercise discipline. Put your own agenda and expectations aside and calm your emotions and internal chatter.

♥ Remain flexible. Having rigid expectations can sabotage productive listening.

♥ Practice patience. It may take your partner time to find comfortable words to verbalize his or her position or feelings.

LIFE DEMANDS CHANGE

Disaster often gives birth to opportunity.

Life has cycles and is about change. Your marriage has, probably, been a significant part of your life's journey. It may have been a time to grow or a time to rest for a while or a time of turmoil that taught tough life lessons. The end of your marriage means losing part of your identity and moving into an unknown future on your own. You are, forever, changed and changing.

Adversity can be a powerful motivation in helping you find your strengths. You have already demonstrated you have the courage and tenacity it takes to redesign your life to better suit your needs and desires. With time, what seems like a disaster may be recognized as an opportunity. Remember, the Chinese character for "crisis" is a combination of two symbols; one for "challenge" and the other for "opportunity."

CELEBRATE YOURSELF AND YOUR SUCCESS

And one day you will hear a laugh you have never heard before.

You are walking into your future with greater wisdom than you have ever had and with the strength and determination it took to get this far. Stay connected with healing energy in a way that works for you. Stay connected to your goals, values, and strengths; to your support systems and spiritual beliefs; and to your future, happening with each step you take. Carry with you the internalized lessons learned from this crisis, leaving the emotional debris of the experience in the past. Use your newly acquired self-knowledge to guide you on your continuing journey of self-discovery and evolution.

As you design a life full of choices suited to your new identity, your sense of well-being will be reflected back to you, generating continued, positive growth. In becoming yourself, you are becoming vital to others who are also finding their way along this path worn by raw emotion and courage. Celebrate your uniqueness. Recognize and cherish your achievements. "Speak them"; speak of your accomplishments aloud, so you will remember and share them with others who need to hear of your successes. Use your pain to keep focused on learning about yourself. Think of it as gift-wrapping. Peeling it away revels the gift of a new you with the vital life force to be who you are meant to be.

As you work through and release the pain, you will shed the part of the old you that is no longer needed. And one day you will hear a laugh you have never heard before. It will surprise, and then, delight you. It came from you, from deep within where there was once only room for heartache. And your laughter will, forever, be an ongoing celebration of your health, joy, and love.

Life can only be understood backwards, but it must be lived forward.
Soren Kierkegaard

What a lovely surprise to finally discover how unlonely being alone can be.
Ellen Burstyn

APPENDIX

A CUSTOMIZING GUIDE
  How To Use
  Specifics To Customize

B GLOSSARY – TERMS OF DIVORCE

C ORGANIZERS
  Action Matters
    How To Start And Proceed
  Money Matters
    Monthly Budget
    Financial Puzzle Pieces
    Wrap It Up Right
  Mind Matters
    Deposition Primer
    Statement Of Client's Rights And Responsibilities
  Agreement Matters
    Pathfinder

D EXHIBITS
  Examples Of Legal Documents
    Summons With Notice
    Verified Complaint
    Order To Show Cause (for pendente lite relief)
    Qualified Domestic Relations Order
    Statement Of Net Worth

The Exhibits are intended to familiarize you with some common legal documents and forms. They are not meant to be working copies. Use the *Money Matters* Organizers to sort out financial data and when you are ready to fill in your Statement of Net Worth, either obtain a working copy from a lawyer or download one from *www.courts.state.ny.us/networth.htm*.

E HELPFUL RESOURCES
  Books
  Web Sites

F INDEX

G BOOST EMPOWERMENT! – TELL YOUR STORY

H EXPRESS ORDER FORM

I DIVORCE GUIDE VOUCHER for $30

An ounce of action is worth a ton of theory.
Ralph Waldo Emerson

Yard by yard, it's very hard. But inch by inch, it's a cinch.
Anonymous

CUSTOMIZING GUIDE

HOW TO USE

Most of the information in *Divorce Empowerment: What You Need To Know, Do, And Say* is applicable to all states. Matrimonial law, however, is state specific. This book presents precise legal information and creates an instructional legal model by using one state, New York, as an example. Cross-references cited in the general text alert you to any information that must be exact for your home state. Use this *Customizing Guide* to adapt specific points, terms, and names introduced in the detailed legal model.

In some states, the terms "divorce" and "dissolution" of the marriage have specific legal connotations. These two terms are used in *Divorce Empowerment* generally and interchangeably, without a specific legal significance intended.

RESOURCES

HELPFUL INTERNET SITES

- *www.divorcesource.com/info/divorcelaws/states.shtml* covers residency requirements, name of the court in which to file to dissolve a marriage, grounds, legal separation, some terminology, property distribution, spousal and child support, and premarital agreements.
- *www.supportguidelines.com* covers child support guidelines and other helpful information, such as state divorce statutes, divorce packets, names of courts and their functions, Child Support Enforcement offices, and State Bar Associations.
- *www.law.cornell.edu/topics/Table_Divorce.htm* is hosted by the Cornell Law School and provides basic data on grounds, residency requirements, child support guidelines, spousal support, and property distribution.

OTHER

- *Laws of the United States: Divorce* by Daniel Sitarz covers grounds, legal separation, residency requirements, name of the court in which to file to dissolve a marriage, property distribution, spousal and child support, and premarital agreements.
- Lawyers who will answer questions or offer an initial free or reasonably priced consultation can be an efficient source for clarifying your state's divorce laws and explaining accepted practices. To benefit most from the time you have with a legal professional, prepare and organize yourself by using this *Customizing Guide* and the general text of *Divorce Empowerment*.
- State Bar Associations may have printed material available upon request.
- Courts sometimes have basic divorce packets available upon request.

SPECIFICS TO CUSTOMIZE

Be aware of specific state requirements, procedures, practices, terminology, and the advantages and disadvantages of taking certain actions. Each item listed in this *Customizing Guide* is in response to a cross-reference cited in the book's general text. Only those chapters containing cross-references, directing readers to the *Customizing Guide*, are listed below. Since some readers may be using *Divorce Empowerment* as a reference tool, looking up select data, this *Guide* is designed to always respond to a cited cross-reference. As a result, some information is intentionally included a number of times.

3 FIRST THINGS FIRST

Be informed about:
- Legal repercussions for a spouse who voluntarily decides to move out of the marital residence.
- Use of "exclusive occupancy" orders, "no prejudice" letters, and pleas of "condonation."
- Emphasis placed on a written chronological marital history and how the data is used.

5 YOUR ROLE

Each state has some demarcation point beyond which the marriage is no longer considered to be legally intact. From that time forward, assets acquired and debts incurred by either spouse are usually viewed by the Court as separate. In New York State, that demarcation line is, almost always, established as of the date legal action is commenced. Know what legal or other action determines this demarcation line in your state, and whether it has an effect on assets and debts acquired, subsequently.

Be familiar with any state laws regarding taping phone communications for the sole purpose of having a record for personal use.

6 FINANCIAL AND PERSONAL DOCUMENTS

Be informed about:
- State regulations regarding joint financial accounts and the removal of items from jointly held safety deposit boxes.
- Under what circumstances restraining orders can be employed.
- What is defined as "separate property" in your state. See the information about the division of property presented in the *Customizing Guide* for *Chapter 13: Division Of Property*.
- Time period your phone company keeps telephone records in its computer and how to obtain records for past billing periods.
- Terminology used in your state to refer to the summary of your expenses, income, assets, and liabilities, sometimes referred to as a "Statement of Net Worth."

Be fully informed about state laws regarding audio- and videotaping of others without their knowledge. Disregarding your state statutes could result in a civil case brought by the injured party, as well as criminal prosecution. About three-quarters of the states allow conversations with others to be recorded without their permission, as long as you are a party in the exchange. Such is the case in New York. In the remaining states, the consent of all parties to a conversation is usually required. At present, some examples of these jurisdictions are Connecticut, Massachusetts, and New Hampshire. Be sure to obtain accurate, current information and advice from a legal professional in your state. It is illegal in all states to record a conversation to which you are not a party or do not have permission to tape.

You may desire to tape phone exchanges to which you are a party to give yourself feedback on how well you are handling divorce-related tasks. If your state prohibits the taping of others without their permission, you might want to set up a tape recorder, not directly connected to the phone, to capture just your part of the exchange.

7 FINDING AND USING INFORMATION

Become informed about:
- Point at which debts incurred by one spouse are no longer considered the responsibility of the other spouse.
- Terminology your state may use that means the equivalent to what has been described in the text for "legal discovery," "interrogatories," and "depositions."
- Time period your phone company keeps telephone records in its computer and how to obtain records for past billing periods.
- How to access public records filed at your County Clerk's Office.
- State regulation of professional private investigators, for example, training and licensing.
- Emphasis placed on a written chronological marital history and how the data is used.

8 SOME LEGAL BASICS

- You must fulfill residency requirements; know what they are.
- Detailed coverage of "grounds" is in *Chapter 10*. Some states have "no fault" criteria upon which to dissolve a marriage.
- Child custody, support, and visitation are covered in greater detail in *Chapter 16*.
- More on what constitutes "separate property" is in *Chapter 13*.

9 FAMILY COURT

This chapter provides a guide for how a court, equivalent to New York's Family Court, might address family-related issues in your state, such as custody, support, and protection. Some courts designed to resolve family-related issues are more consumer friendly than others. A court's atmosphere can influence how available it will be in responding to your needs.

Clarify what you need. Learn which court in your state can address those needs and how you are to proceed, including:

📖 Documentation to provide.

📖 Forms to fill out and file.

📖 Advisability or necessity of having a lawyer.

📖 Steps to take to follow through with your initial action.

10 LEGAL GROUNDS

Often states are referred to as "fault" states or "no-fault" states. Theoretically, fault states require that to legally end a marriage one spouse must prove justified grounds exist. In no-fault states, a marital breakdown of some sort, such as incompatibility, is reason to dissolve the marriage. Examples of those states that use "irreconcilable differences," where neither spouse is considered to be at fault, are California, Illinois, Mississippi, New Hampshire, and Oregon. Other states refer to the no-fault grounds as "irretrievable breakdown of the marriage." Some examples are Connecticut, Florida, Minnesota, Pennsylvania, and Washington.

In reality, all states have some option to allow for the dissolution of a marriage without having to prove fault, such as living apart while complying with the terms of a Separation Agreement for a specific amount of time. Knowing your state's grounds enables you to select the legal option best suited for your situation.

Legal annulments are rare and complicated. To learn what you need to know, a few questions over the phone to a lawyer may give you the necessary state-specific facts.

11 STEPS IN THE DIVORCE PROCESS

To efficiently work with your lawyer, it is important to know state-specific legal facts. Know at what point your state legally recognizes that, henceforth, assets acquired and debts incurred by either spouse are usually viewed as separate. In New York State, this demarcation line is almost always established with the commencement of legal action. In other states, the legal dividing line may be defined as the day a spouse moves out of the residence with no intention of returning or declares the marriage has ended. Knowing your state's law is important, because it may influence you to take certain actions that favorably impact property division and other legal aspects of your case.

Clarify:

📖 Terms used for documents equivalent to New York's Separation Agreement, Settlement Agreement, Stipulation of Settlement, Judgment of Divorce, and Judgment of Separation.

📖 Requirements for each of the above, such as waiting periods and the declaration of "grounds."

Listed below are the terms and names used in the text of *Divorce Empowerment*. Knowing what each refers to will enable you to substitute the appropriate terminology for you state. For example, "petitioner" and "respondent" might be used instead of "plaintiff" and "defendant."

- Pleadings, pleading stage.
- Summons and Complaint (Summons with Notice ,Verified Complaint).
- Answer.
- Name of Court where action is filed (Supreme Court, Superior Court, Family Court, other).
- Pendente lite motions.
- Names of conferences scheduled (Examples: Preliminary Conference, Pretrial Conference).
- Know your rights and role at each conference. For example: Can you be present? What documents must you bring?
- Law guardian. (Note: In many states the terms "law guardian" and "guardian ad litem" are used interchangeably.)
- Discovery, interrogatories, depositions or EBTs (Examination Before Trial), notice of deposition, subpoena power.

Find out state-specific data for the following:
- Are oral stipulations allowed in your area? They are not permitted in some districts and states.
- What are the rules and general outcome about ordering the moneyed spouse to pay the legal fees for the nonmoneyed spouse?
- What is done to minimize "frivolous actions"?

12 PROBLEMS WITH THE LEGAL SYSTEM

Become informed about:
- Policy of awarding legal fees to the financially dependent spouse. In some states, the moneyed spouse can be ordered to pay an amount equal to his or her own legal fees.
- Existence of a "primary care standard," requiring the Court to award custody to the long-term caregiver, unless there is justified cause not to do so.
- Function of law guardians and the quality of their service. You want to be prepared to avoid potential problems.
- Time it takes to receive temporary relief, so you can prepare.
- Measures your state uses to enforce its orders, especially child support orders. (See *Chapter 30*.)
- Your state may use a different name for the equivalent of New York's Department of Social Services, such as Office of Family, Department of Health and Welfare, Department of Human Resources.
- Rights at conferences. It is to your benefit to be present.
- Practice of using oral stipulations. Some districts and states do not allow them.
- Pending reforms or efforts to reform that may influence your case.

13 DIVISION OF PROPERTY

States that are not "equitable distribution" states are "community" states, with the exception of Mississippi which is a "title" state, where each spouse retains the property to which he or she has title. Through its judicial decisions regarding property division, however, Mississippi has adopted a version of "equitable distribution." "Community property" means each spouse shares equally in the income earned and property acquired during the marriage, even when only one spouse supplied the income. Theoretically, property other than separate property is divided equally, but this can be altered by the Court in most community states if there are compelling reasons to make the division more equitable. Community states are Arizona, California, Idaho, Louisiana, Nevada, New Mexico, Texas, Washington, and Wisconsin.

Regardless of whether you live in an equitable distribution state or community state, become informed about what factors the Court considers when distributing property, and what impact fault may have on the Court's decision.

Know what constitutes "separate property" and what is meant by "marital" or "community property" in your state. There are a variety of interpretations. Examples:

📖 Some states consider professional licenses and degrees earned during marriage to be marital and divisible. Most states, however, are reluctant to legally consider licenses and degrees as "property," but do allow for some compensation to a spouse who helped in the acquisition of a license or degree. If a distributive award is not a possibility, the award might be a greater portion of the marital assets or "reimbursement alimony."

📖 Nearly all states consider pensions divisible even though the funds may not yet be available. This is an important issue; pensions are one of the biggest assets.

📖 It is generally accepted that a spouse can contribute to the acquisition and increased value of property without contributing income. A homemaker is seen as contributing to the economic value of the marriage.

Know how the laws of your state apply to valuing a business. For example, is the business considered to be marital or separate property according to your state laws? Know at what point your state legally recognizes a claim for separate property. This may be the date the action is commenced, the date of a particular valuation, or the date of the trial. In New York State, this demarcation line is usually established with the commencement of legal action, but Judges have discretion with regard to certain valuation dates. See the information in the *Customizing Guide* for *Chapter 11: Steps In The Divorce Process*.

14 LET'S LOOK AT THE TAX BITE

Take into account how your state treats capital gains. Federal tax rules are employed differently in the community property states. See the information in the *Customizing Guide* for *Chapter 17: Remember The IRS*.

15 WHO GETS WHAT?

You need to know whether your state legally views pensions and retirement accounts as marital property and divisible with the dissolution of the marriage.

Does your state recognize professional licenses and degrees earned during marriage as marital property and divisible? If not, does it allow for some compensation to the non-licensed spouse who helped in the acquisition of the license or degree? The award might be a greater portion of the marital assets or "reimbursement alimony" where there is too little property for a distributive award.

Know your state's legal interpretation regarding debt payment responsibility. For example, is your separate property protected from being taken by creditors as payment for your spouse's separate debt? Identify debts for which you may be held legally responsible. For example, how do your state courts interpret payment responsibility of medical debts incurred by one spouse?

Know the effect of bankruptcy on any distributive award.

Wills are governed by state law. Learn the specifics for your state.

16 CHILD CUSTODY / SUPPORT / VISITATION

If it applies to your circumstances, become informed about the appropriate procedure to follow to obtain a court order for temporary custody without first filing for divorce.

States award some form of sole or joint/shared custody based on the best interests of the child. Find out:

- What custody arrangements are prevalent in your state and under what conditions.
- Whether your state gives equal consideration to both parents.
- What constitutes the "best interests of the child."
- How parental conduct is viewed by the Court in evaluating parenting ability.
- How much weight is given to the wishes of the child.

Keep current with how your state is ruling on relocation disputes if this is an area that might concern you.

Child custody cases are complicated and Judges rely on others to make evaluations and submit forensic investigative reports. Learn who is involved, their titles (example: probation officer, law guardian, psychiatrist, forensic evaluator), their functions, and who pays the fees involved. Learn as much as you can about the role of the law guardian and forensic evaluator, so you know what to expect and how to prepare.

Learn which courts in your state handle custody and support issues and the appropriate procedure to follow. Carefully consider which court, if there is a choice, would be best for your circumstances.

Know the age at which court-ordered child support ends and under what circumstances. For example, some states require that payments continue to twenty-one, unless the child becomes self-supporting earlier. In other states payments continue only to a child's eighteenth birthday or until high school has been completed. Special rules may apply to disabled or special needs children.

According to federal law, each state is required to have standardized child support guidelines. Some state-mandated guidelines can appear to be a bit complicated. To be able to estimate your child support payments, contact your State Bar Association or State Department of Human Resources and request a copy of the Child Support Guidelines. Become informed about:

- Limit of combined income, if any.
- Method used to determine each parent's portion of the support.
- Amount (percentage or other measure) of income allocated for the number of children involved.
- Expenses included, such as child care, health insurance, and non-reimbursed health care.
- Other expenses approved by state law; for example: private school, special care for the disabled, and special needs of the gifted.

17 REMEMBER THE IRS

Generally, federal tax rules are employed differently in the community property states of Arizona, California, Idaho, Louisiana, Nevada, New Mexico, Texas, Washington, and Wisconsin than they are in equitable distribution states. If you decide to file a separate return while married, work closely with your tax advisor or order *Publication 555, Community Property* from the IRS.

18 ESSENTIAL PRACTICAL CONCERNS

If you anticipate spousal support will be an issue, become familiar with the factors that influence the Court's decision and the type of support generally awarded.

Both COBRA and QMCSO are mandated by federal law and are available in every state.

How are the legal fees of the financially dependent spouse to be paid? Does your Court use discretionary power to award these legal fees by requiring the moneyed spouse pay an amount equal to his or her own legal fees?

20 SELECTING A LAWYER

Know state-specific terminology used for:

- Summons and Complaint.
- Legal devices used in discovery, such as interrogatories, depositions or EBTs, notice of deposition, and subpoena power.

Is an attorney required to provide a written contract specifying what he or she is to do for the client, what is expected of the client in return, and the payment terms? If so, what is it called? Be prepared to negotiate changes and additions that better protect you. See the text of *Chapter 21: Legal Protection* for guidance and suggestions.

Can you request that the moneyed spouse be legally ordered to pay attorney fees for the nonmoneyed spouse? If so, ask your legal counsel what procedure is followed to attain the order. If not, ask what other options may be available regarding the payment of legal fees. For example, your attorney may be willing to wait until the end of the legal proceedings when the legal fees would be available from the property settlement.

21 LEGAL PROTECTION

Does your state have some form of a standardized statement similar to New York's *Statement Of Client's Rights And Responsibilities*, setting forth what you have a right to when retaining legal counsel? You want to know what you and your lawyer are required to do, and what your lawyer is forbidden from doing. If a form stating your rights exists, what is it called? Is your attorney required by law to give you a copy?

If your state requires client-attorney contracts specifying what an attorney is to do and what is expected from the client in return, use the information in *Chapter 21* covering Retainer Agreements in New York to:

- Familiarize yourself with the possible format and content of a client-attorney contract.
- Organize your ideas for changes and additions that help protect you.

If your state does not regulate the legal agreements between matrimonial lawyers and their clients, find out what type of written agreements lawyers in your area offer. The information in *Chapter 21*, covering Retainer Agreements in New York, can be used as a guide for what you might incorporate into such a fee agreement or contract.

If you agree to work with an attorney on a flat fee basis, be sure your agreement spells out what the fee covers and does not cover. You want to know how to proceed if the action were to go beyond what the fee specifically is stated to cover. For example, an uncontested lawsuit may become contested if the parties are unable to agree on an issue.

22 WORKING WITH YOUR LAWYER

If you are unable to pay your lawyer and your business relationship terminates, is the lawyer permitted to hold your file until legal fees owed are paid? If so, you want to protect yourself by maintaining a complete file of your own. It is wise to maintain your own file under any circumstances.

Are attorneys required to itemize their bills? If not, you might want to request your attorney do so; it will help you monitor the legal fees.

If litigation has started and your attorney has indicated to the Court that he or she represents you, are you required to obtain the Court's approval to discharge the lawyer? If so, be informed regarding the procedure to follow.

23 DIVORCE MEDIATION

Be aware of any state laws governing divorce mediation and mediators.

If your state has court-ordered Mandatory Mediation, become well-informed about its purpose and procedures involved, so you will know what to expect and how to benefit.

24 PREPARE FOR SUCCESS

Clarify:
- Terms used for documents equivalent to New York's Separation Agreement, Settlement Agreement, and Stipulation of Settlement.
- Benefits of each type of agreement for your situation.
- Requirements for each, such as waiting periods and the declaration of "grounds."

See information previously presented in the *Customizing Guide*:
- Property division (*Chapter 13*).
- Standardized child support guidelines, "add-ons," and special needs (*Chapter 16*).
- Health insurance and new wills (*Chapters 15, 16* and *18*).
- Spousal support (*Chapter 18*).
- Child custody (*Chapter 16*).

Is there the option of entering into an agreement that legally determines custody, support, and the division of property and past debt, but allows you and your spouse to remain married while living apart?

25 GENERAL FORMAT

Use the information in *Chapter 25* to familiarize yourself with what an agreement can cover even though the accepted format in your state may differ.

26 DESIGN AN AGREEMENT THAT PROTECTS YOU

Use the information in *Chapter 26* for inspiration in structuring an agreement that will better protect you. Some specifics may vary from state to state. Become informed so you can work effectively with your attorney.

Your state may have different terminology to refer to an "Indemnification and Hold Harmless Clause."

Be informed about your state's legal specifics regarding wage withholding of child support payments. It may be a secure method to assure timely payments.

If you are the recipient of maintenance, know whether your state legally interprets cohabitation with a new partner as cause to reduce or eliminate the support.

To best protect yourself, know your state's legal interpretation regarding payment responsibility for your spouse's separate debt. For an example, see the information presented in *Chapter 15* of the *Customizing Guide*.

30 FOLLOWING MARITAL BREAKUP

Know the appropriate court in which to petition for unpaid child support.

Become familiar with the procedures to follow to initiate wage withholding or garnishment and other actions. Wage garnishment is allowed in nearly every state.

What actions (imprisonment, loss of licenses, other) are taken against those found in contempt of court for nonpayment of court-ordered child support?

Does your state allow or encourage some specific practices to help secure delinquent support? Some states allow for the names of parents who have defaulted on child support payments to be publicly known and printed in newspapers. Delaware, Florida, Virginia, Maryland, and Pennsylvania have done so. Alabama's State Department of Human Resources has had a feature on its Web site showing the photographs and names of the state's most wanted child support offenders and how much each owes.

31 LOOKING FORWARD

Find out the specific state laws that pertain to prenuptial agreements.

TERMS OF DIVORCE – GLOSSARY

Names of state-specific legal documents, such as Affidavit of Service, Bill of Particulars, Verified Complaint may differ.

Names of courts in which divorce papers are filed vary among states. For example, the court equivalent to New York's Supreme Court could be named Superior, District, Circuit, Family, Chancery, or something similar. Obtain information on your state court system showing each court and its function.

Names of state agencies and positions will vary, such as the District Attorney in one state may be referred to as the County Attorney in another.

When all is said and done, a lot more is said than done.

Anonymous

GLOSSARY – TERMS OF DIVORCE

Meanings presented in *Terms Of Divorce* focus on how the terms are used relating to marital breakup. New York specific names and terms are indicated as such with "(NYS)." Age and time requirements differ among the states as do names for agencies, officials, and documents. Contact a local Bar Association for state-specific names and requirements to connect with the information presented.

abandonment (NYS) --- legal grounds for divorce when a spouse has left the marital residence without justification or consent, does not intend to return, and has been gone continuously for more than one year.

ACES (Association For Children For Enforcement Of Support) --- largest nonprofit child support group in the nation with chapters in forty-eight states.

action --- a proceeding in Court to demand or protect a party's rights. See: *cause of action, lawsuit.*

active appreciation --- increase in the value of assets as a result of a person's active participation, such as refurbishing rental property or managing investments. See: *passive appreciation.*

addendum --- attachment.

add-ons --- expenses going beyond basic child support, such as child care, education, and health costs that are divided proportionally between the parents and added to the child support amount.

adjournment --- postponement of the proceedings of a case until a specified future time.

adjudicate --- to hear and determine judicially.

adjusted basis --- investment in property, like commercial real estate, determined by adding the cost of improvements to the original cost and subtracting depreciation, usually calculated to determine the taxable gain at disposition. See: *basis, tax basis.*

adultery (NYS) --- grounds for divorce when a married person voluntarily has sex with someone other than his or her spouse.

adversary --- opponent or litigant in a lawsuit.

adversary system --- system of justice in which opposing parties have the opportunity to present their cases before the Court. The assumption is opponents entering this justice system will be represented equally.

AFDC --- See: *Aid to Families with Dependent Children*.

affidavit --- written statement of facts sworn under oath.

Affidavit of Service (NYS) --- certifies the service of any litigation document, such as a Summons with Notice, Summons and Complaint.

after-tax value --- value of an asset after taxes have been paid; real value.

Aid to Families with Dependent Children (AFDC) --- program sponsored by the federal and state governments to provide transitional financial assistance to families with children who are deprived of support because of a parent's death, prolonged absence, incapacity, or unemployment.

alimony --- See: *maintenance*.

allegation --- statement of a party to an action setting forth in a pleading or affidavit what the party intends to prove.

allege --- to assert before proving.

annulment --- legal determination that a marriage is void; it does not and never did exist.

Answer (NYS) --- formal response the defendant makes to the Summons for divorce, separation, or annulment in which he or she admits or denies and/or denies sufficient knowledge or information with regard to the allegations made and may also make counterclaims and affirmative defenses. Same as *Verified Answer*.

antenuptial agreement --- See: *prenuptial agreement*.

appeal --- process in which a higher court, upon request, reviews the decision and order of a lower court to determine whether a reversible error has been made.

appearance --- submission of a party to the jurisdiction of the Court; the required presence at a court hearing either in person or through a lawyer.

appraisal --- procedure used to estimate the fair value of an asset.

appreciation --- increase in value. See: *active appreciation, passive appreciation*.

arbitration --- method of resolving conflicts by submitting them to an impartial person chosen by the parties involved. See: *binding arbitration*.

arrearage --- overdue payments such as child or spousal support; unpaid debt.

assets --- anything owned that has value (property, license, degree, business).

automatic wage deduction --- See: *wage withholding*.

bankruptcy --- a legal proceeding by which an insolvent person or business can obtain relief from having to pay debts. Depending on the type of bankruptcy, the debts are wiped out completely (Chapter 7), partially, or temporarily (Chapter 13 or 11). Court-ordered child and spousal support obligations cannot be discharged by bankruptcy.

basis --- acquisition cost minus depreciation. See: *adjusted basis, tax basis*.

best interests of the child --- foremost consideration of the Court in making decisions about the care of children. This measure is used in custody, abuse, and neglect cases.

bifurcation --- deciding a divorce case in two parts: first, granting the divorce for acceptable legal reasons and then resolving its property, custody, and support issues.

bill of particulars (NYS) --- discovery document used to obtain information about a pleading.

binding arbitration --- conflict resolution method in which parties agree beforehand to comply with the decision of the arbitrator. See: *arbitration*.

brief --- document used to present a party's legal argument to Court, including points of law and legal precedents.

capital gains --- profit from the sale of an investment such as mutual funds, which when held for long-term, may be eligible for preferable capital gain tax treatment. Under certain circumstances, when selling a primary residence an exclusion of $250,000 of the gain is allowed for a person filing alone and an exclusion of $500,000 is allowed if filing jointly. Under certain circumstances, ex-spouses also qualify for this exclusion.

case file --- court file containing papers submitted in a case.

cause of action --- reasons for which a legal action is commenced. See: *action*.

CCCS --- See: *Consumer Credit Counseling Service*.

CDP --- See: *certified divorce planner*.

certified copy --- copy of a document signed and affirmed to be a valid copy of an original by the Clerk of the Court or other authorized individual.

certified divorce planner (CDP) --- specializes in the financial aspects of divorce.

certified financial planner (CFP) --- provides guidance about how to meet life goals through proper financial management.

certified fraud examiner (CFE) --- trained to unravel complicated financial scenarios looking for fraudulent manipulation of assets and liabilities.

CFE --- See: *certified fraud examiner*.

CFP --- See: *certified financial planner*.

change in circumstance (CIC) --- term commonly used for cause to modify an existing court order.

change of venue --- change in the jurisdiction of where the case was brought or is pending, which can be requested by a litigant or done by the Court on its own motion, often because of a bias atmosphere.

Chapter 7, 13, or 11 bankruptcy --- See: *bankruptcy*.

charging lien --- entitles a lawyer the right to be paid from the proceeds of the final divorce settlement.

child abuse --- situation in which a parent or legal caretaker of a child under the age of eighteen inflicts or allows physical or sexual abuse against the child or creates or allows a situation in which there is a risk of physical injury.

child custody --- legal responsibility to physically take care of and make decisions for a minor child.

child neglect --- where a child of less than eighteen years old lacks adequate care and is in danger of or does suffer physical or psychological harm.

Child Protective Services (NYS) --- provides services at the county level to identify cases of suspected child abuse and neglect and intervenes.

Child Protective Services Act of 1973 (NYS) --- a New York State law establishing Child Protective Services in each county to encourage a more thorough reporting of child abuse and neglect and to follow up with appropriate legal action.

child support --- court-ordered monetary support each parent is to pay for their children.

Child Support Enforcement (CSE) Program --- federal/state/local partnership of agencies helping custodial parents with child support issues, especially collecting payments. Individual states develop and operate their programs according to federal law, administered by the Office Of Child Support Enforcement.

child support guidelines --- state-mandated set of rules determining each parent's financial obligation to their children.

Child Support Standards Act (CSSA) (NYS) --- establishes guidelines for the minimum amount of court-ordered child support and other child-related expenses.

CIC --- See: *change in circumstance*.

civil case --- noncriminal lawsuit involving property rights, such as contracts, negligence, divorce.

claim --- demand for or right to something.

COBRA (Consolidated Omnibus Budget Reconciliation Act) --- federal law stipulating that individuals who have been covered by a company's group health plan have the right to remain on the policy for a certain amount of time following the end of their marriages or employment.

COLA --- See: *cost of living adjustment*.

comingled property --- mixing of separate property with marital property, most often causing it to no longer be legally viewed as separate.

community states --- nine states (Arizona, California, Idaho, Louisiana, Nevada, New Mexico, Texas, Washington, Wisconsin) in which property, other than separate property, is theoretically divided equally upon the dissolution of a marriage. In practice, however, individual circumstances often affect a distribution that is equitable.

complainant --- party in an action who initiates the complaint. See: *petitioner, plaintiff*.

complaint (NYS) --- See: *Summons and Complaint, Verified Complaint*.

Compliance Conference (NYS) --- Same as *Pretrial Conference, Trial Readiness Conference (TRC).*

condonation --- act of forgiving a spouse's misconduct, thereby disqualifying the wrongdoing as grounds. For example, having sexual relations with a spouse after learning of adultery forgives the misconduct; as a result, adultery cannot be used as grounds unless both spouses agree to it.

confession of judgment --- an individual's voluntary admission to owing a debt and submission of the matter to the jurisdiction of the Court.

conflict of interest --- when a professional is compromised in impartially performing a service or maintaining confidentiality due to present or previous connections.

Consolidated Omnibus Budget Reconciliation Act --- See: *COBRA.*

constructive abandonment (NYS) --- commonly used legal grounds to dissolve a marriage, alleging a spouse has left the marriage in spirit by refusing without justification to have sexual relations for one or more years.

Consumer Credit Counseling Service (CCCS) --- nonprofit organization offering free or low-cost counseling services to help people analyze and manage their debts.

consumer price index (CPI) --- a measure of the average change in the cost of goods and services over time.

contempt of court --- a willful and deliberate violation of a court order, punishable by the Court. See: *petition of contempt, Order to Show Cause.*

contested divorce --- when parties to the lawsuit cannot agree on how to dissolve their marriage and must litigate some of the issues and rely on the Court to decide them.

contingency fee --- a payment based on a percentage of monetary award received in a case. (In New York, accepting a contingency fee involving the dissolution of a marriage is illegal.)

continuance --- postponement of an action pending in Court to a designated date.

cost of living adjustment --- formulated measure by which court-ordered support payments may be modified to keep up with some change such as inflation.

counsel --- attorney, lawyer.

counterclaim --- allegations filed by the defendant against the plaintiff wherein the defendant asserts his or her claims.

County Clerk's Office (NYS) --- where public records such as deeds, mortgages, judgments, liens, and civil and criminal actions are filed.

court calendar --- schedule of case matters to be heard in the Court.

court order --- Court's written ruling on a disputed issue clarifying the rights and responsibilities of the parties involved and action to be taken.

court reporter --- person who records the testimony during court proceedings and depositions.

CPI --- See: *consumer price index.*

CPS --- See: *Child Protective Services.*

cruel and inhuman treatment (NYS) --- legal grounds for divorce when there is either physical or mental abuse of the degree that makes it unsafe or improper for the parties to reside together as husband and wife.

CSE --- See: *Child Support Enforcement.*

CSS --- Commissioner of Social Services. See: *Department of Social Services.*

CSSA --- See: *Child Support Standards Act.*

custodial parent --- parent who has primary custody of the children and either sole or joint legal custody.

custody --- See: *joint legal custody, joint physical custody, primary custody, residential custody, sole (legal) custody.*

DA --- See: *District Attorney.*

DCIA --- See: *Debt Collection Improvement Act (1996).*

deadlock provision --- sets forth a mutually agreed upon method of dispute resolution regarding issues about which parties cannot agree.

death rights --- right of inheritance to a spouse's estate.

Debt Collection Improvement Act (1996) **(DCIA)** --- authorizes the Department of Treasury to withhold certain federal payments, including federal tax refunds, to cover delinquent child support obligations.

Debt Counselors of America --- nonprofit organization offering free or low-cost counseling services to help people analyze and manage their debts.

decree --- decision or order of the Court. See: *final decree, interlocutory order or decree, judgment, order.*

default judgment --- ruling against a litigant who fails to respond to the other party's action in the time allowed or fails to appear at the hearing.

defendant --- party pleading a defense against the plaintiff's charges. See: *respondent.*

defined benefit plan --- company retirement plan promising to pay a certain amount per month to an employee during retirement. The amount is generally determined by length of employment and a percentage of the salary.

defined contribution plans --- employer sponsored retirement plans such as 401(k), 403(b) and profit sharing plans to which either the employee or employer or both contribute. The investment earnings are not taxed until the money is withdrawn, usually during retirement.

Department of Social Services (DSS) (NYS) --- consists of agencies that focus on the financial, health, and safety needs of people with the purpose of intervening and providing assistance. Example: Child Protective Services.

deposition --- formal method of discovery in which opposing parties answer questions orally under oath in the presence of the lawyers and a court reporter. Same as *examination before trial (EBT).*

depreciation --- expense deduction allowed for tax purposes taken during the period of ownership of capital assets representing an amount for exhaustion.

disbursements --- legal expenses not covered by an attorney's hourly fee, for example, court fees and transcripts and, possibly, long distance phone calls and travel.

disclosure --- See: *discovery*.

discovery --- process of obtaining information concerning the financial value of the marriage and parental fitness when custody is an issue. In cases where there is little disagreement, discovery can be accomplished by personally sharing documents and information. See: *formal discovery*.

discovery stage --- period of time in which opposing parties use informal and formal discovery procedures to obtain necessary information.

discretion of the Court --- See: *judicial discretion*.

dismissal --- termination of a proceeding for specific reasons.

distributive award --- amount of money paid by one spouse to the other to compensate the other spouse for giving up some asset/right, paid either in lump sum or over time.

District Attorney (DA) --- a deputized attorney whose job is to conduct legal proceedings on behalf of the people against those accused of criminal offenses. In some states, the terms Prosecuting Attorney, State's Attorney, County Attorney, or something similar may be used.

divorce decree --- final document signed by the Judge in a divorce action.

docket number --- assigned by the Court to identify a case and all documents relating to it. See: *index number*.

DOD --- date of divorce.

DOM --- date of marriage.

Domestic Relations Law (DRL) (NYS) --- law governing matrimonial actions.

Domestic Relations Law #236 (DRL #236) (NYS) --- See: *Equitable Distribution Law*.

DOS --- date of separation.

DRL (NYS) --- See: *Domestic Relations Law*.

DRL #236 (NYS) --- See: *Equitable Distribution Law*.

DSS (NYS) --- See: *Department of Social Services*.

durable power of attorney --- document granting another individual (called a healthcare proxy, attorney-in-fact, or agent) the legal authority to manage financial affairs and/or make medical decisions for the principal who is unable to do so. A *durable power of attorney* differs from a *power of attorney* in that the former remains in effect in the event the principal becomes incapacitated. See: *power of attorney*.

EBT --- See: *examination before trial, deposition*.

egregious fault --- extremely improper or fraudulent behavior of a party in a divorce action significant enough to have an impact on how the Court decides the ancillary financial and/or custody issues in a case.

emancipation --- point at which a minor is legally considered to be an adult, either by reaching a certain age such as eighteen or twenty-one or by taking a specific action like marrying, joining the armed services, becoming financially self-sufficient, or maintaining a permanent residence separate from parents.

equitable distribution --- power of the Court to use certain criteria in attempting to fairly divide marital assets and liabilities between divorcing spouses.

Equitable Distribution Law (NYS) --- sets forth the general principles for the distribution of property (assets, support, counselor fees) with the dissolution of a marriage; officially referred to as *Domestic Relations Law #236.*

equity --- money value of property in excess of any indebtedness.

estate --- assets and liabilities left by a person at death.

examination before trial (EBT) --- See: *deposition.*

ex parte --- by or for one party.

ex parte motion --- application for relief filed with the Court where no notice is given to the other side, usually when abuse exists or there is fear assets will be or are being hidden, sold, or wasted.

Family Court (NYS) --- authorized to decide custody, support, visitation, and other family-related issues; it does not have the authority to divide marital property or issue divorce decrees.

fault state --- requires a spouse suing to dissolve the marital contract prove the other spouse is legally at fault. New York is a fault state with several fault grounds, but if a married couple lives in substantial compliance with a written Separation Agreement for a year, the divorce can be granted without either spouse being accused of wrongdoing.

Federal Income Tax Offset Program --- administered through the Federal Office of Child Support Enforcement, it provides the state Child Support Enforcement units the means for securing tax refunds of parents who have been proven to owe substantial amounts of back child support.

final decree --- written judicial decision that fully and finally disposes of the litigation.

finding --- a legal determination by the Court.

forensics --- applying scientific knowledge such as financial, medical, or psychological evidence to help solve legal problems.

formal discovery --- process in which opposing parties use legal procedures, such as depositions and interrogatories, to obtain information from each other and third parties regarding the monetary value of the marriage and parental fitness when custody is in dispute. See: *discovery.*

forum shopping --- plaintiff's selection among available choices of the most favorable jurisdiction in which to commence a lawsuit and have the case decided.

401(k) Plan --- See: *defined contribution plans*.

frivolous actions --- legal actions having little or no substance, usually designed to stall the case and wear down the opposition.

garnishment --- a legal proceeding by which a portion of a person's wages or assets is withheld as payment of a debt. See: *wage garnishment*.

goodwill --- value a name, reputation, or celebrity status affords a business or professional position in elevated earning power. The true value of goodwill is difficult to measure and divide with the dissolution of a marriage.

grounds --- acceptable legal reasons to be granted a request to dissolve a marriage.

guardian ad litem (NYS) --- a person appointed to protect the interests of a child or of an adult in civil matters where injury or mental capacity are at issue or to represent the interests of a missing person. (Note: In many states the terms *guardian ad litem* and *law guardian* may be used interchangeably. In New York State the two terms officially differ. See: *law guardian*.)

guardianship --- legal responsibility for a minor or incapacitated adult. The rights and duties may involve making personal decisions, managing property, or both.

HE (NYS) --- See: *Hearing Examiner*.

Head-of-Household --- tax filing status usually allowing for a lower tax rate for an unmarried taxpayer or abandoned spouse who provides more than half the cost of maintaining a household that is the main home for a qualifying person.

healthcare directive --- document setting forth an individual's wishes about what extended medical care should be withheld or provided in the event the person becomes unable to communicate those wishes. Naming an individual, often called a *healthcare proxy*, to be sure those wishes are respected can be included. See: *durable power of attorney, living will*.

healthcare proxy --- person authorized by the principal of a durable power of attorney to make medical decisions for the principal or of a healthcare directive to make sure the principal's wishes are carried out. See: *durable power of attorney, healthcare directive*.

hearing --- court proceeding for the purpose of resolving an issue through testimony, legal arguments and the presentation of evidence.

Hearing Examiner (HE) (NYS) --- legal professional who conducts hearings in place of the Judge. Same as *Judicial Hearing Examiner (JHE)*. See: *Judicial Hearing Officer (JHO)*.

hold harmless --- See: *indemnification and hold harmless clause*.

IAS --- See: *individual assignment system*.

IDVC (NYS) --- See: *Integrated Domestic Violence Court*.

in camera --- in the Judge's chamber, not in public presence.

indemnification and hold harmless clause --- promise of one party to an agreement to assume responsibility for an obligation such as a payment of a debt and to protect the other party from any future loss or expense connected with that obligation.

indemnify --- to insure against loss. See: *indemnification and hold harmless clause*.

index number (NYS) --- assigned to each proceeding started in the Supreme Court to identify the case and all documents related to it. See: *docket number*.

individual assignment system (IAS) (NYS) --- all civil actions are assigned to an individual Judge who handles the case to its conclusion.

Individual Retirement Account (IRA) --- can be divided at divorce or with a legal separation agreement and transferred directly into the other spouse's IRA account without a penalty; penalty-free withdrawals can begin at 59.5 years of age.

injunction --- court order forbidding a party from committing a specific act that is likely to cause harm to another. See: *restraining order*.

Innocent Spouse Exception Law --- legislation designed to relieve one spouse of joint liability for tax, interest, and penalties for items on a joint tax return the other spouse incorrectly reported.

Integrated Domestic Violence Court (IDVC) (NYS) --- established in the Westchester County Supreme Court; one Judge hears all the criminal, family, and matrimonial issues of cases involving domestic violence.

intercept --- a process Child Support Enforcement agencies use to withdraw a portion of payments due to noncustodial parents who are delinquent with court-ordered support payments. Portions of unemployment and disability insurance payments, income tax returns, and lottery gains can be used to pay child support arrearages. See: *Child Support Enforcement (CSE) Program, offset*.

interlocutory order or decree --- provisional judgment directing legal proceedings preliminary to a final decision. See: *pendente lite relief, pretrial order, temporary order*.

interrogatory --- discovery device in which a series of written questions from the adversary must be answered in writing under oath.

intestate --- having died without a valid will.

IRA --- See: *Individual Retirement Accounts*.

irreconcilable differences --- legal grounds for divorce in which neither spouse is at fault, common in many no-fault states. Examples: California, Illinois, Mississippi, New Hampshire, Oregon.

irretrievable breakdown of the marriage --- legal grounds for divorce in which neither spouse is at fault, common in many no-fault states. Examples: Connecticut, Florida, Minnesota, Pennsylvania, Washington.

JHE (NYS) --- See: *Judicial Hearing Examiner*.

JHO (NYS) --- See: *Judicial Hearing Officer*.

joint legal custody --- both parents consult with the goal of making major decisions for minor children. See: *sole (legal) custody*.

joint or shared custody --- arrangement whereby estranged spouses or parents have the legal right to share physical care and decision-making power regarding their children; they may have joint physical custody or joint legal custody or both. See: *joint legal custody, joint physical custody*.

joint physical custody --- minor children reside equally with both parents, for example, alternating weeks. See: *primary custody, residential custody.*

judgment --- formal decision of the Court on a disputed issue determining the rights and responsibilities of the parties involved. See: *decree, final decree, interlocutory order or decree, order, temporary order.*

Judgment of Divorce --- document signed by the Judge granting a divorce.

Judgment of Separation (NYS) --- document signed by the Judge granting a legal separation and deciding custody and support issues but not necessarily the division of marital property.

judicial discretion --- judges' freedom to rule on issues as they think appropriate within the limits of their authority.

Judicial Hearing Examiner (JHE) (NYS) --- Same as *Hearing Examiner (HE)*. See: *Judicial Hearing Officer (JHO).*

Judicial Hearing Officer (JHO) (NYS) --- retired or former New York judge who is designated to perform all judicial tasks in place of a Judge but has no power to hold someone in contempt. See: *Hearing Examiner (HE).*

jurisdiction --- legal authority of the Court to make decisions about a case; geographical area within which the Court's authority is exercised.

juvenile delinquent (NYS) --- person between seven and sixteen who commits an act that would be legally viewed as a crime if committed by an adult.

laches --- undue delay in asserting a right, resulting in a refusal by the Court to allow the requested relief.

law guardian (NYS) --- attorney appointed to represent a child in a custody case.

lawsuit --- See: *action.* Same as *suit.*

legal age --- age at which custody orders no longer apply; for example, eighteen years in New York state, twenty-one in some states. Child support orders apply until the child is considered to be emancipated. See: *emancipation.*

legal custody --- right and obligation of one parent or both to make major decisions regarding minor children.

legalese --- language of the legal profession.

legally separated --- living separately by the terms of a legal agreement or a judgment. See: *Judgment of Separation, Separation Agreement.*

liabilities --- money owed; with divorce or legal separation, both parties will be liable for joint debts until they are paid.

lien --- claim on property by another as security for which a debt must be satisfied or paid.

litigants --- parties involved in a lawsuit: plaintiff and defendant, petitioner and respondent.

litigation --- legal action carried out in the courts to decide unresolved disputes.

living will --- document setting forth a principal's preferences and instructions regarding types of medical treatment and life support procedures. See: *healthcare directive, durable power of attorney*.

long arm statute --- a law that allows one state to claim jurisdiction over a person who lives in another state.

maintenance --- court-ordered monetary support for a spouse or former spouse. Same as *spousal support* or *alimony*.

marital history --- a summary highlighting a spouse's contributions to the economic value of the marriage and as the primary caregiver; it helps to determine equitable distribution of the assets and custody.

marital property --- assets acquired during marriage by either spouse, subject to division with the dissolution of the marriage.

market value --- price that property in its present condition is likely to bring in the open market.

married filing separately --- tax filing status providing the advantage of protecting a married taxpayer from being responsible for what is reported on a spouse's tax return, but having the disadvantage of usually resulting in significantly higher taxes.

mediation --- process in which a separating or divorcing couple works with an impartial third party to negotiate an agreement regarding child support, maintenance, and the division of assets and debts.

minor (NYS) --- person under eighteen years.

minute book --- official record of court proceedings prepared by the Court Clerk.

modification --- a court-ordered change regarding the terms of a previous order.

motion (NYS) --- application to the Supreme Court requesting an order for some particular relief.

motion churning --- tactic used in the judicial process to impose costs on the opposition by excessively litigating.

motion to dismiss or strike --- requests an order to reject or cancel a party's claims, usually due to lack of sufficient evidence.

motion to modify --- requests a change to a previous order, such as child custody or support.

Net Worth Statement (NYS) --- See: *Statement of Net Worth*.

no-fault divorce --- See: *no-fault states*.

no-fault states --- states having no-fault grounds whereby divorce can be granted without one spouse having to prove the other at fault. For examples, see: *irreconcilable differences, irretrievable breakdown of the marriage*.

noncustodial parent --- parent who does not have physical or primary custody of the children.

nonmarital property --- See: *separate property*.

no prejudice letter (NYS) --- legal device stating neither spouse will hold behavior against the other, for example, one will not claim abandonment as grounds for divorce if the other moves out.

notarize --- to verify documents as authentic with the authority and seal of a notary public.

notice of motion --- written notification by one litigant to the other that a hearing is to be held to determine relief requested, such as temporary support and custody.

notice of petition --- written notification by one litigant to the other that a hearing is to be held to determine relief requested, such as temporary support and custody.

OCSE --- See: *Office Of Child Support Enforcement.*

Office Of Child Support Enforcement (OCSE) --- assists state governments in administrating programs through the Child Support Enforcement (CSE) units at the local level. See: *Child Support Enforcement (CSE) Program.*

offset --- portion of a parent's state or federal income tax refund withheld to pay a child support debt.

oral stipulations (NYS) --- oral agreements made before the Judge or in Court that become part of the legal written settlement once dictated into the transcript; not allowed in some jurisdictions.

order --- Court's ruling on a request or disputed issue that either directs the contesting parties to take certain action or establishes their rights and responsibilities. See: *decree, final decree, interlocutory order or decree, judgment.*

Order of Exclusive Occupancy --- court document signed by a Judge giving one spouse the right to live in a residence by excluding the other spouse for a period of time for a valid reason such as abusive behavior.

Order of Protection --- order signed by a Judge intended to protect one party from harassment, assault, molestation, or stalking by the other.

Order to Show Cause --- written application to the Court that requires a party to explain why the requested relief should be allowed or not, often demanding an alleged violator either appear and provide a justified explanation for not obeying a court ruling or be held in contempt of court. See: *petition of contempt, contempt of court.*

party --- person having a direct interest in a legal action such as plaintiff, defendant, petitioner, and respondent.

passive appreciation --- increase in value without active participation, such as the increase in the value of stock due to favorable market conditions. See: *active appreciation.*

payroll deduction --- See: *wage withholding.*

PEBES --- See: *Personal Earnings Benefits Estimate Statement.*

pendente lite --- while the lawsuit is being decided.

pendente lite motion --- See: *temporary motion.*

pendente lite relief --- temporary relief while the lawsuit is being decided, such as support, custody, and restraining a spouse from disposing assets. See: *interlocutory order or decree, pretrial order, temporary order*.

perjury --- intentional falsification of the truth while under oath.

Personal Earnings Benefits Estimate Statement (PEBES) --- The name for this form has changed. See: *Request for Social Security Statement (Form SSA-7004)*.

Person In Need of Supervision (PINS) (NYS) --- a minor under the age of sixteen who is out of control in some way, such as acting dangerously, disobeying authorities, or not going to school.

petition (NYS) --- written application filed with the Family Court requesting particular relief.

petitioner --- party who files a petition with the Court. See: *complainant, plaintiff*.

petition of contempt --- requests an Order to Show Cause. See: *Order to Show Cause*.

physical custody --- right and obligation of one or both parents to provide the primary care and residence for minor children. See: *primary custody, residential custody*.

plaintiff --- party who initiates a lawsuit. See: *complainant, petitioner*.

pleadings --- documents of a lawsuit establishing a plaintiff's cause for the action and the defendant's response, such as Summons, Verified Complaint, Answer, petitions, motions.

pleading stage --- generally, the time period when the Summons and Complaint are served, the Answer is to be received, and temporary motions for interim relief are made.

Poor Person Application (NYS) --- filed with the Court by either the plaintiff or defendant in a divorce action requesting court fees be waived due to lack of sufficient funds.

power of attorney --- document whereby one individual, the principal, authorizes another, the attorney-in-fact or agent, to perform either general or specific legal acts on behalf of the principal. A *durable power of attorney* continues in effect even if the principal becomes incapacitated. See: *durable power of attorney*.

prayer --- plaintiff's request for relief contained in a complaint, petition, or motion.

precedent --- previous judicial decision that serves as a recognized authority in providing guidance for a present decision.

Preliminary Conference (NYS) --- to be held within a certain time of filing the Summons and Complaint for the purpose of resolving disputed issues or establishing a time schedule for the parties involved to do so.

premarital agreement --- See: *prenuptial agreement*.

prenuptial agreement --- legally binding written contract designed and signed by a couple before marrying that details how their assets and liabilities are to be divided in the event of the dissolution of the marriage or death. See: *antenuptial agreement*.

Pretrial Conference (NYS) --- held for the purpose of confirming that discovery has been completed and to schedule a trial date. Same as *Compliance Conference, Trial Readiness Conference (TRC)*.

pretrial order --- grants interim relief while the case is pending. See: *interlocutory order or decree, pendente lite relief, temporary order*.

primary custody --- a minor child primarily resides with one parent. Same as *residential custody*.

pro bono --- for the public good; when an attorney takes a case without compensation.

promissory note --- written agreement in which one party promises to pay another a specific sum of money at an agreed upon time.

pro se --- in one's own behalf; representing oneself in a legal action without an attorney.

QDRO (Qualified Domestic Relations Order) --- court order that directs the pension administrator on how to divide retirement funds between spouses upon the dissolution of their marriage. Under certain conditions a QDRO can be used to collect support.

QMCSO --- See: *Qualified Medical Child Support Order*.

Qualified Domestic Relations Order --- See: *QDRO*.

Qualified Medical Child Support Order (QMCSO) --- court order that grants the parent paying the child's medical expenses the right to deal directly with the child's health care provider and be directly reimbursed.

recusal --- disqualification of a Judge from a case for prejudice or conflict of interest.

referee (NYS) --- Court-appointed officer with the authority to hear testimony and report the findings to the Court.

relief --- legal remedy awarded by the Court to a complainant, petitioner, or plaintiff.

Request for Copy or Transcript of Tax Form (Form 4506) --- to obtain copies of past Income Tax Returns from the Internal Revenue Service.

Request for Social Security Statement (Form SSA-7004) --- to request a Social Security Statement showing earnings history, amount of money paid in, and an estimate of future benefits. See: *Personal Earnings Benefits Estimate Statement (PEBES)*.

residential custody --- See: *primary custody*.

respondent --- person responding to a petition's charges. See: *defendant*.

restraining order --- to prohibit specific actions by one party, such as the withdrawal of funds from marital accounts or the sale of marital property. Often granted pending a hearing and referred to as a *temporary restraining order* or *TRO* until or unless it is made permanent. See: *injunction*.

retainer --- lump sum payment made in advance for legal services to be performed. Usually, it is only a deposit, which will be used by the attorney for services performed and is often followed by periodic payments as services are rendered beyond those covered by the initial retainer.

retainer agreement --- legally binding written contract specifying the obligations of an attorney or law firm to a client, what is expected from the client in return, and the payment terms.

retaining lien --- claim a lawyer may have to a client's file if the working relationship has terminated and the legal fees have not yet been paid. (The file can be held until the fees owed have been paid.)

rules of evidence --- regulates the presentation and admissibility of testimony, documents, and material evidence at depositions and hearings.

satisfaction of mortgage --- document acknowledging the full payment of a mortgage debt, thereby discharging the lien against that person.

SCU --- See: *Support Collection Unit.*

separate property --- property legally recognized as belonging to one spouse alone, such as assets brought to the marriage, gifts from third parties, and inheritances. Most states permit separate property to remain with its owner at the end of a marriage, but some states allow it to be divided equitably along with the marital property.

Separation Agreement (NYS) --- written contract resolving property, custody, and support issues arising from the dissolution of a marriage, and whereby spouses live separately. After living apart for one year according to the terms of the Agreement, either spouse can file for an uncontested divorce.

service (of process) --- officially notifying the opposing party of the pendency of a lawsuit; delivering a pleading or other litigation document.

Settlement Agreement (NYS) --- written agreement resolving property, custody, and support issues arising from the dissolution of a marriage, accompanied by grounds so there is no waiting period required to be divorced.

show cause --- See: *petition of contempt, Order to Show Cause, contempt of court.*

Social Security --- commonly used to refer to programs designed to provide some monthly income to retired or disabled workers or to their dependents.

sole (legal) custody --- minor children reside primarily with one parent and that parent makes major decisions for them. See: *joint legal custody, joint physical custody.*

spousal support --- See: *maintenance.*

Statement Of Client's Rights And Responsibilities (NYS) --- standardized form a lawyer is required by law to give to prospective clients stating rights and responsibilities clients have and what lawyers are required to do and are forbidden from doing.

Statement of Net Worth (NYS) --- snapshot of an individual's or couple's current financial situation showing income, expenses, assets, and liabilities.

statute of limitations --- set time frame within which parties must take legal action to enforce their rights or, thereafter, be excluded from doing so, or within which a person can be held liable for an action or a debt. The statute of limitations for collecting delinquent child support varies among the states.

stay --- a court order suspending the proceedings in a case.

Stipulation of Settlement (NYS) --- a settlement orally agreed to before the Judge and dictated into the record (transcribed by a court reporter), which later becomes a written agreement and is incorporated into the Judgment of Divorce and enforceable as a court order.

subpoena power --- authority to compel a person or a representative of an institution who is not a party to the legal action to appear and give testimony at a deposition or hearing; authority to command a party to an action to produce designated records and documents.

suit --- See: *action*. Same as *lawsuit*.

Summons and Complaint (NYS) --- notifies the defendant of the commencement of the divorce action, states the grounds, details the defendant's wrongdoing, and lists the relief being requested. See: *Summons with Notice, Verified Complaint*.

Summons with Notice (NYS) --- notifies the defendant of the commencement of the divorce action and simply states the grounds and lists the relief being requested. This is a less inflammatory approach of initiating a divorce action than sending a Summons with Complaint, which also includes the details of the allegations. See: *Summons with Complaint, Verified Complaint*.

Support Collection Unit (SCU) (NYS) --- a unit of the Department of Social Services that collects and disburses court-ordered support payments.

Supreme Court (NYS) --- state court having the power to divide marital property and issue divorce decrees; it also has the power to decide custody, support, and visitation issues. See: *Family Court*.

Supreme Court Clerk's Office (NYS) --- provides the clerical services for the Supreme Court and is separate from the County Clerk's Office.

survivor's benefits --- monetary rights of the surviving Alternate Payee to a defined benefit pension plan in the event the Participant dies prior to retirement or before the Alternate Payee dies.

tax basis --- value of property, used to determine taxes owed. See: *adjusted basis, basis*.

temporary motion --- requests some particular interim relief like child support until there is a permanent order, legal separation, or divorce decree resolving the issue. Same as *pendente lite motion*.

temporary order --- results from a temporary motion and directs some specific interim relief, such as custody or support, until there is a permanent order, legal separation, or divorce decree resolving the issue. See: *interlocutory order or decree, pendente lite relief, pretrial order*.

temporary restraining order (TRO) --- issued to prohibit specific actions by one party that cause harm to another such as harassment, violence, or dissipation of marital assets. At a subsequent hearing with both parties present, it is decided whether to make the TRO permanent. See: *restraining order*.

transcript --- official record of proceedings in court or at a deposition.

TRC --- See: *Trial Readiness Conference.*

Trial Readiness Conference (TRC) (NYS) --- Same as *Compliance Conference, Pretrial Conference.*

TRO --- See: *temporary restraining order.*

uncontested divorce --- parties to the lawsuit agree on how to resolve the issues resulting from the dissolution of their marriage without having to litigate any of the issues.

vacate --- to set aside a previous action, to render it void.

venue --- See: *change of venue.*

Verified Answer --- See: *Answer.*

Verified Complaint (NYS) --- document served by the plaintiff on the defendant detailing the reasons for the divorce lawsuit and the relief being sought. See: *Summons and Complaint, Summons with Notice.*

visitation rights --- rights of the noncustodial parent to spend time with his or her children.

wage garnishment --- court-ordered deduction of money from an employee's wages to collect a debt owed either with a one-time lump sum payment or periodical payments over time until the debt is paid. See: *garnishment.*

wage withholding --- deductions from an employee's wages each pay period to cover a financial obligation such as taxes, retirement plan contributions, or health premiums; can be court ordered to collect unpaid child support. Same as *automatic wage deduction* or *payroll deduction.*

waiver --- intentional and voluntary surrender of a known right.

will --- written document that declares how a party wants his or her property disposed of after death and may name a guardian for young children.

without prejudice --- phrase often included in pretrial orders allowing them to be modified later without having to prove a change in circumstances.

writ --- order requiring the execution of a specific act or granting the authority to have it done.

ACTION MATTERS

HOW TO START AND PROCEED

Assess your situation.
Read the *Prelude* and *Chapters 1 – 4.*

- ❏ Discover how to benefit from *Divorce Empowerment*'s fast-find format and reader responsive features.
- ❏ Begin to digest the reality of divorce.
- ❏ Attend to immediate concerns.
- ❏ Start to develop a workable strategy.
- ❏ Move toward resolving marital discord or dissolving the marriage.

Gather information as soon as possible.
Read *Chapters 5 – 7.*

- ❏ Understand your role.
- ❏ Safeguard assets.
- ❏ Find out what financial and personal documents to locate.
- ❏ Design and maintain a filing system.
- ❏ Uncover hidden assets.
- ❏ Begin to organize your written marital history.

Learn legal basics.
Read *Chapters 8 – 10.*

- ❏ Approach the legal process realistically.
- ❏ Learn how to use the Family, Supreme, and Integrated Domestic Violence Courts.
- ❏ Become familiar with legal grounds.

Know the steps in the legal process.
Read *Chapters 11 – 12.*

- ❏ Foresee how the legal system is likely to view your case.
- ❏ Determine your approach and how and when to commence action.
- ❏ Prepare for the three phases of the process.
- ❏ Be aware of the limitations of the judicial system.

Understand property issues.
Read *Chapters 13 – 15.*

- ❏ Anticipate how Equitable Distribution is likely to be applied in your case.
- ❏ Recognize what the Court considers to be a divisible asset.
- ❏ Calculate the real value of the marital property.
- ❏ Devise a negotiating strategy to attain what you need and want.

Cooperate if possible on child, support, and health care issues.
Read *Chapters 16* and *18.*

- ❏ Clarify child support guidelines and extra expenses.
- ❏ Comprehend how custody disputes are handled.
- ❏ Be alert to the impact of bankruptcy on a settlement.

Evaluate tax advantages and disadvantages.
Read *Chapter 17*.

- ☐ Identify your options.
- ☐ Cooperate and share tax savings.

Prepare for your role in negotiations.
Read *Chapter 19*.

- ☐ Master the basics for success.
- ☐ Practice proven techniques.

Decide what type of legal representation you need.
Read *Chapters 20 – 23*.

- ☐ Prepare to interview and select legal counsel.
- ☐ Know your rights and what to include in a Retainer Agreement.
- ☐ Discover how to save time, confusion, and money.
- ☐ Is divorce mediation right for you?

Design an Agreement that protects you.
Read *Chapters 24 – 26*.

- ☐ Accept your role as a key player in designing a settlement.
- ☐ Be familiar with the general format of an Agreement.
- ☐ Include provisions that protect your well-being.

Focus on adjusting and healing.
Read *Chapters 27 – 29*.

- ☐ Heal your body, mind, and heart.
- ☐ Use a variety of methods to release negative energy and enhance healing.
- ☐ Develop a positive strategy for co-parenting.
- ☐ Help your children adjust to what is happening.

Move into your future.
Read *Chapters 30 – 32*.

- ☐ Wrap up the legal and financial aspects.
- ☐ Take action regarding delinquent support payments.
- ☐ Plan for a secure financial future.
- ☐ Enhance your communication style.
- ☐ Recognize your attributes and further refine who you want to be.

MONEY MATTERS

MONTHLY BUDGET

Income and expenses listed in a monthly budget for temporary support may not be the same as those listed to cover expenses following the dissolution of the marriage. Anticipate the decrease and increase in post-marriage income and expenses and factor them into a monthly budget designed to help you plan your future. For example, health insurance is a costly item for which you may be responsible after the marriage ends.

GROSS INCOME

SALARY / WAGES (Including bonuses/ commissions) _____

SELF-EMPLOYMENT _____

OTHER SOURCES

Interest/Dividends _____

Rental Income _____

Pension _____

Trust _____

Social Security _____

Child Support _____

Maintenance _____

Unemployment/Disability _____

Royalties _____

Other _____

TOTAL GROSS INCOME _____

MONTHLY EXPENSES

Divide the amount of any "non-regular expenditure," such as property taxes, and "unusual cost," such as unexpected repairs, by twelve months, so they can be worked into your monthly budget.
PART III - in Chapter 6: "Proposed Budget"

HOUSING (Principal residence/vacation home)

Mortgage/Rent _____

Property Taxes _____

Homeowners/ Renters Insurance _____

General Repairs/ Maintenance (Including service contracts) _____

Unexpected Repairs/ Appliances/Furnishings _____

TOTAL _____

UTILITIES

Oil/Gas/Electric   _____

Garbage Removal   _____

Water   _____

Phone (Home/cell/pager)   _____

TV (Cable/satellite dish)   _____

Internet Service   _____

Other   _____

TOTAL _____

INSURANCE
(Other than homeowners/renters)

Life   _____

Health   _____

Disability   _____

Personal Property   _____

Other   _____

TOTAL _____

AUTO EXPENSES / TRANSPORTATION

Car Payments (Loan/lease) _____

Insurance   _____

Registration/Fees   _____

Gas/Oil/Maintenance   _____

Repairs   _____

Motoring Plan   _____

Commuting   _____

TOTAL _____

PERIODIC PAYMENTS

Credit Card Interest   _____

Personal Loan   _____

Student Loan   _____

Estimated Income Taxes   _____

Prior Existing Maintenance   _____

Prior Existing Child Support   _____

Support of Adult Dependent   _____

TOTAL _____

CHILDREN'S EXPENSES

Day Care/Baby Sitter   _____

Pre-School   _____

Lessons/Tutoring/Equipment   _____

School Lunches   _____

Allowance/Special Events   _____

Summer Camp/Enrichment   _____

Private School/College

Tuition/Fees   _____

Books/Supplies   _____

Transportation   _____

Room/Board   _____

Special Needs (Specify)

_____

_____

_____

TOTAL _____

ADULT EDUCATION EXPENSES

Tuition _____

Books/Fees _____

Transportation/Food _____

TOTAL _____

MEDICAL / DENTAL *
(Expenses not covered by insurance, including deductible and co-payments)

Doctors _____

Dentist/Orthodontist _____

Eye Care _____

Counseling/Therapy _____

Pharmaceutical _____

Hospital _____

Home Care _____

TOTAL _____

* **Amount of total allocated for children**

_____

FOOD / CLOTHING *

Groceries _____

Household Supplies _____

Clothing

Parent _____

Children _____

TOTAL _____

* **Amount of total allocated for children**

_____

ENTERTAINMENT *

Movies/Videos/DVDs _____

CDs/Tapes _____

Live Performances
(Plays/music/dance/sports) _____

Membership Dues _____

Dining Out _____

Books/Magazines/Newspapers _____

Vacations/Family Trips _____

Sporting/Hobby Supplies _____

TOTAL _____

* **Amount of total allocated for children**

_____

MISCELLANEOUS *

Pet Care
(Vet/food/boarding) _____

Personal Health/Beauty Care _____

Professional Services
(Lawyer/accountant/broker/
financial planner) _____

Donations _____

Religious Contributions _____

Professional Dues/Fees _____

Gifts _____

Computer Equipment/Supplies _____

Other _____

TOTAL _____

* **Amount of total allocated for children**

_____

SUMMARY OF EXPENSES

Housing   _____

Utilities   _____

Insurance   _____

Auto Expenses / Transportation   _____

Periodic Payments   _____

Child Care Expenses   _____

Adult Education Expenses   _____

* Amount of total allocated for children

Medical / Dental   *   _____   _____

Food / Clothing   *   _____   _____

Entertainment   *   _____   _____

Miscellaneous   *   _____   _____

TOTAL MONTHLY EXPENSES _____

X 12 Months =

ESTIMATED ANNUAL EXPENSES _____

MONEY MATTERS

FINANCIAL PUZZLE PIECES

Putting the pieces of your financial puzzle together can give you a clear picture of your marriage's monetary value. You play a critical role in gathering the necessary documentation and information. You want to have access to as many, if not all, of the financial facts so you have a valid representation of the financial value of your marriage.
PART III – What Is There And Where Is It?
PART V – Areas Of Concern

Use *Financial Puzzle Pieces* to get organized and stay focused. Mark each item. A suggested code is offered as an example. For further clarification related to an entry, use **W** to designate wife and **H** for husband or **J** for joint.

S = Have in **S**afe place or
    personal file
K = **K**now where to obtain

L = Must **L**ocate;
    do not have.
X = Does not apply

INCOME TAX RETURNS
(Most recent three years)
_____ Federal
_____ State
_____ Local
Returns for earlier years or prior to your marriage may be helpful.
PART III - in Chapter 6: "Financial Records"

LIFE DOCUMENTS
_____ Prior Divorce Settlement
_____ Current Court Orders
_____ Prenuptial Agreement
_____ Trusts
_____ Will
_____ Power of Attorney
_____ Journals
_____ Daily Organizers
_____ Appointment Books

EMPLOYEE PAY AND BENEFITS
_____ Pay Statements (Current year)
_____
_____ Disability/Unemployment/Social
    Security Benefits (Current year)
_____ Auto/Travel Allowances
_____ Bonuses
_____ Deferred Pay
_____ Stock Options
_____ Accumulated Sick Pay
_____ Vacation Pay
_____ Insurance (Medical/disability/life)

BANK RECORDS
(Statements, deposit slips, canceled checks for current year, passbooks)
_____ Checking
_____ Savings
_____ Certificates of Deposit
_____ Credit Union
_____ Children's Custodial Accounts
_____ Children's Accounts

INVESTMENTS / DEBTS
(Statements for current year)
_____ Annuities
_____ Mutual Funds
_____ Stocks/Bonds
_____ Other Investments
_____
_____ Credit Cards/Charge Accounts
_____ Student Loans
_____ Vehicle Loans
_____ Bank Loans
_____ Personal Loans
    (Payable/receivable)

RETIREMENT
_____ Defined Benefit Plan
    (Latest Benefit Statement/copy of
    plan's provisions)
_____ Defined Contribution Plans
    (Latest Statements of Account)
_____
_____ IRA (Latest account statements)
_____

BUSINESS / PROFESSIONAL
_____ Filing Documents
(Proprietorship, LLC, partnership,
corporation)
_____ License
_____ Tax Returns (Last three years)
_____ Accounts Payable/Receivable
_____ Bank Statements (Current year)
_____ Credit Card Statements
(Current year)
_____ Loan Applications or Agreements

PROFESSIONAL PROPERTY
_____ Copyrights/Patents/Royalties
_____ Degrees
_____ Licenses
_____ Contracts
_____ Other

REAL ESTATE RECORDS
_____ Deeds
_____ Mortgages (Residence/other)
_____ Original documents
_____ Monthly statements
(Current year)
_____ Fair Market Values (Appraisals)
_____ Repairs/Improvements
_____ Closing Documents

INSURANCE POLICIES
_____ Health
_____ Life
_____ Disability
_____ Homeowners/Renters
_____ Umbrella/Liability
_____ Vehicles
_____ Personal Property
_____ Commercial

SAFETY DEPOSIT BOX
_____ Inventory of Contents
_____ Copies of Documents

PERSONAL PROPERTY
(Titles, receipts, appraisals, photographs)

MISCELLANEOUS
_____ Household Items
(Itemized list)
_____ Other

VEHICLES
_____ Automobiles

_____ Recreational

_____

COLLECTIONS
_____ Jewelry
_____ Musical instruments
_____ Tools and machines
_____ Art
_____ Other

_____

_____

SEPARATE PROPERTY
_____ Gifts

_____

_____ Inheritances

_____

_____ Personal injury awards
_____ Premarital property

_____

_____ Litigation claims
(Action pending)

STATEMENT OF NET WORTH
_____ Listing Assets/Liabilities
and Expenses/Income
(Lawyers often provide forms with
which they are most comfortable)

STATEMENT OF INCOME / EXPENSES
_____ Monthly Budget
APPENDIX – Money Matters: Monthly Budget
_____ Bills/Receipts

MONEY MATTERS

WRAP IT UP RIGHT

Follow through with legal and financial tasks to be certain the terms of your Agreement are put in place.
PART IX - in Chapter 30: "Wrap Up Documents"

RETIREMENT ASSETS

☐ Have assets been transferred according to the QDRO?

INVESTMENT FUNDS

☐ Are IRAs, bonds, and mutual funds transferred correctly in your name?

REAL ESTATE

Obtain evidence for each property.
☐ Deeds/leases in name of new owner/tenant.
☐ New deeds recorded with the County as public records.
☐ Title insurance and survey.
☐ Previous closing statements and appraisals.
☐ All keys.
☐ Warranties (Appliances, equipment, other).
☐ Contracts (Furnace, yard work, other).

SATISFACTION OF MORTGAGE

Have evidence for each property.
☐ Has your name been removed from any liens for which you are no longer responsible?
☐ Has a Satisfaction been recorded with the County as a public record?

DEPOSIT ACCOUNTS

(Checking, savings, CDs, credit union)
☐ Recorded correctly in your name?
☐ Joint accounts closed?

INCOME TAXES

☐ Clarify filing status.
☐ Know whether you are required to pay quarterly estimated income taxes.

VEHICLES

(Cars, recreational, other)
☐ Registration and keys.
☐ Title in correct name.
☐ Insurance cards in correct name.

DEBTS

☐ Be sure debts your ex-spouse agreed to pay are being paid in a timely fashion.
PART IX - in Chapter 30: "Ongoing Concerns"

ESTATE PLANNING DOCUMENTS

Write or rewrite.
☐ Will.
☐ Trusts.
☐ Durable Power of Attorney.
☐ Healthcare Directive.

INSURANCE POLICIES

Be sure to have adequate coverage.

HEALTH

☐ COBRA – required paperwork has been submitted.
☐ Own plan (If not under COBRA).
☐ Children's plan.
(Be sure it is in effect if your ex-spouse covers the children on his / her policy)

LIFE

Are the beneficiaries correct?
☐ Your policy.
☐ Ex-spouse's policy.
_____ Evidence of existence.
(To assure support payments)
_____ Payments up to date.

DISABILITY

☐ Your policy.
☐ Ex-spouse's policy.
_____ Evidence of existence.
(To assure support payments)
_____ Payments up to date.

OTHER

☐ Homeowners or Renters.
☐ Vehicles.
☐ Personal Property.

MISCELLANEOUS

☐ Frequent flyer miles.
☐ Season tickets and memberships.
☐ Other.

RECORD KEEPING SYSTEM

☐ If you do not already have one, design a system to organize the financial and other records and documents of your family's life.
PART IX - in Chapter 30: "Record Keeping / Filing System"

Fear is a fine spur.
Irish Proverb

It is a good answer that knows when to stop.
Italian Proverb

MIND MATTERS

DEPOSITION PRIMER

YOU HAVE THE RIGHT TO

→ Ask that questions be repeated and clarified.

→ Have an answer read back to you if needed.

→ Read documents about which you are being asked questions.

→ Consult privately with your attorney but try to do so between questions or at breaks.

→ Request a break when you need a few minutes to regain your strength or focus.

PREPARATION

Go over strategy with your attorney and be clear about your goals. Be aware that if during the deposition your lawyer instructs you not to answer a question, there is probably good reason, even if you feel your answer would help your case. Your legal counsel may see something in the question that you cannot.

Be candid with your lawyer. The truth is likely to surface in some form. Prepare how to handle aspects of the case or your prior behavior about which you are uncomfortable or embarrassed.

Practice answering the types of questions you expect to be asked. Some questions may be complicated or have parts.

Learn some simple breathing exercises or self-suggestion techniques to enable you to stay calm, alert, and focused. You want to perform at your best.

If you feel the need to have notes or a brief chronology with you at the deposition, have it reviewed and approved by your lawyer. Anything you consult during the questioning is to be made available to the opposing attorney upon request.

Anticipate that you are going to have to remain calm and respectful under stressful conditions. Be prepared for the possibility that the opposition may try to ruffle or even anger you. It works to your benefit to remain courteous and in control.

The opposing attorney is likely to suggest there are inconsistencies in your testimony with previous testimony or with the contents of documents. Discuss how to handle this eventuality with you lawyer and be prepared to state something to the effect that you are giving your best recollection.

DURING EXAMINATION

Listen carefully; be certain you understand each question; ask for clarification when needed.

Pause briefly before answering each question. It gives you time to think, and your attorney time to formulate an objection if necessary.

Speak clearly; your answers are being recorded by a court reporter.

Stop answering a question as soon as your lawyer starts to speak; he or she may have an objection.

Do not let yourself be rushed. Take time to formulate your answers, especially to complicated questions. The transcript does not reflect time or pauses.

Keep responses simple; answer only what is asked; do not offer additional information.

Yes and no are acceptable answers, but when this short answer works to your disadvantage, you have the right to add an explanation.

If you do not know an answer, say so. Do not guess. Do not express opinions.

Do not offer to look up or obtain data, unless it has been previously approved by your attorney.

Remain quiet but listen to exchanges between attorneys. What your lawyer is saying may heighten your awareness to the complexity of the question. It may be leading somewhere you had not initially anticipated. Request that the question be read again before restructuring your answer.

If interrupted by the opposing attorney while you are answering, remain respectful and when he or she finishes insist upon completing your answer before moving on to the next question.

Be alert to the words *Isn't it a fact...?* Be certain you completely agree before answering affirmatively.

Do not let yourself be manipulated by silence following a short answer. Do not say more because it appears to be expected. Be vigilant of any subtle techniques to get you to say more than is necessary to answer the question.

The opposing attorney may use a variety of manipulative techniques in questioning you. At times the approach may be pleasant and cordial while at other times, abrasive or provocative. Remain businesslike; your spouse's attorney is not your friend. He or she is trying to do the best for a client and you are not that client. Do not try to please or impress with your answers. Also stay calm and focused when you feel you are being provoked.

Keep in mind that the adversarial techniques used may sacrifice some accuracy in the drive to win. Do not assume the opposing lawyer's description of the contents of a document or of prior testimony is accurate. Before answering, give yourself time to think and your lawyer time to object. Ask to see the document. If you feel you need to read more than just the statement to which the attorney is referring, take the time to read as much of the document as necessary. If you do not remember the document or what someone else meant by it, say so. Do not guess or interpret.

STATEMENT OF CLIENT'S RIGHTS AND RESPONSIBILITIES

Your attorney is providing you with this document to inform you of what you, as a client, are entitled to by law or by custom. To help prevent any misunderstanding between you and your attorney please read this document carefully.

If you ever have any questions about these rights, or about the way your case is being handled, do not hesitate to ask your attorney. He or she should be readily available to represent your best interests and keep you informed about your case.

An attorney may not refuse to represent you on the basis of race, creed, color, sex, sexual orientation, age, national origin or disability.

You are entitled to an attorney who will be capable of handling your case; show you courtesy and consideration at all times; represent you zealously; and preserve your confidences and secrets that are revealed in the course of the relationship.

You are entitled to a written retainer agreement which must set forth, in plain language, the nature of the relationship and the details of the fee arrangement. At your request, and before you sign the agreement, you are entitled to have your attorney clarify in writing any of its terms, or include additional provisions.

You are entitled to fully understand the proposed rates and retainer fee before you sign a retainer agreement, as in any other contract.

You may refuse to enter into any fee arrangement that you find unsatisfactory.

Your attorney may not request a fee that is contingent on the securing of a divorce or on the amount of money or property that may be obtained.

Your attorney may not request a retainer fee that is nonrefundable. That is, should you discharge your attorney, or should your attorney withdraw from the case, before the retainer is used up, he or she is entitled to be paid commensurate with the work performed on your case and any expenses, but must return the balance of the retainer to you. However, your attorney may enter into a minimum fee arrangement with you that provides for the payment of a specific amount below which the fee will not fall based upon the handling of the case to its conclusion.

You are entitled to know the approximate number of attorneys and other legal staff members who will be working on your case at any given time and what you will be charged for the services of each.

You are entitled to know in advance how you will be asked to pay legal fees and expenses, and how the retainer, if any, will be spent.

At your request, and after your attorney has had a reasonable opportunity to investigate your case, you are entitled to be given an estimate of approximate future costs of your case, which estimate shall be made in good faith but may be subject to change due to facts and circumstances affecting the case.

You are entitled to receive a written, itemized bill on a regular basis, at least every 60 days.

You are expected to review the itemized bills sent by counsel, and to raise any objections or errors in a timely manner. Time spent in discussion or explanation of bills will not be charged to you.

You are expected to be truthful in all discussions with your attorney, and to provide all relevant information and documentation to enable him or her to competently prepare your case.

You are entitled to be kept informed of the status of your case, and to be provided with copies of correspondence and documents prepared on your behalf or received from the court or your adversary.

You have the right to be present in court at the time that conferences are held.

You are entitled to make the ultimate decision on the objectives to be pursued in your case, and to make the final decision regarding the settlement of your case.

Your attorney's written retainer agreement must specify under what circumstances he or she might seek to withdraw as your attorney for nonpayment of legal fees. If an action or proceeding is pending, the court may give your attorney a "charging lien," which entitles your attorney to payment for services already rendered at the end of the case out of the proceeds of the final order or judgment.

You are under no legal obligation to sign a confession of judgment or promissory note, or to agree to a lien or mortgage on your home to cover legal fees. Your attorney's written retainer agreement must specify whether, and under what circumstances, such security may be requested. In no event may such security interest be obtained by your attorney without prior court approval and notice to your adversary. An attorney's security interest in the marital residence cannot be foreclosed against you.

You are entitled to have your attorney's best efforts exerted on your behalf, but no particular results can be guaranteed.

If you entrust money with an attorney for an escrow deposit in your case, the attorney must safeguard the escrow in a special bank account. You are entitled to a written escrow agreement, a written receipt, and a complete record concerning the escrow. When the terms of the escrow agreement have been performed, the attorney must promptly make payment of the escrow to all persons who are entitled to it.

In the event of a fee dispute, you may have the right to seek arbitration. Your attorney will provide you with the necessary information regarding arbitration in the event of a fee dispute, or upon your request.

Receipt Acknowledged:

_____   _____   _____
Attorney's Signature   Client's Signature   Date

AGREEMENT MATTERS

PATHFINDER

Design an agreement that protects you. Detailed suggestions and guidelines are described in *PART VII – Legal Agreements*. Use this Organizer to stay focused.

PART VII - Chapter 24: Prepare For Success
Chapter 25: General Format
Chapter 26: Design An Agreement That Protects You

PROPERTY DIVISION

Determine ownership status, who is to be responsible for specific expenses or liens, and who is to be the recipient of any income.

MARITAL RESIDENCE

PART V - in Chapter 15: "Principal Residence"
PART VII - in Chapter 25: "Property Division"

☐ Address, tax map number, mortgage information.
☐ Ownership status: co-owned, sold, and transferred.

LEASES

☐ Remove name.
☐ Distribute security deposits.

OTHER REAL PROPERTY

PART V - Chapter 13: Division Of Property
Chapter 14: Let's Look At The Tax Bite
Chapter 15: Who Gets What?
PART VII - in Chapter 25: "Property Division"

☐ Ownership status.
☐ Responsibility for expenses.
☐ Recipient of income.

LIENS

PART VII - in Chapter 26: "Property"

☐ Remove your name from any liens on property transferred to the other party.

OTHER PROPERTY

PART V - Chapter 13: Division Of Property
Chapter 14: Let's Look At The Tax Bite
Chapter 15: Who Gets What?

☐ Bank accounts: savings, checking, CDs.
☐ Vehicles: cars, boats, other.
☐ Professional licenses, degrees, goodwill.
☐ Royalties, copyrights, patents.
☐ Defined benefit pension plans, IRA accounts, profit sharing, 401(k), other defined contribution plans, stocks, bonds.
☐ Personal property: furniture, tools, equipment, jewelry, club memberships, art collections, frequent flyer miles, other.
☐ Private businesses.
☐ Custodial accounts.
☐ Money awards.
☐ Other.

PENSION

Precisely detail the division of the pension; it is one of the most valuable assets. The Qualified Domestic Relations Order (QDRO) distributes the pension according to the written terms of your Agreement.

PART V - in Chapter 15: "Pension"
PART VII - in Chapter 26: "Property: Pension"
APPENDIX – Exhibits: Qualified Domestic Relations Order

❐ Amount or portion the Alternate Payee is to receive.

❐ Method of calculating payments.

❐ Time period of payments.

❐ Be sure the Alternate Payee is allowed to borrow from the plan if the Participant has the right to do so.

❐ Include wording so the Alternate Payee can share in any monetary incentive accompanying early retirement.

❐ State that the Alternate Payee is to be allowed to take money from the plan at the earliest retirement age, usually fifty-five years, even if the Participant does not retire at that age.

❐ Assure that the Alternate Payee is to receive "death benefits" in the event the Participant dies before the earliest retirement age:

  ↪ Specify the death benefit options the Participant is required to choose, or that

  ↪ Life insurance on the Participant is to guarantee the Alternate Payee's portion of the pension.

CUSTODY AND VISITATION / ACCESS RIGHTS

CUSTODY ARRANGEMENT

PART V - Chapter 16: Child Custody / Support / Visitation
PART VII - in Chapter 25: "Custody And Access Rights"

❐ Sole, joint or variation.

❐ Custody arrangement to be followed in the event of the death or incapacitation of one or both parents.

PARENTAL RESPONSIBILITIES

PART V - Chapter 16: Child Custody / Support / Visitation
PART VII - in Chapter 26: "Custody And Visitation / Access"

❐ Name the parent, if not both, with whom the children are to live.

❐ With joint decision making, list the major decisions:

  ↪ Choice of health care professionals.

  ↪ Type of health care.

  ↪ Religious training.

  ↪ Participation in enrichment programs.

  ↪ Schools attended.

  ↪ Summer camps.

  ↪ Vacation and school trips.

  ↪ Time limits for the completion of parentally financed education and/or training.

  ↪ Management of the children's careers, incomes, and investments.

  ↪ Other.

❐ Set forth your plan to keep each other informed regarding:

  ↪ Injury or serious illness.

  ↪ General health and well-being.

↪ Location of the children.
↪ Notices about child-related events and activities.
↪ Information, records, and reports from professionals.

OTHER

PART V - in Chapter 16: "Relocation Disputes"
PART VII - in Chapter 26: "Custody And Visitation / Access"

❏ Which parent, if not both, is to be kept informed and involved on a regular basis by professionals and others overseeing the children's activities:
   ↪ Medical treatments and reports.
   ↪ School conferences.
   ↪ Back-to-school activities.
   ↪ Interim reports, report cards.
   ↪ Recitals, sporting events.
❏ Establish the terms whereby a parent can permanently relocate.

VISITATION / ACCESS SCHEDULE

PART V - in Chapter 16: "Visitation"
PART VII - in Chapter 25: "Visitation / Access"
*   in Chapter 26: "Custody And Visitation / Access"*

A detailed schedule helps to establish a stable routine.

❏ Which weekends, including times of commencement and conclusion of visits.
❏ Special days, including with whom the days are to be spent and specific time of starting and ending the visits.
❏ Extended visitation during summer vacations.
❏ Visitation schedule for other people important in the children's lives.
❏ Reasonable, unobstructed mail, e-mail, and telephone contact.
❏ Access to a child during a period of serious illness.

Determine:

❏ Who is to provide the transportation for visits.
❏ How to arrange for temporary schedule changes and makeup visits.

DEADLOCK PROVISION

PART VII - in Chapter 26: "Deadlock Provision / Arbitration Clause"

❏ Anticipate the need to modify the Agreement in the future.

CHILD SUPPORT

BASIC CHILD SUPPORT

PART V - in Chapter 16: "Child Support"
PART VII - in Chapter 25: "Child Support"
*   in Chapter 26: "Child Support"*
APPENDIX – Customizing Guide

Payments of the noncustodial parent are described:

❏ How much.
❏ When.
❏ Where.

METHOD OF PAYMENT
PART VII - in Chapter 26: "Child Support"
- ☐ Personal check or money order.
- ☐ Voluntary account deduction.
- ☐ Wage deduction.

ANNUAL INCREASE
PART VII - in Chapter 26: "Child Support"
- ☐ Specific percentage.

HOW OTHER EXPENSES ARE TO BE COVERED
PART V - in Chapter 16: "Child Support"
PART VII - in Chapter 26: "Child Support"
- ☐ Children's extended visits.
- ☐ Telephone costs for child-parent communication.
- ☐ Long distance travel expenses for visitation.
- ☐ Increased costs when a child receives a driver's license.
- ☐ Higher education expenses.
- ☐ Extras during the younger years.
- ☐ Medical expenses not covered by insurance.
- ☐ Increasingly expensive needs as children grow older.

EMANCIPATION
PART V - in Chapter 16: "Child Support"
PART VII - in Chapter 26: "Child Support"
- ☐ What constitutes emancipation for each child.

HEALTH INSURANCE
PART V - in Chapter 18: "Health Care"
PART VII - in Chapter 25: "Child Support"
*   in Chapter 26: "Child Support"*
- ☐ Identify the parent responsible for health insurance coverage.
- ☐ Define under what circumstances coverage is to be terminated.
- ☐ Specify type of coverage.
- ☐ Medical plan documentation is to be shared.
- ☐ Parents are to cooperate in filling out forms and exchanging reimbursement information.
- ☐ Proof is to be made available that the agreed upon coverage is in effect.
- ☐ If insurance is not maintained in full force, the recipient parent may acquire a policy for the children and the cost is to be reimbursed by the payer.

DOCUMENT SPECIAL NEEDS
- ☐ Request necessary education, therapy, and medical attention.

PROVIDE FINANCIAL SECURITY
PART V - in Chapter 15: "Your Will"
PART VII - in Chapter 26: "Child Support"
APPENDIX – in Agreement Matters: Pathfinder – "Life And Disability Insurance"
- ☐ Write a new will.
- ☐ Life insurance.
- ☐ Disability insurance.

DEADLOCK PROVISION
PART VII - in Chapter 26: "Deadlock Provision / Arbitration Clause"
- ☐ Anticipate the need to modify the Agreement in the future.

SPOUSAL MAINTENANCE

BASICS ABOUT PAYMENTS
PART V - in Chapter 18: "Maintenance"
PART VII - in Chapter 25: "Spousal Maintenance"
- ☐ Lump sum or periodic.
- ☐ Payment intervals and amount.
- ☐ Duration of support.
- ☐ Penalties for late payments.
- ☐ Location where payments are to be sent.

METHOD OF PAYMENT
PART VII - in Chapter 26: "Spousal Maintenance"
- ☐ Personal check or money order.
- ☐ Voluntary account deduction.
- ☐ Wage deduction.

TAX CONSEQUENCES
PART V - in Chapter 17: "Support Payments" and "Options With Tax Consequences"
PART VII - in Chapter 26: "Options And Their Consequences"
- ☐ If it is decided that payments are to be taxable income to the recipient and tax deductible to the payer, determine how the tax savings are to be shared.

MODIFICATION AND TERMINATION
PART VII - in Chapter 25: "Spousal Maintenance"
in Chapter 26: "Spousal Maintenance"
- ☐ Agree on a schedule or index for automatic increases or decreases.
- ☐ Determine under what circumstances payments are to be modified or terminated.

MEDICAL COVERAGE
PART V - in Chapter 18: "Health Care"
PART VII - in Chapter 25: "Spousal Maintenance"
in Chapter 26: "Spousal Maintenance"
- ☐ Identification of insurance policy.
- ☐ Coverage and duration.
- ☐ Responsibility for the cost of the policy and deductible amounts.
- ☐ Parties are to cooperate regarding the application of forms and reimbursement information.
- ☐ Proof that the agreed upon coverage is in effect (to be made available upon request).
- ☐ If the party providing the health insurance were to change jobs, he or she is to make the benefits of any insurance plan offered by the new employer available to the ex-spouse or obtain substantially equivalent insurance through other sources.
- ☐ If insurance is not maintained in full force, the recipient may acquire a policy and the cost is to be reimbursed by the payer.

LIFE AND DISABILITY INSURANCE
APPENDIX - in Agreement Matters: Pathfinder – "Life And Disability Insurance"
- ☐ To be maintained on the payer with the recipient as beneficiary of the life insurance policy.

DEADLOCK PROVISION
PART VII - in Chapter 26: "Deadlock Provision / Arbitration Clause"
- ☐ Anticipate the need to modify the Agreement in the future.

RESPONSIBILITY FOR DEBTS

PART VII - in Chapter 25: "Responsibility For Debts"
in Chapter 26: "Debts And Liabilities"

☐ Identify creditors and specify balance due to each.

☐ Name party responsible for paying each debt and state commencement date.

☐ Have your name removed from any lien on property transferred to the other party.

☐ To be certain the debt is paid, you might want to assume the responsibility of doing so in exchange for a greater share of the marital property.

☐ Include an Indemnification and Hold Harmless Clause.

INCOME TAXES

FILING STATUS

PART V - in Chapter 17: "Advantages To Working Together"
PART VII - in Chapter 26: "Income Taxes"

☐ Specify filing status to be used until the legal Agreement is finalized and:

↪ How the tax deficiency is to be paid or the refund distributed for a joint return.

↪ Which parent is to claim the children as dependents and get credit for the mortgage interest, real estate taxes, and child care credit if filing separately.

☐ Specify past filing status and:

↪ Who is responsible for paying any deficiency, interest, or penalties that may arise.

↪ That each party is to provide necessary records and documents if there is an audit.

EXEMPTIONS AND CREDITS

PART VII - in Chapter 26: "Income Taxes"

☐ If you agree to give up an exemption to the other parent to generate a shared tax savings, do so for only one year at a time.

☐ Clearly state in your Agreement that the transfer of this exemption is to be reviewed annually and will be in effect for only one year in duration if not renewed.

☐ You may also want to include that your consent to waive the tax exemption is contingent on the payer being current with all support obligations.

DEADLOCK PROVISION

PART VII - in Chapter 26: "Deadlock Provision / Arbitration Clause"

An audit on your joint returns covering the previous three tax years or more may be conducted.

☐ Consider submitting disagreements about deficiencies, interest, penalties, or the distribution of refunds to arbitration.

HOLD HARMLESS CLAUSE

PART VII - in Chapter 26: "Income Taxes"

☐ Agree to abide by an Indemnification and Hold Harmless Clause in the event there is an audit revealing deficiencies.

LIFE AND DISABILITY INSURANCE

BASICS

PART VII - in Chapter 25: "Life And Disability Insurance"

Identify insurance policies of each party:

☐ Amount.

☐ Duration.

☐ Beneficiary.

☐ Person responsible for paying premium.

☐ Name of insurance company.

SUPPORT PAYMENT ASSURANCE

PART VII - in Chapter 25: "Life And Disability Insurance"
in Chapter 26: "Support Payment Assurance"

Spousal and child support payments end with the death of the payer.

☐ When securing child support, include:

↪ Beneficiary status is to terminate with the emancipation of the children.

↪ Amount of reduction in insurance payable to the recipient with the emancipation of each child.

☐ When securing spousal support, specify:

↪ Whose life is being insured.

↪ Who is responsible for paying the premiums.

↪ Under what circumstances maintaining the recipient as beneficiary is no longer an obligation (for example, remarriage).

↪ Whether the recipient of the support is to be the irrevocable beneficiary or owner of the policy.

↪ If your spouse will not agree to your being the owner of the policy or the irrevocable beneficiary, specify what evidence you need to receive periodically as proof the insurance is in effect.

↪ State that you have the right to pay the premiums yourself if there is a lapse in payment.

↪ Make lapsed premium payments "a charge and lien" against the other party's estate.

OPTIONS AND THEIR CONSEQUENCES

PART VII - in Chapter 26: "Options And Their Consequences"

Be prepared to make wise decisions about:

☐ Possibility of Bankruptcy.

☐ Accepting a Property Settlement as a Trade for Maintenance.

☐ Accepting Maintenance Payments as a Trade for Child Support.

I was married by a judge. I should have asked for a jury.

Groucho Marx

SUPREME COURT OF THE STATE OF NEW YORK
COUNTY OF _____

--X   Index No._____
                  Date Summons Filed: _____

                  Plaintiff designates _____
                  County as the place of trial.
                  The basis of venue is
                  Defendant's residence.

          Plaintiff,

    -against-   **SUMMONS WITH NOTICE**

                  Defendant resides at:

          Defendant.   _____
                  _____
                  _____

--X

ACTION FOR A DIVORCE

To the above named Defendant:

     YOU ARE HEREBY SUMMONED to answer the complaint in this action and to serve a copy of your answer on Plaintiff's Attorney within twenty (20) days after the service of this summons, exclusive of the day of service, where service is made by delivery upon you personally within the state of New York, or within thirty (30) days after completion of service where service is made in any other manner. In case of your failure to appear or answer, judgment will be taken against you by default for the relief demanded in the complaint.

Dated:

                  _____

NOTICE: The nature of this action is to dissolve the marriage between the parties on the grounds of the cruel and inhuman treatment, the abandonment and/or the constructive abandonment of the Plaintiff by the Defendant. The relief sought is:

A judgment of absolute divorce in favor of the Plaintiff dissolving the marriage between the parties in this action. The nature of the ancillary relief demanded is:

1) Granting Plaintiff custody of the infant issue;

2) Granting exclusive use and occupancy of the marital residence to Plaintiff;

3) Granting equitable distribution of the marital assets;

4) Granting Plaintiff title to separate property and any appreciation thereon;

5) Directing Defendant to pay child support and other child related expenses pursuant to the Domestic Relations Law Section 240 including but not limited to school tuition and expenses, unreimbursed health expenses;

6) Awarding Plaintiff a distributive award based upon the dissipation by Defendant of marital assets;

7) Directing Defendant to pay spousal maintenance to the Plaintiff;

8) Granting Plaintiff title and exclusive use of a vehicle;

9) Directing Defendant to maintain health, life, disability, automobile insurance for the benefit of the Plaintiff and the children and to pay all unreimbursed expenses;

10) Directing Defendant to pay Plaintiff's counsel fees, accountant fees, appraisal fees and any other necessary expert fees, costs, and disbursements;

11) Such other and further relief.

SUPREME COURT OF THE STATE OF NEW YORK
COUNTY OF _____

---X   Index No.

                    Plaintiff,

                                                              VERIFIED COMPLAINT

          -against-
                                                              ACTION FOR DIVORCE

                    Defendant.

---X

          The Plaintiff, by his/her attorneys, _____, complaining
of the Defendant, alleges the following:

          FIRST: The parties are over the age of 18 years.

          SECOND: The Plaintiff has resided in New York State for a continuous period
in excess of two years immediately preceding the commencement of this action.

          THIRD: The Plaintiff and Defendant were married on _____, in City
of _____, County of _____,
State of New York.

          The marriage was <u>not</u> performed by a clergyman, minister or leader of the
Society for Ethical Culture.

          FOURTH: There are two children of the marriage, namely:

                    <u>Name – Date of Birth – Address</u>

          There is no other child as a result of this marriage, and no other child is
expected.

          The Plaintiff resides at _____.
The Defendant resides at _____.

The parties are covered by the following group health plans:

Plaintiff

Group Health Plan: NONE

Defendant

Group Health Plan: _____
Address: _____
Identification Number: _____
Plan Administrator: _____
Type of Coverage: _____
The Defendant has no other group health plans.

FIFTH: The grounds for divorce are as follows: Commencing on or about _____, and continuing for a period of more than one (1) year immediately prior to the commencement of this action, the Defendant refused to have sexual relations with the Plaintiff despite the Plaintiff's repeated requests to resume such relations. The Defendant does not suffer from any disability which would prevent him from engaging in sexual relations with the Plaintiff. The refusal to engage in sexual relations was without cause or justification and occurred at the marital residence at _____.

SIXTH: There is no judgment in any court for a divorce and no other matrimonial action for divorce between the parties is pending in this Court or in any other court of competent jurisdiction.

WHEREFORE, the Plaintiff demands judgment against the Defendant, dissolving the marriage between the parties to this action, and granting the following relief:

That the Plaintiff and Defendant shall have joint custody of the children of the marriage, _____, born on _____, and _____, born on _____, however, the children shall reside with the Plaintiff.

That the Defendant shall have reasonable rights of visitation away from the custodial residence.

That the Family Court shall have concurrent jurisdiction with the Supreme Court with respect to any future issues of maintenance, child support, custody and visitation.

That the Defendant shall pay to the Plaintiff, through the Support Collection Unit for _____ County, _____ per week for child support.

That the Defendant shall provide health insurance benefits to the Plaintiff and the children.

That the Defendant shall pay all unreimbursed medical expenses of the Plaintiff and the children.

That the Plaintiff may resume use of her maiden name _____, or any former surname.

That the Court grant such other and further relief as the Court may deem just and proper.

The parties have divided up the marital property, and no claim will be made by either party under equitable distribution.

Dated: _____

_____
Attorney for Plaintiff

VERIFICATION

STATE OF NEW YORK, COUNTY OF _____, ss.

I, _____, am the Plaintiff in the action for a divorce. I have read the foregoing Complaint and know the contents thereof. The contents of the Complaint are true to my knowledge, except as to those matters therein stated to be alleged upon information and belief, and as to those matters, I believe them to be true.

_____
Plaintiff

Subscribed and sworn to before me on

_____, _____.

_____
Notary Public

My commission expires on _____.

At a Matrimonial Term of the Supreme Court held in and for the State of New York, County of _____ at

_____

_____ on the

_____ day of _____.

PRESENT: HON. _____
J.S.C.

---X

<table>
<tr><td></td><td>Index No. _____</td></tr>
<tr><td>Plaintiff,</td><td> **ORDER TO SHOW CAUSE** </td></tr>
<tr><td>-against-</td><td></td></tr>
<tr><td>Defendant.</td><td></td></tr>
</table>

---X

Upon the affidavit of _____ sworn to the _____ day of _____, the affirmation of _____, dated the day of _____, the Summons entitled "ACTION FOR A DIVORCE," and the exhibits annexed thereto, and upon all the pleadings and proceedings heretofore had herein,

LET the Defendant, _____, or his attorney, Show Cause at a matrimonial Term of this Court, located at _____ on the _____ day of _____, _____, at 9:30 o'clock in the forenoon of that day, or as soon thereafter as counsel can be heard why an Order should not be made and entered granting the following relief:

a)   An Order granting pendente lite custody of the infant issue of the marriage, to wit: _____ , born _____ and _____ born _____ , to Plaintiff pursuant to Domestic Relations Law Section 240 (1) (a);

b)   An Order, pursuant to Domestic Relations Law Section 240 (1) (b), granting temporary child support in the amount of Eight Hundred ($800.00) Dollars per week as and for the support of _____ and _____ ;

c)   An Order, pursuant to Domestic Relations Law Section 234, granting exclusive use and possession of the marital residence, located at _____ , to the Plaintiff pending the final determination of the above entitled action for divorce;

d)   An Order granting that Defendant pay directly the monthly payments on the marital residence, including but not limited to mortgage, real estate taxes, utilities, which include electric/gas and telephone, maintaining the homeowner's insurance, reasonable and necessary home repairs and cable television, as well as maintaining all automobile insurance;

e)   A Temporary Restraining Order, pursuant to Domestic Relations Law Section 234, prohibiting Defendant from removing property from the marital residence and from further removing any funds from joint and/or marital bank accounts, whether maintained in his name alone, or jointly with another, in any bank, wherever situated and restraining Defendant from encumbering, pledging, selling or otherwise transferring any and all assets, both marital and separate property, taken by the Defendant from the joint and/or marital bank accounts, and further if any such transfers have either taken place or are the subject to pending contract or legal action, that the proceeds received from such transfers be placed in an interest-bearing escrow account pending the outcome of this action for divorce;

f)   An Order, pursuant to Domestic Relations Law, prohibiting Defendant from removing any stocks, bonds or other assets, whether maintained in his name alone, or jointly with another, in any bank or financial institution, wherever situated and restraining Defendant from encumbering, pledging, selling or otherwise transferring any and all stocks, bonds and other assets, taken by the Defendant, and further if any such transfers have either taken place or are the subject to pending contract or legal action, that the proceeds received from such transfers be placed in an interest-bearing escrow account pending the outcome of this action for divorce;

g)   An Order, pursuant to Domestic Relations Law Section 236, Part B, directing Defendant to continue to provide policies of health and dental insurance providing benefits for health and hospital care, dental and related services for the Plaintiff and the infant issue of the marriage, pendente lite, and to further provide for all out-of-pocket and unreimbursed medical expenses;

h)   An Order, pursuant to Domestic Relations Law Section 236, Part B, directing Defendant to purchase, maintain or assign a policy of insurance on the life of Defendant in the sum of _____ Dollars and to designate Plaintiff as the beneficiary of said policy; and

i)   Pursuant to Domestic Relations Law Section 237, an award of favor of the attorneys for Plaintiff and directing Defendant to pay the sum of _____ Dollars as and for attorneys' fees, pendente lite, with leave to the firm to make application for a further award at the appropriate time;

j)   For such other and further relief as the court may seem just and proper;

LET service of a copy of this order and the papers upon which it is granted, together with the attached Summons with Notice in an Action for Divorce, by personal service, be made upon _____ , Defendant, on or before the _____ day of _____ , _____ , be deemed good and sufficient service.

HON. _____

J.S.C.

At the Matrimonial/IAS Part _____ of the New York
Supreme Court at the Courthouse, _____
County, on _____.

PRESENT: HON. _____
                            J.S.C.

---X   Index No. _____

              Plaintiff,

                                                         QUALIFIED DOMESTIC
                                                         RELATIONS ORDER

        -against-

        Defendant.

---X

        WHEREAS, ("Alternate Payee") and ("Participant") have separated
and their marriage has been dissolved; and

        WHEREAS, Participant is a participant in the following qualified
retirement plan (the "Plan"):

        Plan name:
        Company name:
        Trustee of the Plan:
        Administrator of the Plan:

        NOW, THEREFORE:
        1. This instrument is intended to qualify as a Qualified Domestic
Relations Order ("QDRO") as defined in Section 414(p) of the Internal Revenue Code
of 1986, as amended (the "Code") and Section 206(d)(3)(B) of the Employee
Retirement Income Security Act of 1974, as amended ("ERISA"), and shall be
administered and interpreted in conformity with the Code and ERISA.

        2. This Court shall retain jurisdiction to amend this Order for the
purpose of maintaining its qualification as a QDRO.

        3. As a division of property pursuant to this Order, the Plan shall cause
the amount set forth below to be assigned the Alternate Payee:

OPTION I: The sum of $ _____.

OPTION II: The sum of $ _____ plus any allocable earnings or losses on
said amount (based of the Participant's current investment elections) from
_____ to the date such sum is transferred to the Alternate
Payee's new account established under the Plan.

OPTION III: _____ percent of the Participant's "total account balance" under the Plan as of the close of business on _____ plus any allocable earnings or losses on said amount (based of the Participant's current investment elections) from _____ to the date such sum is transferred to the Alternate Payee's new account established under the Plan.

Said amount shall be transferred from the Participant's total account under the Plan to a new account under the Plan for the name of the Alternate Payee.

4. Said amount credited to the Alternate Payee's account under the Plan shall be paid to the Alternate Payee in the form of a single lump-sum payment as soon as reasonably possible after the Administrator of the Plan determines that this Order, or any modification of the Order, is a QDRO.

5. In the event of the death of the Alternate Payee prior to the distribution of all of the amount assigned the Alternate Payee by this Order, the Plan shall hold the balance of the account of the Alternate Payee pending further order of the Court. The Court reserves jurisdiction to make appropriate modifications to this Order in such event, with the goal of permitting the amount of the Alternate Payee's account to be distributed to the estate of the Alternate Payee, while protecting the Participant from any requirement to pay taxes on the amount distributed to the estate of the Alternate Payee.

6. The address of the Participant and Alternate Payee may be changed from time to time by written notice to the Administrator of the Plan and the other party. The following current information pertains to the Participant:

        Name:
        Address:
        Soc. Sec. No.:
        Date of Birth:

The following current information pertains to the Alternate Payee:

        Name:
        Address:
        Soc. Sec. No.:
        Date of Birth:

IT IS SO ORDERED.

Dated: ENTER:

                                            _____
                                              J.S.C.

IT IS SO STIPULATED AND APPROVED AS TO FORM AND CONSENT:

Dated: _____

Dated: _____

_____ COURT of the state of _____

COUNTY OF _____   Index No._____

---X

         Plaintiff,

    - against -

         Defendant.

---X

STATEMENT OF NET WORTH (DRL §236)

Date of commencement of action _____

STATE OF _____ COUNTY OF _____SS.:

_____, the (Petitioner) (Respondent) (Plaintiff) (Defendant) herein, being duly sworn, deposes and says that the following is an accurate statement as of _____, of my net worth (assets of whatsoever kind and nature and wherever situated minus liabilities), statement of income from all sources, and statement of assets transferred of whatsoever kind and nature and wherever situated:

I. FAMILY DATA

(a) Husband's Age _____ (b) Wife's Age _____
(c) Date Married _____ (d) Date of Separation _____
(e) Number of dependent children under 21 years _____
(f) Names and Ages of Children

    _____
    _____
    _____

(g) Custody of Children _____Husband _____Wife
(h) Minor Children of Prior Marriage: _____Husband _____Wife
(i) (Husband)(Wife) (paying)(receiving) $_____ as alimony (maintenance) and/or $_____ child support in connection with prior marriage
(j) Custody of Children of Prior Marriage:
    Name _____
    Address _____
(k) Is marital residence occupied by Husband_____ Wife_____ Both_____
(l) Husband's Present Address _____
    Wife's Present Address _____
(m) Occupation of Husband _____ Occupation of Wife _____
(n) Husband's Employer _____
(o) Wife's Employer _____
(p) Education, training and skills (Include dates of attainment of degrees, etc.)
    Husband _____
    Wife _____
(q) Husband's Health _____
(r) Wife's Health _____
(s) Children's Health _____

II. EXPENSES

II. **EXPENSES**: (You may elect to list all expenses on a weekly basis or all expenses on a monthly basis, however, you must be consistent. If any items are paid on a monthly basis, divide by 4.3 to obtain weekly payments; if any items are paid on a weekly basis, multiply by 4.3 to obtain monthly payment. Attach additional sheet, if needed. Items included under "Other" should be listed separately with separate dollar amounts.)

    Expenses listed [ ] weekly   [ ] monthly

(a) Housing

  1. Rent _____   4. Condominium charges _____
  2. Mortgage and amortization _____   5. Cooperative apartment maintenance _____
  3. Real estate taxes _____

                                 Total: Housing $_____

(b) Utilities
   1. Fuel oil _____ 2. Gas _____ 3. Electricity _____ 4. Telephone _____ 5. Water _____
                                                              Total: Utilities $_____

(c) Food
   1. Groceries _____ 2. School lunches _____ 3. Lunches at work _____
   4. Liquor/alcohol _____ 5. Home entertainment _____ 6. Other (_____) _____
                                                              Total: Food $_____

(d) Clothing
   1. Husband _____ 2. Wife _____ 3. Children _____ 4. Other (_____) _____
                                                              Total: Clothing $_____

(e) Laundry
   1. Laundry at home _____ 2. Dry cleaning _____ 3. Other (_____) _____
                                                              Total: Laundry $_____

(f) Insurance
   1. Life _____ 2. Homeowners/Tenants_____ 3. Fire, theft and liability _____
   4. Automotive _____ 5. Umbrella policy _____ 6. Medical plan _____
   7. Dental plan _____ 8. Optical plan _____ 9. Disability _____
   10. Worker's Compensation _____ 11. Other (_____) _____
                                                              Total: Insurance $_____

(g) Unreimbursed Medical
   1. Medical _____ 2. Dental _____ 3. Optical _____ 4. Pharmaceutical _____
   5. Surgical, nursing, hospital _____ 6. Other (_____) _____
                                                              Total: Unreimbursed Medical $_____

(h) Household Maintenance
   1. Repairs _____ 2. Furniture, furnishings, housewares _____ 3. Cleaning
   supplies _____ 4. Appliances, including maintenance _____ 5. Painting _____
   6. Sanitation/carting _____ 7. Gardening/landscaping _____ 8. Snow removal _____
   9. Extermination _____ 10. Other (_____) _____
                                                              Total: Household Maintenance $_____

(i) Household Help
   1. Babysitter _____ 2. Domestic (housekeeper, maid, etc.) _____ 3. Other (_____) ____
                                                              Total: Household Help $_____

(j) Automotive
   Year _____ Make _____ Personal _____ Business _____
   Year _____ Make _____ Personal _____ Business _____
   Year _____ Make _____ Personal _____ Business _____
   1. Payments _____ 2. Gas and oil _____ 3. Repairs _____ 4. Car wash _____
   5. Registration and license_____ 6. Parking and tolls _____ 7. Other _____
                                                              Total: Automotive $_____

(k) Educational
   1. Nursery and pre-school _____ 2. Primary and secondary _____ 3. College _____
   4. Post-graduate _____ 5. Religious instruction _____ 6. School transportation _____
   7. School supplies/books _____ 8. Tutoring _____ 9. School events _____
   10. Other (_____) _____
                                                              Total: Educational $_____

(l) Recreational
   1. Summer camp _____ 2. Vacations _____ 3. Movies _____ 4. Theatre, etc. _____
   5. Video rentals _____ 6. Tapes, CDs, etc. _____ 7. Cable television _____ 8. Team
   sports _____ 9. Country/pool club _____ 10. Health club _____ 11. Sporting
   goods _____ 12. Hobbies _____ 13. Music/dance lessons _____ 14. Sports
   lessons _____ 15. Birthday parties _____ 16. Other (_____) _____
                                                              Total: Recreational $_____

(m) Income Taxes
    1. Federal _____ 2. State _____ 3. City _____ 4. Social Security and Medicare _____
                                            Total: Income Taxes $_____

(n) Miscellaneous
    1. Beauty parlor/barber _____ 2. Beauty aids/cosmetics, drug items _____
    3. Cigarettes/tobacco _____ 4. Books, magazines, newspapers _____ 5. Children's
    allowances _____ 6. Gifts _____ 7. Charitable contributions_____ 8. Religious
    organization dues _____ 9. Union and organization dues _____ 10. Commutation
    and transportation _____ 11. Veterinarian/pet _____ 12. Child support payments (prior
    marriage) _____ 13. Alimony and maintenance payments (prior marriage) _____
    14. Loan payments _____ 15. Unreimbursed business expenses _____
                                       Total: Miscellaneous $_____

(o) Other: 1. (_____) _____ 2. (_____) _____
    3. (_____) _____ 4. (_____) _____   **Total: Other $_____**

                        TOTAL MONTHLY EXPENSES: $_____
                        TOTAL ANNUAL EXPENSES: $_____

III. GROSS INCOME: (State source of income and annual amount. Attach additional sheet, if needed).
    (a) Salary or wages: (State whether income has changed during the year preceding date of this affidavit _____. If so, set forth name and address of all employers during preceding year and average weekly wage paid by each. Indicate overtime earnings separately. Attach previous year's W-2 or income tax return.)

    _____   _____
    _____

    (b) Weekly deductions:
        1. Federal Tax   _____
        2. New York State Tax   _____
        3. Local Tax   _____
        4. Social Security   _____
        5. Medicare   _____
        6. Other Payroll Deductions (Specify)   _____
    (c) Social Security Number _____
    (d) Number and Names of Dependents claimed: _____
    (e) Bonus, Commissions, Fringe Benefits (use of auto, memberships, etc.)   _____
    (f) Partnership, Royalties, Sale of Assets (income and installment payments)   _____
    (g) Dividends and Interest (state whether taxable or not)   _____
    (h) Real Estate (income only)   _____
    (i) Trust, Profit Sharing and Annuities (principal distribution and income)   _____
    (j) Pension (income only)   _____
    (k) Awards, Prizes, Grants (state whether taxable or non-taxable)   _____
    (l) Income from Bequests, Legacies and Gifts   _____
    (m) Income from all other sources
        (including alimony, maintenance or child support from prior marriage)   _____
    (n) Tax preference items:
        1. Long-term capital gain deduction   _____
        2. Depreciation amortization or depletion   _____
        3. Stock options - Excess of fair market value over amount paid   _____
    (o) Other Household Member's Income   _____
    (p) Social Security   _____
    (q) Disability Benefits   _____
    (r) Public Assistance   _____
    (s) Other   _____

                        TOTAL MONTHLY INCOME: $_____
                        TOTAL ANNUAL INCOME: $_____

IV. ASSETS (If any asset is held jointly with spouse or another, so state, and set forth your respective shares. Attach additional sheets if needed.)

A. Cash Accounts

Cash

1.1 a. Location _____
    b. Source of funds _____
    c. Amount $_____

                                        Total: Cash $_____

Checking Accounts

2.1 a. Financial Institution _____
    b. Account Number_____
    c. Title holder _____
    d. Date opened _____
    e. Source of funds _____
    f. Balance $_____
2.2 a. Financial Institution _____
    b. Account Number_____
    c. Title holder _____
    d. Date opened _____
    e. Source of funds _____
    f. Balance $_____

                                    Total: Checking $_____

Savings Accounts (Individual, Joint, Totten Trusts, CDs, Treasury Notes)

3.1 a. Financial Institution _____
    b. Account Number _____
    c. Title holder_____
    d. Type of Account _____
    e. Date opened _____
    f. Source of funds _____
    g. Balance $_____
3.2 a. Financial Institution _____
    b. Account Number _____
    c. Title holder _____
    d. Type of Account _____
    e. Date opened _____
    f. Source of funds _____
    g. Balance $_____

                                     Total: Savings $_____

Security Deposits, Earnest Money, etc.

4.1 a. Location _____
    b. Title owner_____
    c. Type of Deposit _____
    d. Source of funds _____
    e. Date of deposit _____
    f. Amount $_____

                          Total: Security Deposits, etc. $_____

Other

5.1 a. Location _____
    b. Title owner _____
    c. Type of Deposit _____
    d. Source of funds _____
    e. Date of deposit _____
    f. Amount $_____

                                        Total: Other $_____

                              Total Cash Accounts: $_____

B. Securities

Bonds, Notes, Mortgages

1.1 a. Description of Security _____
     b. Title holder _____
     c. Location _____
     d. Date of acquisition _____
     e. Original price or value _____
     f. Source of funds to acquire _____
     g. Current value $_____

Total: Bonds, Notes, etc. $_____

Stocks, Options, etc.

2.1 a. Description of Security _____
     b. Title holder _____
     c. Location _____
     d. Date of acquisition _____
     e. Original price or value _____
     f. Source of funds to acquire _____
     g. Current value $_____

2.2 a. Description of Security _____
     b. Title holder _____
     c. Location _____
     d. Date of acquisition _____
     e. Original price or value _____
     f. Source of funds to acquire _____
     g. Current value $_____

2.3 a. Description of Security _____
     b. Title holder _____
     c. Location _____
     d. Date of acquisition _____
     e. Original price or value _____
     f. Source of funds to acquire _____
     g. Current value $_____

Total: Stocks, Options, etc. $_____

Broker Margin Accounts

3.1 a. Name and address of Broker_____
     _____
     b. Title holder _____
     c. Date account opened _____
     d. Original value of account _____
     e. Source of funds _____
     f. Current value $_____

Total: Margin Accounts $_____

Total Value of Securities: $_____

C. Loans to others and Accounts Receivable

1.1 a. Debtor's name and address _____
     _____
     b. Original amount of loan or debt _____
     c. Source of funds from which loan made or origin of debt
     _____
     d. Date payment(s) due _____
     e. Current amount due $_____

1.2 a. Debtor's name and address _____
     b. Original amount of loan or debt _____
     c. Source of funds from which loan made or origin of debt
     _____

d. Date payment(s) due _____

e. Current amount due $_____

Total: Loans and Accounts Receivable $_____

D. Business Interests

1.1   a. Name and address of business _____

      b. Type of business (corporate, partnership, sole
         proprietorship or other) _____

      c. Your capital contribution _____

      d. Your percentage of interest _____

      e. Date of acquisition _____

      f. Original price or value _____

      g. Source of funds to acquire _____

      h. Method of valuation _____

      i. Other relevant information _____

      j. Current net worth of business $_____

Total: Value of Business Interest $_____

E. Cash Surrender Value of Life Insurance

1.1   a. Insurer's name and address _____

                                                       _____

      b. Name of Insured _____

      c. Policy Number _____

      d. Face amount of policy _____

      e. Policy owner _____

      f. Date of acquisition _____

      g. Source of funding to acquire _____

      h. Current cash surrender value $_____

Total: Value of Life Insurance $_____

F. Vehicles (automobile, boat, plane, truck, camper, etc.)

1.1   a. Description _____

      b. Title owner _____

      c. Date of acquisition _____

      d. Original price _____

      e. Source of funds to acquire _____

      f. Amount of current lien unpaid _____

      g. Current fair market value $_____

1.2   a. Description _____

      b. Title owner _____

      c. Date of acquisition _____

      d. Original price _____

      e. Source of funds to acquire _____

      f. Amount of current lien unpaid _____

      g. Current fair market value $_____

Total: Value of Vehicles $_____

G. Real Estate (including real property, leaseholds, life estates, etc.
at market value -- do not deduct any mortgage)

1.1   a. Description _____

      b. Title owner _____

      c. Date of acquisition _____

      d. Original price _____

      e. Source of funds to acquire _____

      f. Amount of mortgage or lien unpaid _____

      g. Estimated current market value $_____

1.2 a. Description _____
     b. Title owner _____
     c. Date of acquisition _____
     d. Original price _____
     e. Source of funds to acquire _____
     f. Amount of mortgage or lien unpaid _____
     g. Estimated current market value $_____

Total: Value of Real Estate $_____

H. Pensions & Trusts (pension, profit sharing, legacies, deferred compensation, etc.)

1.1 a. Description of trust _____
     b. Location of assets _____
     c. Title owner _____
     d. Date of acquisition _____
     e. Original investment _____
     f. Source of funds _____
     g. Amount of unpaid liens _____
     h. Current value $_____
1.2 a. Description of trust _____
     b. Location of assets _____
     c. Title owner _____
     d. Date of acquisition _____
     e. Original investment _____
     f. Source of funds _____
     g. Amount of unpaid liens _____
     h. Current value $_____

Total: Vested Interest in Trusts $_____

I. Contingent Interests (stock options, interests subject to life estates, prospective inheritances, etc.)

1.1 a. Description _____
     b. Location _____
     c. Date of vesting _____
     d. Title owner _____
     e. Date of acquisition _____
     f. Original price or value _____
     g. Source of funds to acquire _____
     h. Method of valuation _____
     i. Current value $_____

Total: Contingent Interests $_____

J. Household Furnishings

1.1 a. Description _____
     b. Location _____
     c. Title owner _____
     d. Original price _____
     e. Source of funds to acquire _____
     f. Amount of lien unpaid _____
     g. Current value $_____

Total: Household Furnishings $_____

K. Jewelry/Art /Antiques (only if valued at more than $500)

1.1 a. Description _____
     b. Title owner _____
     c. Location _____
     d. Original price or value _____
     e. Source of funds to acquire _____

      f. Amount of lien unpaid_____

      g. Current value $_____

1.2 a. Description _____

      b. Title owner _____

      c. Location _____

      d. Original price or value _____

      e. Source of funds to acquire _____

      f. Amount of lien unpaid _____

      g. Current value $_____

                                          Total: Jewelry/Art/etc. $_____

L. Other Assets (tax shelter investments, collections, judgments, causes of action, patents, trademarks, copyrights, and any other asset not hereinabove itemized)

1.1 a. Description _____

      b. Title owner _____

      c. Location _____

      d. Original price or value _____

      e. Source of funds to acquire _____

      f. Amount of lien unpaid _____

      g. Current value $_____

1.2 a. Description _____

      b. Title owner _____

      c. Location _____

      d. Original price or value _____

      e. Source of funds to acquire _____

      f. Amount of lien unpaid_____

      g. Current value $_____

                                          Total: Other $_____

                                       TOTAL ASSETS: $_____

V. LIABILITIES

A. Accounts Payable

1.1 a. Name and address of creditor _____

      _____

      b. Debtor _____

      c. Amount of original debt _____

      d. Date of incurring debt _____

      e. Purpose _____

      f. Monthly/other periodic payment _____

      g. Amount of current debt $_____

1.2 a. Name and address of creditor _____

      _____

      b. Debtor _____

      c. Amount of original debt _____

      d. Date of incurring debt _____

      e. Purpose _____

      f. Monthly/other periodic payment _____

      g. Amount of current debt $_____

                                Total: Accounts Payable $_____

B. Notes Payable

1.1 a. Name and address of note holder _____

      _____

      b. Debtor _____

      c. Amount of original debt _____

      d. Date of incurring debt _____

      e. Purpose _____

f. Monthly/other periodic payment _____

g. Amount of current debt $_____

1.2 a. Name and address of note holder _____

_____

b. Debtor _____

c. Amount of original debt _____

d. Date of incurring debt _____

e. Purpose _____

f. Monthly/other periodic payment _____

g. Amount of current debt $_____

Total: Notes Payable $_____

C. Installment Accounts Payable (security agreements, chattel mortgages)

1.1 a. Name and address of note holder _____

_____

b. Debtor _____

c. Amount of original debt _____

d. Date of incurring debt _____

e. Purpose_____

f. Monthly/other periodic payment _____

g. Amount of current debt $_____

1.2 a. Name and address of note holder _____

_____

b. Debtor _____

c. Amount of original debt _____

d. Date of incurring debt _____

e. Purpose_____

f. Monthly/other periodic payment _____

g. Amount of current debt $_____

Total: Installment Accounts $_____

D. Brokers' Margin Accounts

1.1 a. Name and address of broker _____

_____

b. Debtor _____

c. Amount of original debt _____

d. Date of incurring debt _____

e. Purpose _____

f. Monthly/other periodic payment _____

g. Amount of current debt $_____

Total: Brokers' Margin Accounts $_____

E. Mortgages on Real Estate

1.1 a. Name and address of mortgagee _____

_____

b. Address of property mortgaged _____

_____

c. Mortgagor _____

d. Original debt _____

e. Date of incurring debt _____

f. Monthly/other periodic payment _____

g. Maturity date _____

h. Amount of current debt $_____

1.2 a. Name and address of mortgagee _____

_____

b. Address of property mortgaged _____

_____

c. Mortgagor _____

  d. Original debt _____

  e. Date of incurring debt _____

  f. Monthly/other periodic payment _____

  g. Maturity date _____

  h. Amount of current debt $_____

                                        Total: Mortgages Payable $_____

F. Taxes Payable

1.1 a. Description of tax _____

  b. Amount of tax _____

  c. Date due _____

                                           Total: Taxes Payable $_____

G. Loans on Life Insurance

1.1 a. Name and address of insurer _____

  _____

  b. Amount of loan _____

  c. Date incurred _____

  d. Purpose _____

  e. Name of borrower _____

  f. Monthly/other periodic payment _____

  g. Amount of current debt $_____

                                     Total: Life Insurance Loans $_____

H. Other Liabilities

1.1 a. Description _____

  b. Name and address of creditor _____

  _____

  c. Debtor _____

  d. Original amount of debt _____

  e. Date incurred _____

  f. Purpose _____

  g. Monthly/other periodic payment _____

  h. Amount of current debt $_____

                                      Total: Other Liabilities $_____

                                           TOTAL LIABILITIES: $_____

NET WORTH

  TOTAL ASSETS: $_____

  TOTAL LIABILITIES: **(minus)**   ($_____)

  NET WORTH: $_____

VI. ASSETS TRANSFERRED

List all assets transferred in any manner during the preceding three years, or length of the marriage, whichever is shorter (transfers in the routine course of business which resulted in an exchange of assets of substantially equivalent value need not be specifically disclosed where such assets are otherwise identified in the statement of net worth).

Description of Property Transferred	To Whom Transferred & Relationship	Date of Transfer	Value
_____	_____	_____	_____
_____	_____	_____	_____
_____	_____	_____	_____
_____	_____	_____	_____

VII. SUPPORT REQUIREMENTS

(a) Deponent is at present (paying)(receiving) $_____ per (week)(month), and prior to separation (paid)(received) $_____ per (week)(month) to cover expenses for _____

_____ These payments are being made (voluntarily) (pursuant to court order or judgment) (pursuant to separation agreement), and there are (no) arrears outstanding (in the sum of $_____ to date).

(b) Deponent requests for support of each child $_____ per (week)(month). Total for children $_____.

(c) Deponent requests for support of self $_____ per (week)(month).

(d) The day of the (week)(month) on which payment should be made is _____.

VIII. COUNSEL FEE REQUIREMENTS

(a) Deponent requests for counsel fee and disbursements the sum of $_____.

(b) Deponent has paid counsel the sum of $_____ and has agreed with counsel concerning fees as follows:

_____

_____

(c) There is (not) a retainer agreement or written agreement relating to payment of legal fees. (A copy of any such agreement must be annexed.)

IX. ACCOUNTANT AND APPRAISAL FEES REQUIREMENTS

(a) Deponent requests for accountants' fees and disbursements the sum of $_____. (Include basis for fee, e.g., hourly rate, flat rate)

(b) Deponent requests for appraisal fees and disbursements the sum of $_____. (Include basis for fee, e.g., hourly rate, flat rate)

(c) Deponent requires the services of an accountant for the following reasons:

_____

_____

(d) Deponent requires the services of an appraiser for the following reasons:

_____

_____

X. OTHER DATA

Other data concerning the financial circumstances of the parties that should be brought to the attention of the Court are:

_____

_____

_____

_____

The foregoing statements and a rider consisting of _____ page(s) annexed hereto and made part hereof, have been carefully read by the undersigned who states that they are true and correct.

_____

Name

Petitioner/Plaintiff   Respondent/Defendant

Sworn to before me this _____ day of _____ , 200__

_____

Notary Public

_____

Attorney Name and Address

CLIENT CERTIFICATION

I, _____, HEREBY CERTIFY, under penalty of perjury, that I have carefully read and reviewed the annexed document and that all information contained in that document is true and accurate in all respects to the best of my knowledge and understanding.

I FURTHER CERTIFY, under penalty of perjury, that neither my attorney, nor anyone acting on my attorney's behalf, was the source of any of the information contained in the annexed document; that I provided all of the information contained in the annexed document to my attorney; and that I understand that my attorney, in executing the Attorney Certification required by 22 NYCRR 202.16(e), is relying entirely upon the information provided by me and upon my certification that all such information is true and accurate.

I FURTHER CERTIFY that the annexed document includes all information which I provided my attorney which is relevant to such document and that my attorney has not deleted, omitted or excluded any such information.

Dated: _____, _____

_____
Name

HELPFUL RESOURCES

BOOKS

Crazy Time: Surviving Divorce And Building A New Life by Abigail Trafford. Validates the powerful feelings that arise when a marriage ends by identifying the emotional phases connected with it from crisis, through reaction, to recovery.

Dinosaurs Divorce: A Guide For Changing Families by Marc Tolon Brown, Laurence Krasny Brown. A practical communication tool for parents to help four to eight year old children understand their feelings and encourage them to work in a positive manner with the changing family arrangement.

Divorce And Money: How To Make the Best Financial Decisions During Divorce by Violet Woodhouse. Comprehensive reference educating and offering advice about how to protect financial well-being.

Getting The Love You Want: A Guide For Couples by Harville Hendrix, Ph.D. Concentrates on the theory and practice of how to create a mature relationship in which the legitimate needs of each partner are satisfactorily met.

Getting To Yes: Negotiating Agreement Without Giving In by Roger Fisher, William Ury. Concise guide on negotiation techniques that emphasizes the importance of focusing on interests rather than positions, keeping emotions out of the transactions, and looking for options where there is mutual benefit.

Getting Up, Getting Over, Getting On: A Twelve Step Guide To Divorce Recovery by Micki McWade. Succinctly and effectively guides readers through an approach to healing using the Twelve Step philosophy.

Helping Your Kids Cope With Divorce The Sandcastles Way by M. Gary Neuman, Patricia Romanowski. Insightful coverage of effective, empathetic communication techniques to use with children that enhance understanding and family bonds, and thereby help children cope with divorce.

It's Not Your Fault, Koko Bear: A Read-Together Book For Parents And Young Children During Divorce by Vicki Lansky. Creative communication tool for parents to help children (age three to eight) accept their feelings about divorce and be assured it is not their fault.

Mars And Venus Starting Over: A Practical Guide For Finding Love Again After A Painful Breakup, Divorce, Or The Loss Of A Loved One by John Gray. An effective, supportive guide that focuses on releasing negative emotions, healing pain, and reconnecting with love.

Mom's House, Dad's House: A Complete Guide For Parents Who Are Separated, Divorced, Or Remarried by Isolina Ricci, Ph.D. Provides realistic advice on how to minimize the negative impact of divorce on children while creating and maintaining two stable homes.

Rebuilding: When Your Relationship Ends by Bruce Fisher, Robert E. Alberti. Explores the natural emotions that accompany the loss of a love relationship and presents a nineteen-step rebuilding model for divorce recovery.

Spiritual Divorce: Divorce As A Catalyst For An Extraordinary Life by Debbie Ford, Neale Donald Walsh. Offers insight and encouragement on how to use the pain of divorce as a catalyst to learn and grow, ultimately creating an experience of gain instead of loss.

The Unexpected Legacy Of Divorce: A 25 Year Landmark Study by Judith S. Wallerstein, Julia M. Lewis, Sandra Blakeslee. A perceptive twenty-five-year study of the impact on children who grew up in divorced families or families that stayed unhappily together.

WEB SITES

www.adr.org – Information on arbitration and local offices of the American Arbitration Association. See *Part VII* – in *Chapter 26: "Deadlock Provision / Arbitration Clause."*

www.backgroundcheckgateway.com – Provides tips and guidance for searching public records and locating hard-to-find information and people.

www.bankrate.com – Variety of information and tips on financial topics such as types of loans and rates, credit problems, refinancing, insurance, and financial planning.

www.childsupport-aces.org/ – Information about legal rights and solutions for child support problems.

www.consumercredit.com – For a fee, the American Consumer Credit Counseling, Inc. helps clients regain financial control through debt management.

www.courts.state.ny.us/networth.htm – To download a working copy of a Statement of Net Worth.

www.divorcesource.com/info/divorcelaws/states.shtml – Covers grounds, legal separation, residency requirements, name of the court in which to file to dissolve a marriage, some terminology, property distribution, spousal and child support, and premarital agreements.

www.dos.state.ny.us/ – (New York State Department of State) Provides access to some public records such as business entities and licenses.

www.equifax.com – To obtain a copy of credit report.

www.experian.com – To obtain a copy of credit report.

www.irs.gov – See *Part III* - in *Chapter 6: "Income Tax Returns"* and *Part V* - in *Chapter 17: "Support Payments"* and *"Exemptions And Credits."*

www.kbb.com – To find private sale and trade-in values of vehicles. See *Part VI* - in *Chapter 22: "Be Prepared And Alert."*

www.law.cornell.edu/topics/Table_Divorce.htm – Hosted by the Cornell Law School; provides basic data on grounds, residency requirements, child support guidelines, spousal support, and property distribution.

www.lawinfo.com/barassoc.html – Links to state and local state Bar Associations; other features include FAQs and discussion groups.

www.makinglemonade.com – Focuses on all aspects of single parenting; numerous helpful links.

www.mediators.org – Sponsored by the Association for Conflict Resolution; referral list; some information about requirements. See *Part VI - in Chapter 23: "Selecting A Mediator."*

www.nccs.org – (National Credit Counseling Services) Debt counseling; online financial tools to calculate loan and credit card payoff; bankruptcy information.

www.njapm.org – (New Jersey Association of Professional Mediators) Lists names of participating mediators and contact information.

www.nolo.com – Information on many divorce-related issues such as custody, financial decisions and planning, mediation, and wills and estate planning.

www.nysmediate.org – (New York Council on Divorce Mediation) Lists participating mediators by county and links to dispute resolution organizations.

www.palidan.com/statebar.htm – Inclusive directory of local and state Bar Associations. If your county or local area is not included refer to a local phone book.

www.ssa.gov – Social Security information and forms. See *Part V - in Chapter 15: "Pension."*

www.supportguidelines.com – Covers child support guidelines and other helpful information, such as state divorce statutes, divorce packets, names of courts and their functions, Child Support Enforcement offices, and State Bar Associations.

www.supportkids.com – Private company assisting in the collection of delinquent court-ordered child support in exchange for a percentage of the amount successfully collected.

www.transunion.com – To obtain copy of credit report.

We are our perceptions.

INDEX

A

abandonment, 17-18, 57-59, 268
    constructive abandonment, 59
ACES (Association For Children For
    Enforcement Of Support), 196
action for divorce, [*See* commencement
    of lawsuit, Summons and Complaint,
    Summons with Notice]
Action for Separation, 63
Action Matters Organizer, 7, 245-246
adjusted basis, 84
adjustment:
    children, 11-12, 183-184
    personal, 9-10, 11
    rebuilding, 171-172, 205-206
    See also: co-parenting, healing, Life
        Mural Ceremony, power of
        positive thinking, reactions to
        divorce, strategy
adultery, 18, 57-59, 64
adversarial legal system, 7, 10-11, 73,
    119, 130, 256
Agreement Matters Organizer, 259-265
agreements to end marriage, [*See* legal
    agreements]
alimony, [*See* maintenance]
anger, 6, 22-23, 109, 111, 169, 174, 176,
    179
annulment, 10, 53, 60, 218
Answer, 65
anxiety, 22, 109, 183, 197
appreciation, 82, 90, 203, 268
    active, 45, 81-82
    passive, 81
assets:
    dissipation of, 28, 35, 38, 79-80, 105
    hidden, 40-44
    post-divorce, 189-191
    protection of, 28-29, 31-33, 61-62,
        64-65, 200-202, 218
    restraining orders, 28, 31, 33,
        41-42, 62, 66, 216, 274-275

    true value of, 83-85, 91-92, 101, 220
    See also: bankruptcy, businesses,
        comingling property,
        commencement of lawsuit,
        degrees, equitable distribution,
        financial records, goodwill,
        licenses, marital property,
        prenuptial agreements, principal
        residence, retirement plans,
        separate property
attorneys:
    attributes, 117-118
    bills / fees, 106-107, 129-130, 150
    firing of, 130-31
    initial consultation, 118-120
        First Meeting Data Organizer,
            118-119, 120, 127
    interview questions, 120-122
    locating, 115-116
    quality of service, 115
    working with, 127-131
    See also: client's rights, professional
        conduct, Retainer Agreement

B

bank accounts, 31, 34, 41
bankruptcy, 92, 104, 106, 107-108, 156,
    164-165, 221, 293
best interests of the child, 96-97, 221
bifurcation, 130
budget, 36-37
    Monthly Budget, 247-250
businesses, 35-36, 42-43, 82, 91

C

capital gains, 83-84, 101
CCCS, [*See* Consumer Credit Counseling
    Service]
CDP, [*See* certified divorce planner]
celebrity status, 81-82, 91-92, 200-201

certified divorce planner (CDP), 102, 107, 153
certified financial planner, 106
certified fraud examiner (CFE), 42, 82
CFP, [*See* certified financial planner]
charging lien, 107, 123, 125, 126, 131, 258
Child Protective Services, 55
children, 11-12,
     safety, 17-18, 21, 29, 53, 55
     See also: custody, child support
child support, 50, 54, 99-100, 147-148, 159-160, 165, 219, 221-222
     delinquent payments, 75, 193-196, 225
     payment assurance, 163-164, 190
     See also: *Reinisch v. Reinisch, Rohrs v. Rohrs*
Child Support Enforcement (CSE) Program, 75, 193-195, 215, 293
Child Support Standards Act (CSSA), 52, 99-100, 147
client's rights, 75, 123-124
     See also: *Statement Of Client's Rights And Responsibilities*
COBRA (Consolidated Omnibus Budget Reconciliation Act), 106, 161, 189, 222, 253
COLA, [*See* cost of living adjustment]
collections, 30, 33, 128, 146, 252
college expenses, 100, 107, 157
     See also: *Reinisch v. Reinisch, Rohrs v. Rohrs*
comingling property, 81-82, 201, 203
commencement of lawsuit:
     advantages of, 28, 33, 40, 61-63, 216, 218
     effect on assets / debts, 27, 32, 39, 62, 64, 79, 81, 90, 216, 218
     procedure, 64-67, 70, 95-96, 144
     requirements, 49-50
communication, 12
     as co-parents, 182, 184-185
     new relationships, 206-210
     with children, 11-12, 183-184, 185-186

community property states, 220, 222
complaint, [*See* Verified Complaint]
condonation, 18, 59, 216
confession of judgment, 124, 258
Consolidated Omnibus Budget Reconciliation Act, [*See* COBRA]
constructive abandonment, 57, 59
Consumer Credit Counseling Service (CCCS), 32
contempt of court, 66, 196, 225
     See also: Order to Show Cause
contested divorce, 10-11, 38, 50, 63, 69-70, 95-96
     See also: custody: contested
contingency fee, 123, 126
co-parenting:
     communicating with:
          children, 183-184, 185-186
          other parent, 184-185
     goals, 181-182, 192-193
cost of living adjustment, 100, 105-106, 161
counterclaim, 65
County Clerk's Office, 42-44, 71, 116, 190, 217
court calendar, 51, 130, 134
court orders, 55-56, 62-63, 144, 216
     enforcement of, 75, 144, 193-196, 219
     See also: oral stipulations, Order of Protection, QDRO, QMCSO, restraining orders, temporary orders
court reporter, 44, 68, 256
CPS, [*See* Child Protective Services]
credit, 13, 32, 43
     cards, 31-32, 35
     investigating, 39-40
     See also: debts
cruel and inhuman treatment, 59-60
CSE, [*See* Child Support Enforcement]
CSSA, [*See* Child Support Standards Act]
custodial parent, 184
     See also: child support, custody, *Reinisch v. Reinisch, Rohrs v. Rohrs*

custody, 50
  amicable, 95
  arrangements, 96
  contested, 29, 37-38, 45-46, 69,
    74-75, 96-98, 120-222
  desertion, 54
  leaving the residence, 17-18, 98
  relocation, 97, 157-158
  visitation / access, 100, 147,
    156-158

D

deadlock provision / arbitration clause,
  153-154, 158, 160, 161
death rights, 80, 100, 150, 163,
  202-203
  See also: will
debt, 27-28, 32, 34, 41-43, 92, 142, 149,
  162, 192, 194, 221, 225, 251, 264,
  286-289
  See also: bankruptcy,
    commencement of lawsuit,
    credit, liens
deeds, 35, 42-43, 129, 154-155, 190, 252,
  253
defendant, 50, 64-66, 69, 196, 219,
  267-289
  See also: respondent, Exhibits
defined benefit plan, 35, 88, 89, 128,
  146, 251
defined contribution plans, 35, 88, 89,
  251
degrees, 45, 51, 62, 80, 81, 82, 91-92,
  128, 146, 201, 220, 221, 252, 279
Department of Social Services (DSS), 75,
  219
deposition, 42, 44, 68-69, 137, 219
  See also: *Deposition Primer*, stages
    of divorce process
Deposition Primer, 255-256
depression, 169, 174
disbursements, 125, 268, 289
discovery, 28, 41, 44, 66-70, 119, 129,
  137
  disclosure, 136-137, 151
  See also: *Deposition Primer*

distributive award, 92, 106, 220, 221,
  268
divorce file, 28-30, 129, 131, 223
  See also: *Financial Puzzle Pieces*,
    retaining lien
documents, [*See* information and
  documents, Statement of Net Worth]
Domestic Relations Law, 57, 61-63,
  79-80, 268, 273-275
DSS, [*See* Department of Social
  Services]
durable power of attorney, [*See* power of
  attorney]

E

EBT, [*See* examination before trial]
emancipation, 147-148, 150, 159,
  221-222
emotions:
  damaging effects of, 174-175
  grounds and, 58
  negotiations and, 109
  releasing, 176-177
  working with attorney, 115
  See also: adjustment, healing,
    reactions to divorce, specific
    emotions (ex. fear)
equitable distribution, 79-80, 142, 220,
  268, 271
  See also: assets
equity credit lines, 32
estate planning, 190-191
  See also: death rights, will
ex parte motion, 66
examination before trial (EBT), 68
  See also: deposition
Exhibits:
  Order To Show Cause (for pendente
    lite relief), 273-275
  Qualified Domestic Relations Order,
    277-278
  Statement Of Net Worth, 279-290
  Summons With Notice, 267-268
  Verified Complaint, 269-271

F

faith, 6, 170, 177, 303
Family Court, 62, 66, 75, 96, 97-99, 105,
194, 196, 217-218, 270
how to use, 56
pros and cons, 55
services, 53-55
See also: child support: delinquent
payments
fault states, 57, 218
fear, 22, 109-110, 169-172, 174, 176,
180, 184, 186
Federal Income Tax Offset Program, 194
filing system, 29-30, 191-192
financial planning, 107, 292
Financial Puzzle Pieces, 251-252
financial records, 27-46, 87-93, 189-192,
216-217
See also: *Financial Puzzle Pieces*,
Monthly Budget, Statement of Net
Worth, *Wrap It Up Right*
First Meeting Data Organizer, 118-120,
127
forensics, 66, 71, 74-75, 82, 97-98, 221
forgiveness, 175, 176-179
forum shopping, 61
401(k) Plan, 83, 84, 89, 200
frivolous actions, 71, 219

G

garnishment of personal property, 194
See also: wage garnishment, wage
withholding
goodwill, 51, 91-92, 146
grounds, 18, 49-50, 57-60, 63-65, 68,
141, 215, 218, 268, 270
guardian ad litem, [*See* law guardian]
guilt, 169, 174-175, 176-177, 179

H

Head-of-Household, 103, 162, 189
healing:
coping with damaging emotions,
174-180
self-awareness, 205-206, 210-211

sharing grief, 115, 173-174
See also: forgiveness, Life Mural
Ceremony, power of listening,
power of positive thinking
health, 21-23, 142, 169-171, 196-197
See also: adjustment, healing,
insurance
health insurance, [*See* insurance]
healthcare directive, 191, 253
hearings, 67, 70, 75-76, 126, 219
Family Court, 56, 96
pendente lite motions, 65-66
Preliminary Conference, 66-67
Pretrial Conference, 69-70
hidden assets, 40-44
hold harmless, [*See* indemnification and
hold harmless clause]
How To Start And Proceed, 7, 245-246
IDVC, [*See* Integrated Domestic
Violence Court]
imprisonment, 57, 58, 60, 196, 225
income tax returns, [*See* taxes]
indemnification and hold harmless
clause, 155, 162, 163, 224
Individual Retirement Account (IRA),
34, 35, 83, 89, 91, 101, 146, 189
inflation: effect of, 88, 92, 107
child support, 100
maintenance, 105-106, 161
information and documents:
filing systems, 29-30, 191-192
gathering and using, 27-30, 31-38,
39-46
See also: Organizers
injunction, [*See* restraining order]
Innocent Spouse Exception Law, 104
insurance:
disability and life, 35, 65, 88, 90, 93,
100, 105, 149-150, 156, 160,
163-164, 189, 190-192, 202
health, 149, 159, 161, 189, 222
responsibility for, 36, 65, 107, 143,
148, 248, 253
See also: *Agreement Matters*
Organizer, COBRA, Exhibits,
QMCSO
Integrated Domestic Violence Court
(IDVC), 76

interrogatory, 68-69
　　See also: stages of divorce process
investments, 33, 35, 157, 251
　　See also: *Agreement Matters*
　　　Organizer, Exhibits
IRA, [*See* Individual Retirement
　　Accounts]
irreconcilable differences, 57, 218
irretrievable breakdown of the marriage,
　　57, 218
IRS (Internal Revenue Service), 34,
　　83-85, 101-104, 220, 222, 292

J

joint accounts, 31-33, 39-40, 189
Judgment of Divorce, 10, 62-63, 69, 218
Judgment of Separation, 10, 50, 57, 63,
　　144, 218
judgments, [*See* court orders, temporary
　　orders]
judicial bias, 74
judicial discretion, 51-52, 74, 92,
　　106-107, 119, 196, 203, 220, 222
jurisdiction, 50, 52, 53, 61-62, 69, 73, 76
　　See also: Exhibits

L

law guardian, 66, 74-75, 97-98, 119, 219,
　　221
laws change, 51-52, 91, 103
lawyers, [*See* attorneys]
legal agreements, 10-11, 60, 62-63, 69,
　　141, 144, 224
　　basic preparation, 142-143
　　common Articles, 145-151
　　what to include, 153-165
　　See also: Action for Separation,
　　　Agreement Matters Organizer,
　　　Judgment of Divorce, Judgment of
　　　Separation, oral stipulations,
　　　prenuptial agreements, Retainer
　　　Agreement, Separation
　　　Agreement, Settlement
　　　Agreement, Stipulation of
　　　Settlement, *Wrap It Up Right*

legal fees, 65, 70, 74, 106-107, 118,
　　121-122, 123-124, 219, 222-223
　　See also: charging lien, contingency
　　　fee, disbursements, Exhibits,
　　　Retainer Agreement, retainer fee
legal process:
　　brief overview, 10-11
　　options, 61-63, 218-219, 224-225
　　reality of, 5-7, 49, 73-76, 115-120,
　　　130-131, 141-144
　　See also: commencement of lawsuit,
　　　legal agreements, stages of divorce
　　　process, *Statement Of Client's*
　　　Rights And Responsibilities
legalese, 10, 49, 145
liabilities, [*See* debts]
licenses, 45, 51, 62, 75, 80-82, 91-92,
　　195, 201, 220-221, 225, 252, 292
liens, 43, 92, 124, 154-155, 162, 190,
　　253
　　See also: charging liens, Exhibits,
　　　retaining liens, security lien
life insurance, [*See* insurance]
Life Mural Ceremonies, 178-180
living will, [*See* healthcare directive]

M

maintenance: 263
　　duration, 105
　　modification, 148,161, 225
　　payment assurance, 163-164
　　payments, 148-149, 160-161
　　qualifying factors, 38, 105
　　special concerns, 105-106, 164-165
　　tax issues, 102-104, 106, 148,
　　　161-162
　　temporary, 105
　　See also: bankruptcy, Exhibits
marital history, 19, 45-46, 217
marital property, 45, 62, 79-82, 91, 142,
　　221
married filing separately, 103
material possessions, 17, 33, 35, 146, 252
mediation, 133-134, 224
　　interviewing and selecting, 134-135
　　pros and cons of, 136-137
Monthly Budget, 247-250

mortgage, 42-43, 45, 84, 87, 92, 124, 146, 154-155, 252, 258
motion churning, 130
mourning, 5, 11, 169, 173, 181

N

negotiating, 44, 61, 69, 109-111, 125-126, 143, 223
Net Worth Statement, [*See* Statement of Net Worth]
no prejudice letter, 17-18, 216
no-fault divorce, [*See* no-fault states]
no-fault states, 58-59, 218
noncustodial parent, 184
    See also: child support, custody, *Reinisch v. Reinisch, Rohrs v. Rohrs*
nonmarital property, [*See* separate property]

O

OCSE, [*See* Office Of Child Support Enforcement]
Office Of Child Support Enforcement (OCSE), [*See* Child Support Enforcement (CSE) Program]
oral stipulations, 69-70, 76, 219
order of exclusive occupancy, 17, 216
Order of Protection, 17, 53, 56
Order to Show Cause, 62, 65-66, 75, 196
    See also: contempt of court, Exhibits
orders, [*See* court orders]
organization, [*See* filing system, Organizers]
Organizers:
    Action Matters, 245-246
    Agreement Matters, 259-265
    Financial Puzzle Pieces, 251-252
    First Meeting Data, 118-119
    Mind Matters, 255-258
    Monthly Budget, 247-250
    Wrap It Up Right, 253

P

Pathfinder, 259-265

payroll deduction, [*See* wage withholding]
PEBES, [*See* Personal Earnings Benefits Estimate Statement]
pendente lite motions, 62, 65-66, 75, 105
    See also: restraining orders, temporary orders
pendente lite relief, 273-275
    See also: restraining orders, temporary orders
pensions, [*See* retirement plans]
perjury, 35, 74, 119, 130
Person In Need of Supervision (PINS), 54
Personal Earnings Benefits Estimate Statement (PEBES), [*See* Request for Social Security Statement (Form SSA-7004)]
personal records, 37-38
petition, 54-56, 66, 75, 105, 194-196, 219, 225
    See also: pendente lite motions
petitioner, 56, 219
    See also: plaintiff
plaintiff, 60, 61-62, 63, 64-66, 69, 219
    See also: Exhibits, petitioner
pleadings, 64-67, 219, 273
post-divorce:
    financial and legal tasks, 189-197, 199-200
    new relationships, 205-210
    staying organized, 191-192
    Wrap It Up Right, 253
    See also: estate planning, prenuptial agreements
power of attorney, 28, 190-192
power of listening, 209-210
power of positive thinking, 170, 177-178
Preliminary Conference, 66-67, 69, 70, 219
prenuptial agreements, 81, 200-203, 225
    discussion of, 202-203
    legality of, 202
    protection without, 203
    what to include, 201-202
Pretrial Conference, 69-70, 219

primary caregiver, 45, 74, 92, 95, 98, 201
principal residence, 17, 87, 88, 101, 127, 146, 216
private investigator, 40, 42, 43, 44, 195, 217
pro se, 56, 116-117
professional conduct, 73-74, 119, 130-131
promissory note, 124, 258
property, [*See* assets]
public records, 42-43, 116, 190, 217, 292
Push-Ups For Change, 23-24

Q

QDRO (Qualified Domestic Relations Order), 87-91, 108, 121, 155-156, 194-195, 260
    See also: Exhibits
QMCSO, [*See* Qualified Medical Child Support Order]
Qualified Domestic Relations Order, [*See* QDRO]
Qualified Medical Child Support Order (QMCSO), 106, 222

R

reactions to divorce:
    of other people, 12-13
    personal, 5-7, 9-13, 169
reality of divorce, 3, 5-7
    financial, 79-80
    legal, 10-11, 49, 61-63, 73-76, 95-96, 106-107
    personal involvement, 27-29, 109-111, 117-122, 125-126, 127-131, 141-143
recusal, 74
reform, 76, 123-124, 219
Reinisch v. Reinisch, 51-52
relief, [*See* temporary orders]
relocation, 65, 97, 157-158, 221
Request for Copy or Transcript of Tax Form (Form 4506), 34
Request for Social Security Statement (Form SSA-7004), 88-89
resentment, 22, 109, 174-177, 179

residency requirements, 49
    See also: commencement of lawsuit
respondent, 54, 56, 219
    See also: defendant
restraining orders, 28, 31, 33, 42, 62, 66, 93, 216, 274-275
Retainer Agreement, 119, 122, 123-126, 127, 129, 131, 223, 257-258
retainer fee, 118, 123-125, 127, 223, 257
    See also: Retainer Agreement
retaining liens, 124, 126, 129
retirement plans:
    dividing with QDRO, 89-91, 121, 155-156, 194-195, 221
    documentation, 35, 42, 87-88, 189
    taxes on, 83-84, 91, 101
Rohrs v. Rohrs, 51-52

S

safety deposit boxes, 32-33, 216
satisfaction of mortgage, 190, 253
security lien, 124, 258
separate property, 34, 45, 51, 61-62, 79-82, 200-203, 216, 218, 220-221, 252, 268, 274
Separation Agreement, 10, 50, 57, 60, 62-63, 141, 144, 145, 218, 224
service (of process), 64
Settlement Agreement, 10, 62-63, 141, 218, 224
shame, 169, 174-175, 177
show cause, [*See* contempt of court, Order to Show Cause]
Social Security, 88-89, 106, 191, 281
spousal support, [*See* maintenance]
stages of divorce process:
    discovery, 28, 41, 44, 66-70, 129, 137, 219
        See also: *Deposition Primer*
    pleading, 64-67, 219, 273
    trial, 70
Statement Of Client's Rights And Responsibilities, 123-124, 223, 257-258
Statement of Net Worth, 31, 36, 41, 51, 65, 67, 82, 151, 216, 292
    Exhibits, 279-290

Stipulation of Settlement, 10, 62-63, 141, 218, 224
strategy:
    financial, 13, 27-30, 79-80, 199-200, 251-252
    How To Start And Proceed, 245-246
    legal, 17-19, 49, 61-63, 95-96, 115, 127-128, 141-144
    personal, 13, 17-19, 21-24, 171-172, 205-206
    See also: co-parenting, healing, negotiating, *Pathfinder*
stress, 5-6, 21-22, 111, 169-171, 173, 182-183, 196-197, 255
subpoena power, 38, 41, 68-69, 87, 219
Summons and Complaint, 50, 64-65, 66, 119, 219
    See also: Summons with Notice, Verified Complaint
Summons with Notice, 50, 64, 219
    See also: Exhibits, Summons with Complaint, Verified Complaint
Supreme Court, 50, 57, 53-55, 62, 66, 76, 97-99, 219, 270
survivor's benefits, 90, 191

T

tape recording, 18, 30, 38, 184, 216-217
tax basis, [*See* adjusted basis]
taxes: 292
    business, 35-36, 41, 195
    capital gains, 83-85, 101, 220
    community states, 222
    distributive awards, 92
    exemptions and credits, 103, 163
    filing status, 103, 149, 162-163, 189
    Innocent Spouse Exception Law, 104
    IRA transfers, 89, 91
    maintenance, 102, 161, 164-165
    post-divorce, 189, 199-200
    property, 36, 87, 146
    refunds, 149
        offset to cover delinquent child support, 75, 194

returns, 34, 41
sale of principal residence, 101
support payments, 102
    options, 104, 106, 148, 161, 164-165
temporary orders, 53-54, 56, 62, 64-66, 75, 96, 105, 219, 221
temporary restraining order (TRO), [*See* restraining order]
titles, 35, 80-81, 190, 220, 253
transcript, 34, 69, 71, 76, 256
Trial Readiness Conference (TRC), [*See* Pretrial Conference]
TRO, [*See* temporary restraining order]

U

UCC (Uniform Commercial Code) records, 43
uncontested divorce, 10, 61, 62-63, 95-96

V

Verified Answer, [*See* Answer]
Verified Complaint, 50, 64-65, 66, 119, 219
    See also: Exhibits, Summons and Complaint
Visitation / access rights, 50, 53, 96-98, 100, 147, 156-158, 270

W

wage garnishment, 194, 225
    See also: garnishment of personal property
wage withholding, 193-194, 225
    See also: garnishment of personal property
will, 80, 93, 100, 160, 190-191, 221, 224, 293
    See also: death rights
without prejudice, 17-18, 66, 216
Wrap It Up Right, 253

BOOST EMPOWERMENT !

TELL YOUR STORY

APPEAR In the NEXT EDITION of

DIVORCE EMPOWERMENT
What You Need To Know, Do, And Say

Inspire Others • Share Useful Tips • Positive Techniques • Turning Point Tales

How Did You...?		
Muster Strength	Nourish Hope / Faith	Locate Information
Maintain Balance	Obtain Support	Surmount Obstacles
Refine Skills	Sustain Focus	Endure Setbacks
	Use the Internet	Triumph

Guidelines

- To be considered for publication your submission must be clearly written, typed (double spaced), concise (no more than 300 words), and signed.
- Include your signature and state of residence with the statement: *I understand and accept the terms of the Caveat and grant PowerWise Books permission to use my submission.*

Submit

Mail: PowerWise Books, PO Box 162, Putnam Valley, NY 10579

Fax: (845) 526-2737

E-mail at: *www.divorce-guide.com*

Contact Data – Optional

Name _____

Organization / Company _____

Address _____

City _____ State _____ Zip _____

Fax _____ E-mail _____

Caveat

- By submitting your signed article you agree to grant PowerWise Books permission to use it.
- PowerWise Books reserves the right to edit submissions for clarity and brevity and to print them in less than their entirety.
- Published anecdotes are to be identified only by the contributor's first name or initials and state of residence.
- No other recognition and no monetary compensation are to be rendered.

PowerWise Books

Weaving Wisdom Into Power

EXPRESS ORDER FORM

Give

DIVORCE EMPOWERMENT
What You Need To Know, Do, And Say

to Colleagues, Clients, and Friends

Inquire about "Bulk Rate Discount"

Mail: PowerWise Books, PO Box 162, Putnam Valley, NY 10579

Fax: (845) 526-2737

E-mail at: *www.divorce-guide.com*

Include Payment

_____ Number of copies x $21.95 $_____

New York residents – Sales Tax for your locality   _____

Shipping and handling for one book is $4.95   _____

Include $1.95 for each additional book   _____

                                  Total $_____

☐ Check or money order payable to **PowerWise Books**

☐ VISA Card # _____ Expiration Date _____

Name as printed on card _____

Signature _____

Money Back Guarantee on direct orders.
Return unblemished copy with receipt within four months of purchase.

Ship To

Name _____

Organization / Company _____

Address _____

City _____ State _____ Zip _____

Fax _____ E-mail _____

PowerWise Books

Weaving Wisdom Into Power

DIVORCE GUIDE VOUCHER for $30

Use toward Consultation with a Divorce Guide professional
$90 Value for $60

Learn about Divorce Guide at *www.divorce-guide.com*

TO SCHEDULE AND USE VOUCHER

1. **Photocopy** this form; fill in necessary data.
2. **Attach** original sales receipt for this book.
3. **Submit** payment of $60.
   _____ Check or money order – payable to "Divorce Guide, Inc"

   _____ VISA # _____ Expiration Date _____

   Name as printed on card _____

   Signature _____
4. **Mail** to Divorce Guide, Inc., PO Box 162, Putnam Valley, New York 10579.
5. **Contact Information** – Needed to Schedule and Confirm Your Appointment
   Name _____

   Time Available _____

   E-mail Address or Fax Number _____
6. **Preference:** Consult with the Author _____ or with an Associate _____

RELEVANT INFORMATION

Length of Marriage _____

Children – Ages / Special Needs _____

Major Concerns _____

_____
_____
_____

Fifty-minute consultations are scheduled according to schedule availability. Money back guarantee. The Divorce Guide Voucher is honored ONLY WHEN the original sales receipt is enclosed. Otherwise, the regular fee applies. Payment terms connected with voucher are to be honored throughout 2003. Thereafter, check *www.divorce-guide.com* for updated fee information and special considerations.

Divorce Guide, Inc
Have the Divorce Guide
By Your Side

●

(845) 526-8000
(845) 526-2737 Fax
www.divorce-guide.com